AF291768

CHANEL

ICONS OF FASHION

Michael O'Neill

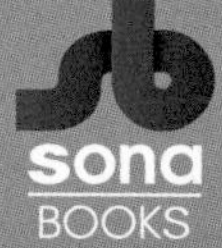
sona
BOOKS

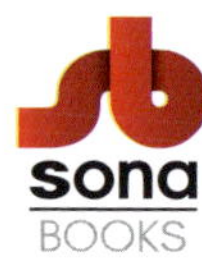

sona
BOOKS

First Published Danann Media Publishing Limited 2023
WARNING: For private domestic use only, any unauthorised Copying, hiring,
lending or public performance of this book is illegal.

CAT NO: SON0560

Photography courtesy of

Getty images:

Guy Marineau/WWD/Penske Media
Fine Art Images/Heritage Images
Victor Virgile/Gamma-Rapho
Erick Pasquier/Gamma-Rapho
Brissand/AFP
Michel Artault/Gamma-Rapho
Dickson Lee/South China Morning
Post

Hulton-Deutsch Collection/Corbis
ullstein bild
Bettmann
Patrick Kovarik/AFP
Keystone-France/Gamma-Rapho
Bertrand Rindoff Petroff
Stephane De Sakutin/AFP
Sasha/Hulton Archive

Hulton Archive
New York Times Co
Phillips/Topical Press Agency/Hulton
Archive
FPG/Hulton Archive
Apic
Bertrand Rindoff Petroff

Alamy:

Dzmltry Kliapitski
Everett Collection Historical
f8 archive
Pictorial Press Ltd
Lordprice Collection
Photo 12
Doug Peters

Sipa US
olga Yastremska
Antiqua Print Gallery
Abaca Press
Grzegorz Czapski
Keystone Press
Lebrecht Music & Arts

flab
GRANGER – Historical Picture Archive
Radu Bercan
Album
Xinhua
Phil Rees

Other images, Wiki Commons

Book design by Darren Grice at Ctrl-d
Cover design by caroleschillingdesign
Editor Carolyn McHugh
Additional writing by Carolyn McHugh
Proof reader Finn O'Neil

Made in EU.
ISBN: 978-1-917259-27-9

CONTENTS

ICON OF A GOLDEN AGE

"When one makes up one's mind to tell the truth,
one has to go all the way."

French fashion designer Coco Chanel presented the world with many contradictory and intriguing faces. Celebrated as a couturière to Hollywood stars, and a successful businesswoman, she was also, less famously, an abandoned child, a drug user, mistress to aristocrats, and rumoured to be an antisemitic and secret Nazi collaborator. As she moved in high circles, counting political leaders, dominant cultural figures and royalty among her friends and acquaintances, none were aware of her rags to riches past.

Always hiding herself and afraid her secrets would come out; this ruthlessly ambitious woman invented a version of herself which became a worldwide fashion icon. The designs of the woman who was never able to anchor her love in a marriage have become embedded into her era as no others; Chanel No.5 perfume, the little black dress, the Chanel tweed suit, the 2.55 handbag.

But for all her deceit, subterfuge and ruthless self-interest, she possessed the great gift of understanding what women wanted. Using clothes to express her own desires and through her own life-style choices, she first embodied the aspirations of French women in the 1920s – an age when they were longing to throw off the shackles of the Belle Epoque and the boa-constrictor of male domination that saturated every aspect of their lives.

In those days, any woman who dared to express artistic talent was expected to marry and allow herself to be subsumed into her husband's professional and domestic needs. Coco Chanel showed that there was another life waiting for women if they had the courage to rebel. 'Be who you are', she advised, 'Not who the world wants you to be'.

The story of how Coco Chanel, a woman of immense incongruities, orchestrated her rise from poverty to world fame is, of course, fascinating and full of half-truths and red herrings; how could it be otherwise, for that is precisely how she wanted it to be.

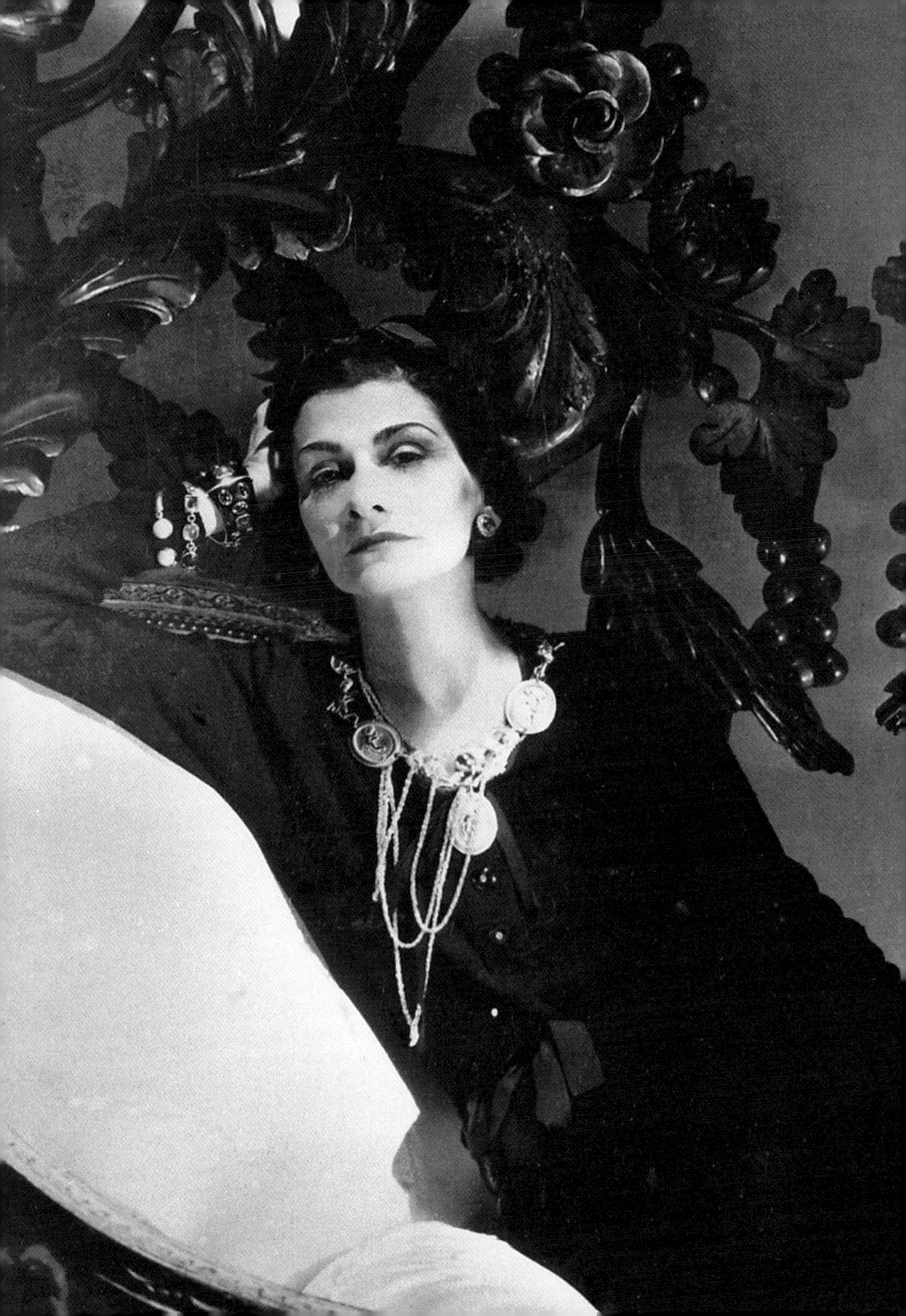

THE UNEASY CHILDHOOD 1883–1904

"Arrogance is in everything I do. It is in my gestures, the harshness of my voice, in the glow of my gaze, in my sinewy, tormented face."

Coco Chanel was born Gabrielle Bonheur Chanel in a poorhouse in the market town of Samur, Maine-et-Loire in western France, on 19 August 1883. Her 20-year-old mother, Eugénie Jeanne Dévolle, was a laundry woman from farming stock, while her father, 28-year-old Albert Chanel was an itlnerant street vendor, away at the time of Coco's birth. Her parents weren't married, despite already having another daughter, one-year-old Julia, making the sisters illegitimate – a stigma that weighed heavily in those times.

So it's hardly surprising that as an adult Coco invented and re-invented the early years of her life , with the true facts surrounding her birth – illegitimacy and impoverished circumstances – becoming her first 'secrets'.

She had a helping hand in deliberately obfuscating her past when her father's surname was misspelled on her birth certificate as Chasnel. Later in life, as Coco, she would talk of being born in a hospital (and even, on occasion, on a train) rather than mention the poorhouse. She also suggested the name given to her, 'Gabrielle Bonheur', was that of the nun who acted as midwife.

The origins of the name Coco are as nebulous as much else in her life; her father, not having been involved in choosing it, apparently didn't think much of the name Gabrielle. He would call her 'Little Coco', and from then on, 'I was simply Coco', she said. Not that Albert seemed to care a great deal about any of the children, despite Coco's desire to imagine herself as his favourite child. Redrawn in her adult life as an 'adoring' father, Coco gave no hint that her father might not have even liked her, nor any of his other children, nor even wanted to have any in the first place.

Coco was followed into her impoverished world by four other siblings: Alphonse, in 1885, Antoinette in 1887, Lucien in 1889 and Augustin in 1891, although Augustin did not survive infancy. Albert did finally marry Eugénie in 1884 when Coco was just over a year old, although before long, he would absent himself again.

ABOVE: Gabrielle 'Coco' Chanel as a young girl

The memories that the adult Gabrielle allowed to seep through to the public from her childhood are sketchy and generally unreliable. She preferred to keep her mother Eugénie at a shadowy distance, as a woman in ill-health who died of tuberculosis, whilst Coco (then aged 11, not six as she later maintained) and her sisters had been farmed out to an uncle in Brive-la-Galliarde in the south-west of France. She would present her father as a character seemingly pieced together from fairy tales and longings, as an absent, but loving and protective, prince in disguise.

Albert was not around when his 32-year-old wife died in 1895, returning only to sort the children out before vanishing to America. He sent the boys to work as free farmhands with a peasant family, while palming the girls off on the nuns of the Sacred Heart of Mary in Aubazine, who 'cared for' orphaned and abandoned girls.

Coco romantically whitewashed her father's disappearance as 'going to seek his fortune', but the hurt she felt at that time, which infused her life with the 'aunts', as the nuns became in the retelling, could not be prevented from bubbling to the surface in later life. Coco confessed that she 'fed on sorrow and horror. I wanted to kill myself', after the crushing realisation that 'my father had ruined my mother', that she was being called, 'an orphan', and was unloved.

Coco would speak of being beaten by the nuns, but alongside these punishments, the nuns taught her how to sew, embroider and iron – skills that would change her destiny.

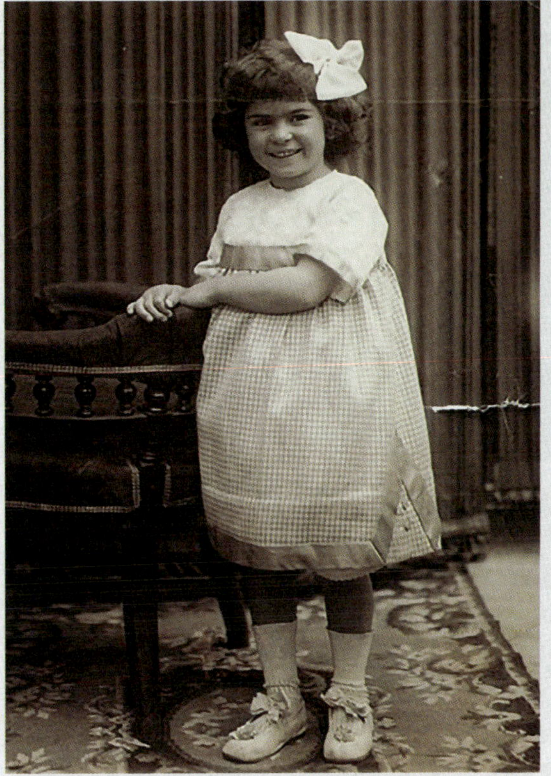

And this skill was further advanced during the latter years of her time with the nuns of Aubazine when Coco came to know one of her real aunts, Louise, her father's sister. Louise lived in Varennes-sur-Allier and, married but childless, would invite Coco to visit.

Coco's father never visited her at the Abbey, and she would remain more or less incarcerated with her 'aunts' – the nuns – until she was 18. However, as an adult, Coco would say that Albert had visited her; but this 'fantasy father' was a man who was redeemed in her telling of the story as having left his insupportable life for a better one. It was completely understandable for her that he could

'I don't know anything more terrifying than the family'

COCO CHANEL

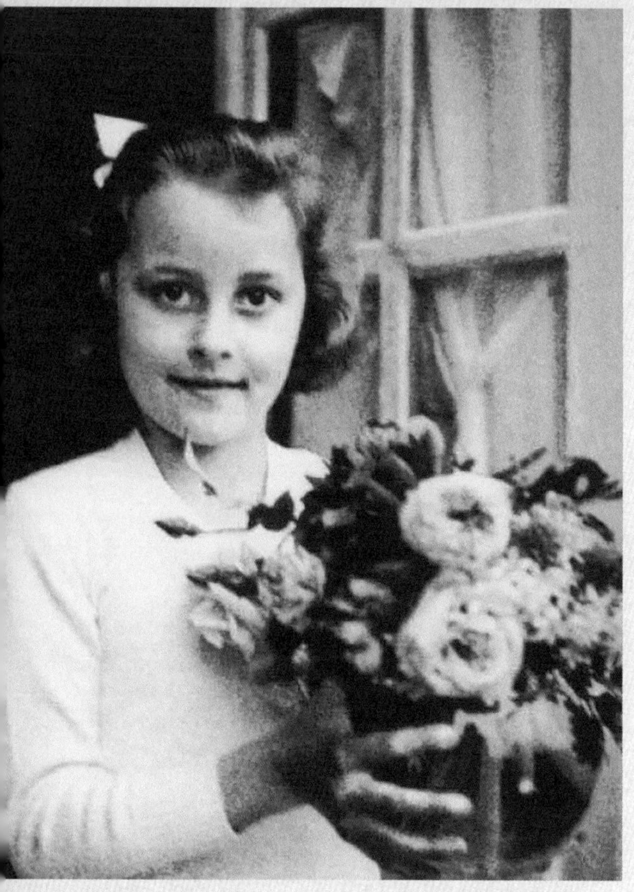

not rescue her, and after all, what really mattered was that she was loved by him, being the girl who brought 'the good days, fun, happiness' to his existence.

But in truth, she had a sorrowful existence treading the stone floors inside the gloominess of the Abbey at Aubazine, sleeping in an iron bed beneath the crucifixes, with some Victorian novels as her only entertainment.

Her sister Julia's sad reality was an illegitimate son – there were later unsubstantiated rumours that he actually belonged Coco – and then suicide. The reason? Coco spoke little about Julia, suggesting her sister was a jilted lover and therefore took a blade to her wrists. With so little information, speculation took root, and the cause of Julia's death was variously thought to be tuberculosis, or even freezing to death in the snow. Coco at first took the boy, André Palasse, under her wing, though his presence was unwanted later, for obvious reasons as a witness to the past, and he was sent to an English boarding school.

In later life, Coco would visit the Abbey and make donations, but never stayed long within its sombre walls. As an adult, she would talk about the crude clothing she was forced to wear by the nuns, although, once again, it's impossible to sift fact from fiction; no doubt the orphaned girls were chastely dressed as befitted their lot in life. Coco would say she had constantly tried to find ways around the clothing rules but was thwarted by the nuns in her attempts to wear clothes that would make her stand out from the other girls, with whom she never felt, nor acknowledged, any affinity.

Her 18th birthday signalled the end of Coco's time at the Abbey, because only girls who wanted to give themselves to the Lord were permitted to remain. But Coco had not quite escaped the religious orders, for she was then sent to the sisters of the Notre Dame school in Moulins, little more than 30kms from her Aunt Louise's house.

Notre Dame was a religious institution run by canonesses. Coco would say that she was admired here for her talent of singing and playing the organ, rather than the more likely fact being that she was sneered at as a peasant girl in hand-me-down clothes. But one thing that was true was that

ABOVE: Young Coco Chanel

she spent time at Notre Dame honing her budding talents as a seamstress.

Her only escape from an otherwise dreary grey life and its extension into one of servitude, which she was expected to enter, came from the romantic novels which she read so avidly. Those stories helped not only to sweeten her days under both nuns and canonesses, but also to provide the ground rules for the future Coco who was to emerge from the chrysalis of her unloved past, blinking into a glittering and colourful future.

Another motif Coco took from her childhood into adult life was the camellia flower. Coco would often recall that as a naive 13-year-old, her 'aunts' had taken her to Paris to see a play at the theatre. 'La Dame aux Camélias', from the novel of the same name by Alexandre Dumas. Coco saw her life being played out in front of her, she said in later life, but as that alone wasn't a sufficiently dramatic account, she 'sobbed her way through the entire performance', eliciting complaints from others in the audience.

Other versions of the theatre visit exist, of course, but the flower itself remained constant, indelibly imprinted into her past and present. It would flourish on embossed buttons, spread over shoes and bags, weave through her prints and its shape glow from pearls or diamonds. The white, odourless flower was omnipresent even in her home, surging from her chandeliers and the Chinese black ebony coromandel screens that she loved '... since I was 18 years old... I nearly fainted with joy when... I saw a coromandel for the first time'.

When her time at Notre Dame was over, she went to live with Aunt Louise and her aunt's husband, Paul Costier, and Adrienne, Louise's much younger sister who was just a year older than Coco. Both Coco and Adrienne soon found employment as seamstresses in a drapers shop in the town at the Rue de l'Horloge. They also assisted in the shop, selling clothes to the local gentry. Coco eventually left her aunt's home to take up residence in a room above the shop, working at the weekends, altering the uniforms of cavalry officers.

It was now that Coco's reality and fantasy began to fuse. The soldiers she had dreamed of and read about in novels truly did enter the girls' lives to take them around town and to concerts in the park in Moulins. Fascinated by the excitement the performers generated, by the life exploding around her, she determined to become part of it and get onto the stage herself, eventually succeeding and entertaining spectators with songs, one of which was titled, 'Qui qu'a vu Coco dans l'Trocadéro?' (Who has seen Coco on the Trocadero?), and another, 'Ko Ko Ri Ko'.

It is perhaps more likely that she began to be associated with the name Coco at this time, rather than having been given it by her father. But because the adult Coco refused to acknowledge that she had ever sung on stage, she had no choice but to come up with another explanation for the name. Thus the star was humbly reborn.

'My life didn't please me, so I created my life'

COCO CHANEL

FOLLOWING THE RULES 1904–1909

"It's not the appearance, it's the essence. It's not the money, it's the education. It's not the clothes, it's the class."

Coco's entrée into the glamorous salon life she would one day dominate came in 1904 when she was 21 and met the 24-year-old cavalry officer Étienne Balsan in Moulin.

Her relationship with Balsan showed her where her sexual allure, in tandem with ambition, could lead her. Throw in her previous shame and fear of a return to poverty and it was a combustible, potent mix.

Balsan was from an entirely different background than Coco, having been educated at an English boarding school. He had inherited a share of his father's successful textile business when he was just 18 but, having no desire to continue the family trade, he joined the Chasseurs d'Afrique in Algiers, a light cavalry regiment. He was stationed in Moulins while serving with the 10th Regiment of chasseurs à cheval, and crossed paths with Coco when they were both out and about the town, in places such as the Grand Café and La Rotonde where Coco sang.

The pair became lovers and Coco moved in with him, living as one of his mistresses, when Balsan bought a country estate, Royallieu in Compiègne to the north-east of Paris, after completing his military service.

No wilting wallflower, Coco had already come to understand the rules of the game that women needed to play in her era; use or be used. She was evidently prepared to play the game, despite being one among a string of women Balsan would entertain. Although Coco was a permanent 'accoutrement' at Royallieu, she shared him with his other main lover, the beautiful and renowned courtesan and actress Émilienne d'Alençon. The two women were quite different. Émilienne wore the finest fashions, while Coco was more often dressed plainly for horse-riding or in simple country suits with a straw boater, set very low on her head.

Quite how an impoverished girl from Paris slotted into the domestic arrangements at Royallieu can be gleaned neither from Étienne, who nobly never spoke about his time with Coco, nor from Coco herself. Her recollections were of a house where societal mores were dispensed with, indeed scorned, amongst the favoured wealthy, but in

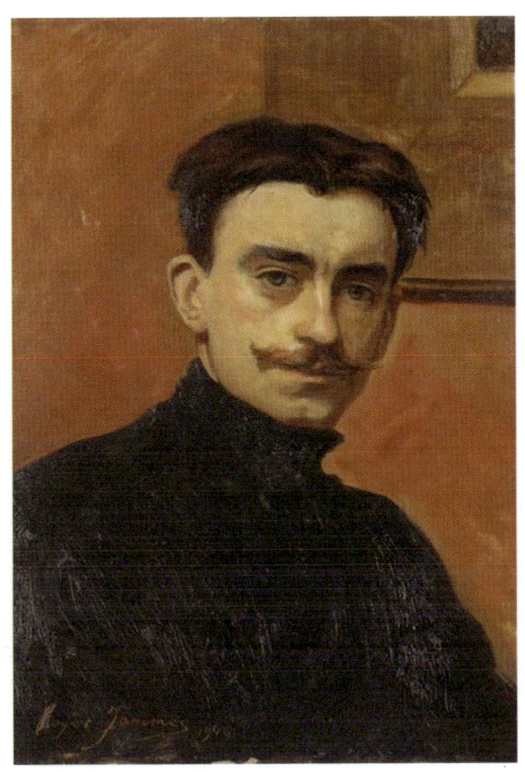

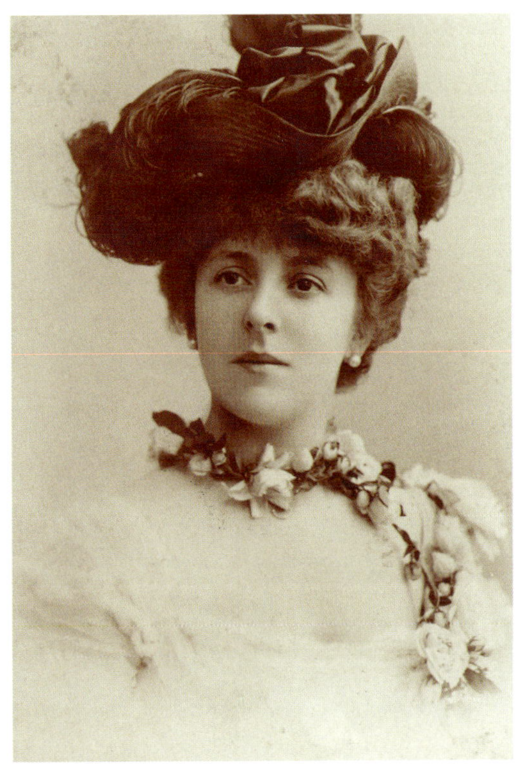

which others, servants and Coco included, were expected to know their place.

On occasions miserable, tear-stained and homesick, she is said to have told Émilienne, who seemingly not viewing her as a rival, became her friend, 'I'm neither happy nor unhappy – I'm hiding. It's like home here, only better'.

Coco stayed at Royallieu for six years, never likely to break into the glamorous salon on an equal footing with the other glitterati of the era. She appeared not to try to compete with the other guests in the fashion stakes, eschewing the elaborate costuming they loved in favour of her own androgynous invention, an 'exotic gamine' on the run, clothed in male neckties, straw boaters and plain white shirts.

Her perseverance with this twilight existence at Royallieu did eventually bring dividends however when she met a wealthy 28-year-old Englishman who would become central to her life and future success – Arthur 'Boy' Capel.

Later described as '... intellectual, politician, tycoon, polo-player and the dashing lover and sponsor of the fashion designer Coco Chanel', Boy Capel might seem an even more unlikely companion to the impoverished waif lingering in Royallieu than Étienne Balsan.

TOP LEFT: Étienne Balsan
TOP RIGHT: Émilienne d'Alençon

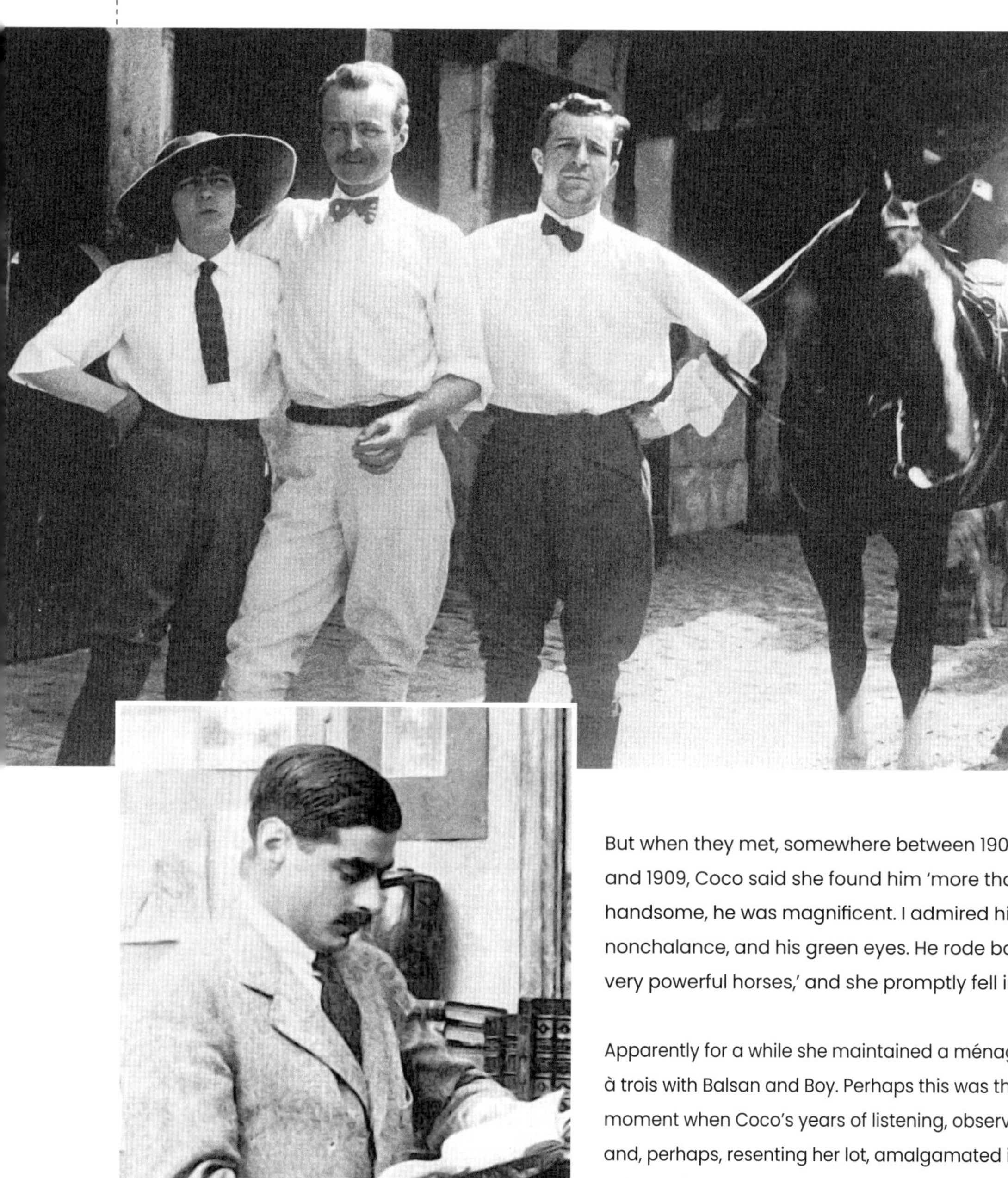

But when they met, somewhere between 1908 and 1909, Coco said she found him 'more than handsome, he was magnificent. I admired his nonchalance, and his green eyes. He rode bold and very powerful horses,' and she promptly fell in love.

Apparently for a while she maintained a ménage à trois with Balsan and Boy. Perhaps this was the moment when Coco's years of listening, observing and, perhaps, resenting her lot, amalgamated into a determination never again to allow herself to be mistreated by those with power and influence. Perhaps she went further and resolved to reverse the roles, so that she herself become the user, the abuser, possibly, of friendships and those with great influence.

ABOVE: Boy Capel
TOP: Gabrielle 'Coco' Chanel with Étienne Balsan (center) at Château de Royallieu

'Not to feel love is to feel rejected regardless of age'

COCO CHANEL

The emerging relationship was given the Coco treatment and consequently swathed in a mist drawn up out of her conjurer's hat, which masks the reality. Sometimes Coco would recall feeling confused, nonchalant about Boy's constant love dalliances. At other times anger and trepidation can be detected through her declarations of tolerance, and statements that 'there were tears and quarrels' as she, Boy and Balsan attempted to sort out their odd threesome. Or were they all confused? Did Balsan truly pledge to kill himself as the trio dined amicably together? While Coco was always clear that she had never loved Balsan, had she truly needed to ignore his pleas not to leave her as she hurriedly caught a train to Paris and Boy's arms? Had she honestly ever felt that she should kill herself and 'set them both free'?

Around this turning point in her progress to the top, Coco allows that convenient haze covering her past to dissipate gradually, as the realities become far more intriguing than a make-believe history could ever be.

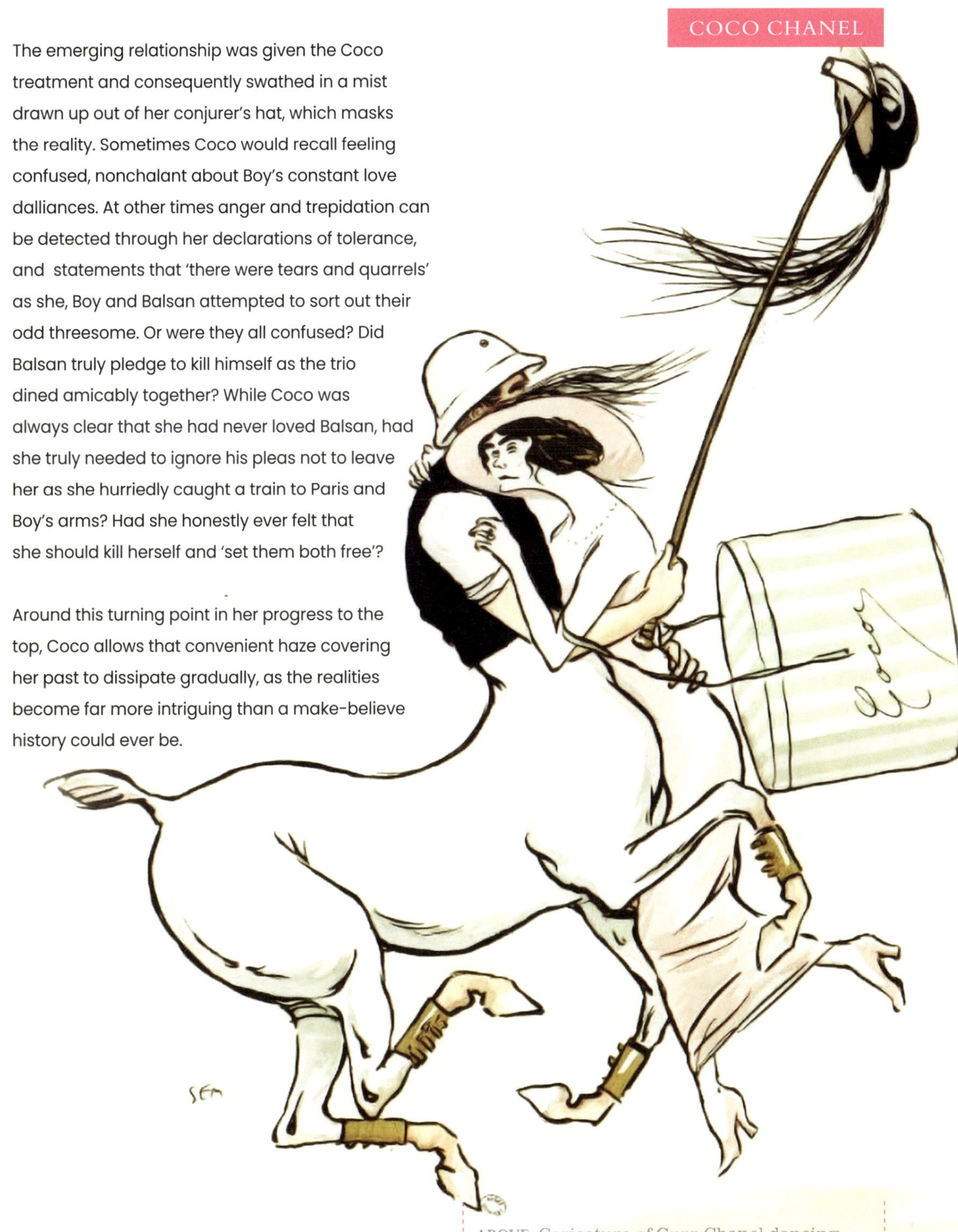

ABOVE: Caricature of Coco Chanel dancing with Boy Capel in "Tangoville sur mer"

SUCCESS IN PARIS 1909–1917

"How many cares one loses when one decides not to be something but to be someone."

Whatever the exact circumstances of her relationships with Balsan and Capel, and despite their other infidelities, both her lovers proved that they were prepared to go the extra mile for her, more so than if she were simply a pretty plaything, by supporting her business ambitions.

Coco had dreams of starting her own business selling her self-designed hats – she was already making them for the women she knew, some of whom were actresses and who appeared on stage and in periodicals wearing Coco's creations.

Having shared her affections, the two men now shared the burden of setting her up as a milliner, with Balsan putting his Parisian apartment at her disposal and Boy providing the funding.

As she looked back at the period, gratitude to them both seemed to take second place to Coco's expressed sense of unease about herself and just how the two men saw the future of their cosy trio. She worried too about Boy's inability to pass by a pretty face without becoming involved, despite her protestations to the contrary when she said; 'I couldn't have cared less whether he was unfaithful'.

Perhaps it was true. Perhaps Coco was too engrossed in her unexpected, new-found good fortune to worry for long about anything or anyone. Certainly now her simple, chic little hats, which sat so comfortably lightly on the wearer's head, began to make waves in society and cause consternation amongst established couturiers. The women who dressed to be noticed were now flocking to her door.

Soon Coco could no longer cope with the demand, working from the Paris apartment, and Boy's ever-open coffers funded her move to 21 Rue Cambon. With a door sign announcing 'Chanel Modes', Coco opened for business here on 1 January 1910.

Boy and Coco were glamour personified, and her ideas and business expanded exponentially. She advertised her designs by wearing them herself as often as possible as she moved around Paris, a slim and eye-catching figure. She summoned her sisters to work with her as demand grew.

RIGHT: Coco Chanel, circa 1910

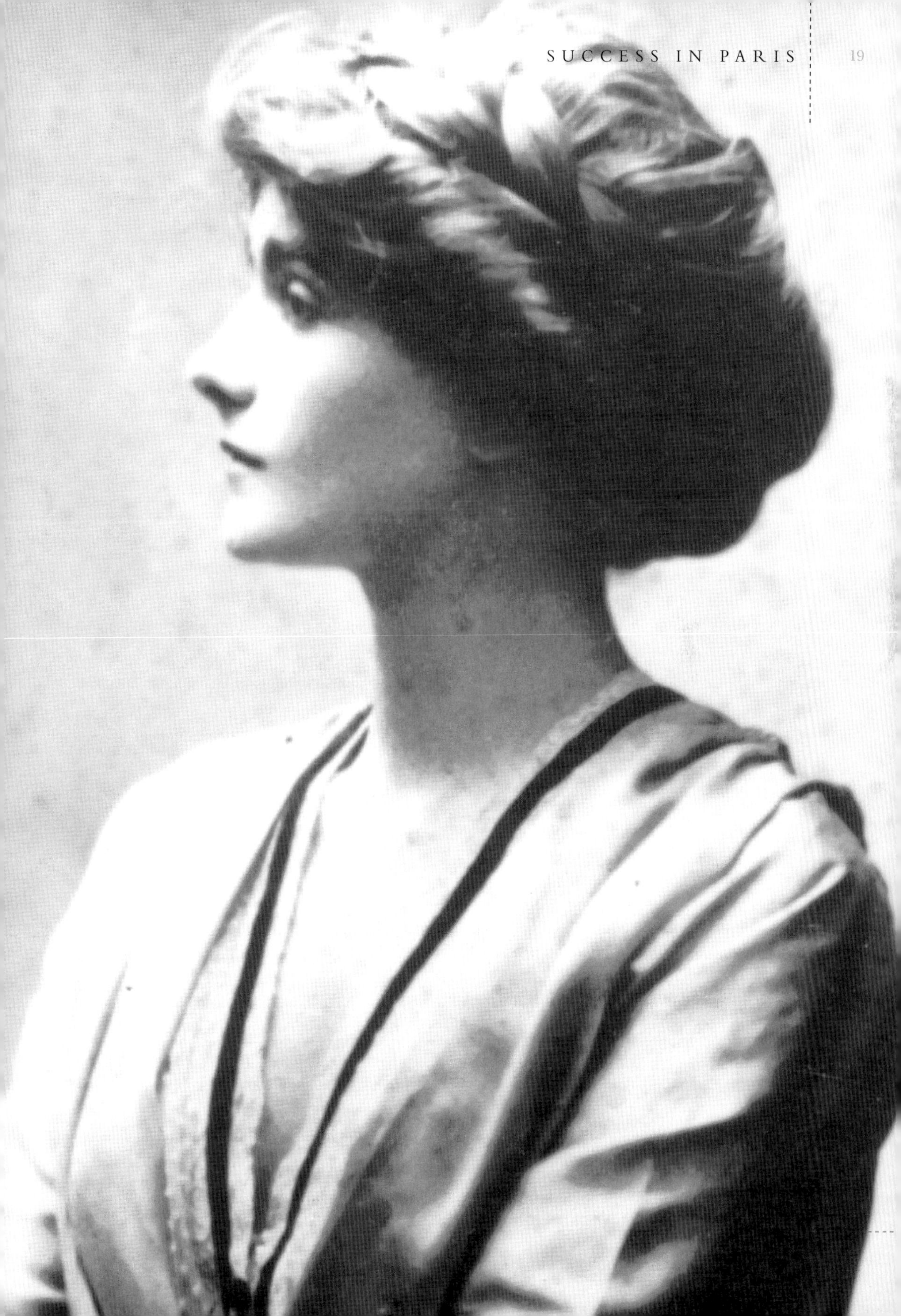

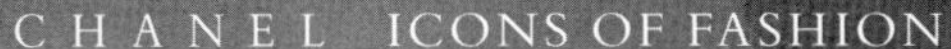

Clothes were added to her range, some inspired by Boy's blazers, others by the English sportswear and masculinity of his general attire. Her dreams were rapidly materialising. All, that is, except for one; Boy would never marry her, a fact she had long understood. 'He was my father, my brother, my entire family', she is quoted as saying later in life. If she is to be believed, the strain of the uncertainty of their relationship was ever present, despite her extraordinary success, and she remembered that she 'often fainted'.

But Boy loved her, whatever her version of their relationship, and he was adept at dealing with his fragile girlfriend. Indeed, she ascribed to him the power of healing her weak nerves, merely by his reassuring her that she could faint whenever and wherever, he would always be there. Which, of course, he was not. He had his own life to lead. Now as for evermore Coco would need to sustain herself emotionally. No lover ever asked her, or persuaded her, to marry.

Yet for all her success, it came as a shock to her when she discovered that what she had thought was a profitable enterprise was, in fact, being bankrolled by Boy Capel. The knowledge that she was still a kept woman made her even more determined to succeed in business and become truly independent. Already hard-headed and calculating, Coco improved her business skills and within 12 months she had turned things around so that she no longer needed Boy to prop up her business affairs. In later years she revelled in recalling that afterwards Boy told her, almost sadly, 'I thought I gave you a plaything; I gave you freedom'.

Now a woman of truly independent means, Coco could afford to send her nephew, André Palasse,

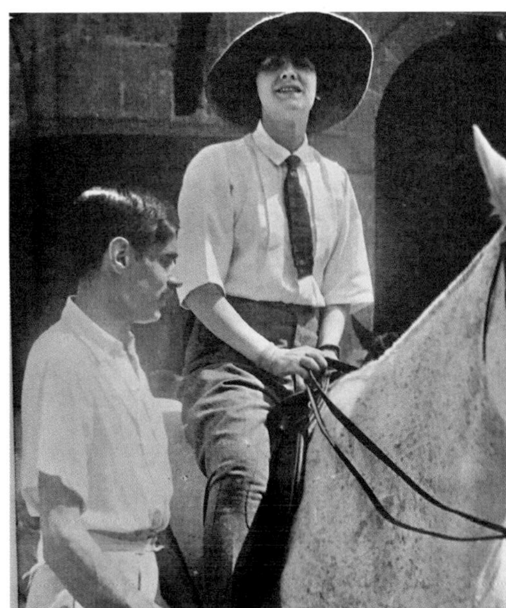

Julia's son – if indeed that's what he was – to boarding school in England. This was the perfect place for him to pick up a cut-glass English accent which would match the emotional and personal distancing required for Coco to maintain the construct that was her imaginary past.

Coco's new premises had opened at an inauspicious time; tension in Europe was increasing as the summer passed and there was talk of war. Boy became a captain in the British Army, and suggested that, to be on the safe side, Coco consider moving to Deauville on the northern French coast.

This she did, complete with her milliners, accepting Boy's help to fund the move. She rented a shop, named 'GABRIELLE CHANEL' between the casino and the fashionable Hotel Normandy. Deauville was a playground for the wealthy, so with European aristocrats and glamorous society women in plentiful supply, Coco set about winning them over.

ABOVE: Coco with Boy Capel, at his stables
LEFT: Coco Chanel, 1910

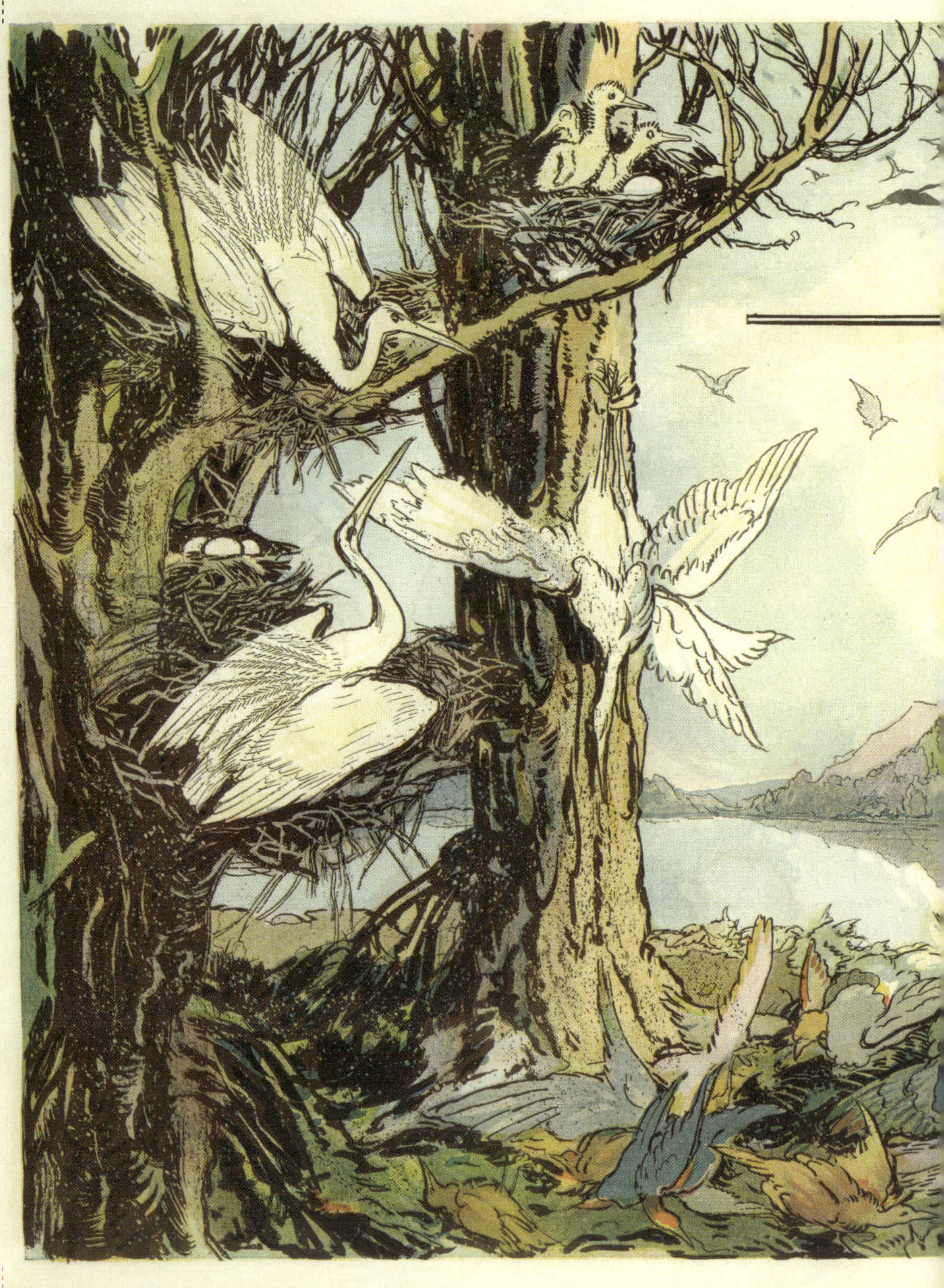

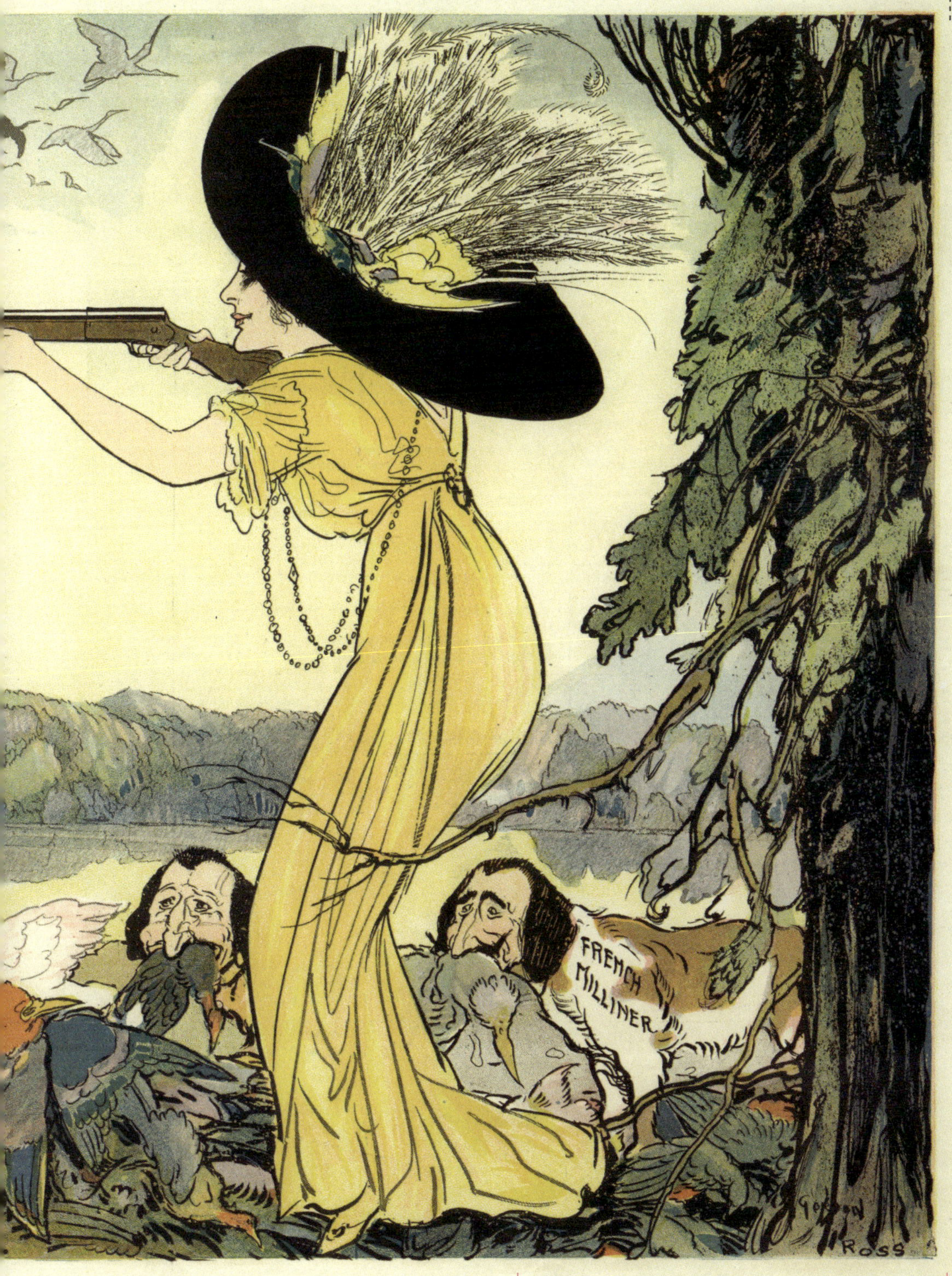

ABOVE: "The woman behind the gun" illustration shows a woman, believed to be Coco Chanel, 1911

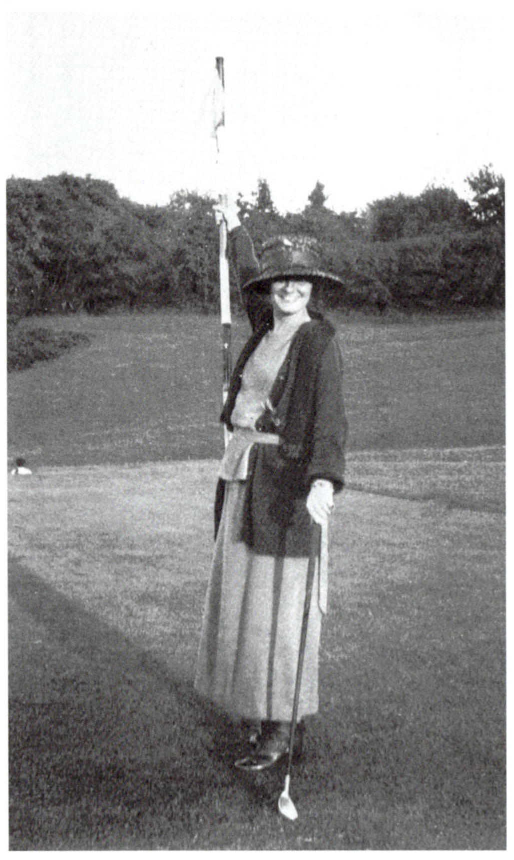

Inspired by her new surroundings, Coco was particularly taken with the beige colour of the wide Deauville beaches, and is quoted as mentioning that she liked beige, it was 'her' colour and one that would never go out of fashion. She gained fresh creative ideas from the maritime environment and the simplicity and utilitarian nature of the sailors' clothing, which reminded her of the clothing of the working people in whose milieu she had spent her young life.

So, true to her motto that one should be able to walk, dance and even ride in a well-cut dress – the corner-stone belief upon which rested her empire – she wasted no time in designing new outfits.

But as the First World War began and the Germans powered towards Paris, textiles came to be in short supply. Undaunted, Coco resorted to using something that was plentiful; jersey, a material which fishermen had used as underclothing. The rumour was that she had been handed a large polo jersey one day during a polo match and became aware of the elasticity and comfort it offered.

INSPIRED BY RIDING

Horse racing was a great attraction in Deauville, where Boy had stables. Having learned to ride during her time at Royallieu with Balsan, Coco was an accomplished horsewoman – she even bought a horse and rode races. Rather than sit side saddle, as most women did, Coco rode like a man, legs astride the horse's back.

Her hobby brought her into contact with others in the equestrian world; from wealthy riders to more humble stable lads and all their clothing – the flat hats, the caps, cravats, jodhpurs and jackets – gave her design inspiration. Even the padded under-saddle blankets fired her creativity, as the padding feature would reappear later in her famous padded handbags.

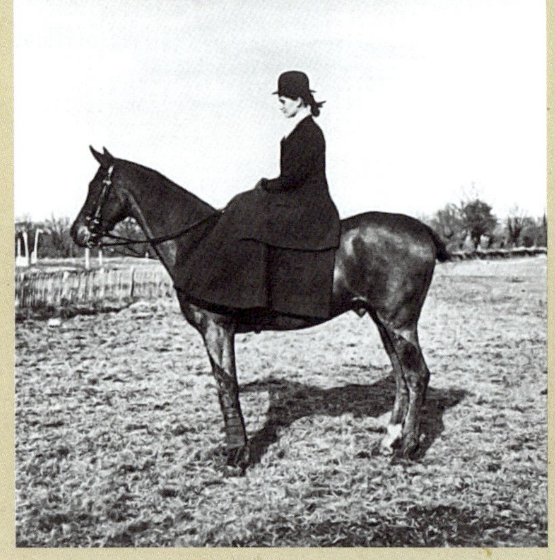

ABOVE: Coco Chanel, playing golf, circa1910

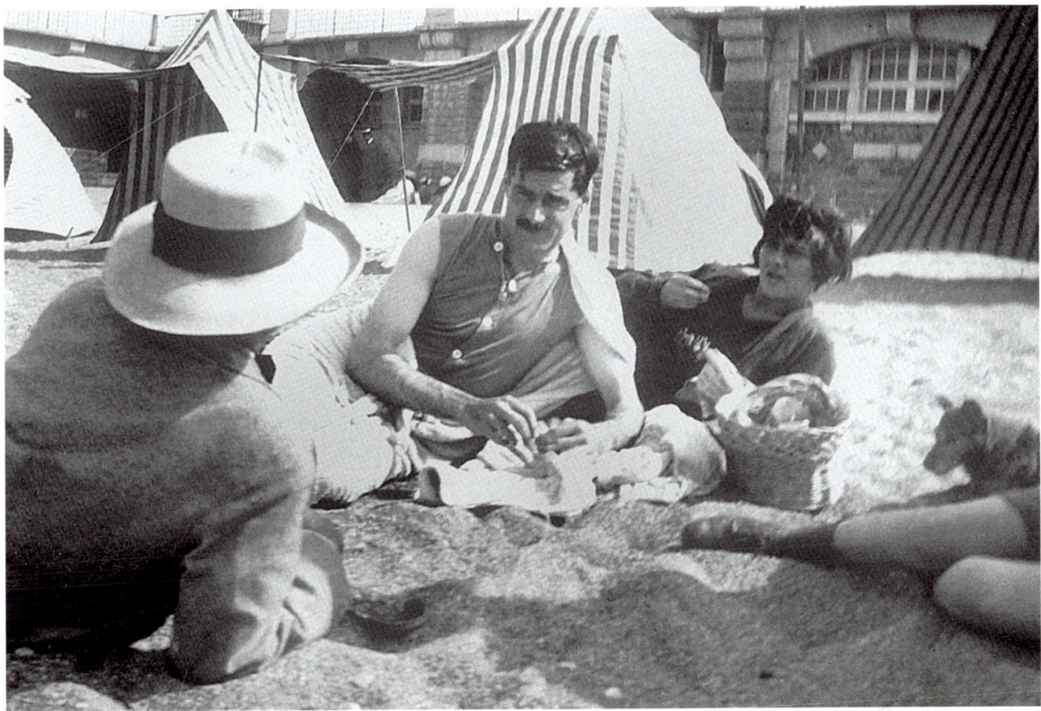

Her first iconic designs were about to be born.

Using jersey, she fashioned her androgynous collections; polo shirts, jodhpurs, short pleated skirts, and light and airy beach 'pyjamas'. It was also in Deauville, that Coco designed her famous Breton-striped marinière sweater, and sportswear such as yachting pants.

Sales were good, possibly because the ascetic, though still chic, jersey creations seemed appropriately humble enough to wear in wartime. Besides which, it was very practical for anyone engaged in war work, too. True to one of her later maxims, 'Since everything is in our heads, we had better not lose them', Coco was again proving to be expert at seizing opportunities whilst others took their foot off the accelerator.

While the business did well, Coco did worry about her brothers, Alphonse and Lucien, who were now in the French Army. But, ever positive, she wrote to them saying; 'Don't be too anxious, perhaps everything will finish sooner than we think'.

By the time the war did end in 1918, Coco emerged ahead of the pack. From her initial position of subservience, she had grown strong and developed a ruthless ambition that would brook no obstacles. She sensed that the idea of a woman being merely the over-ornamented armband of the male ego belonged to another age; one that she and many other women could not wait to see consigned to the history books.

And Coco Chanel was going to be at the forefront of the headlong charge into modernity.

ABOVE: Coco Chanel and her lover Arthur "Boy" Capel (centre) on the beach in Saint Jean de Luz in 1917

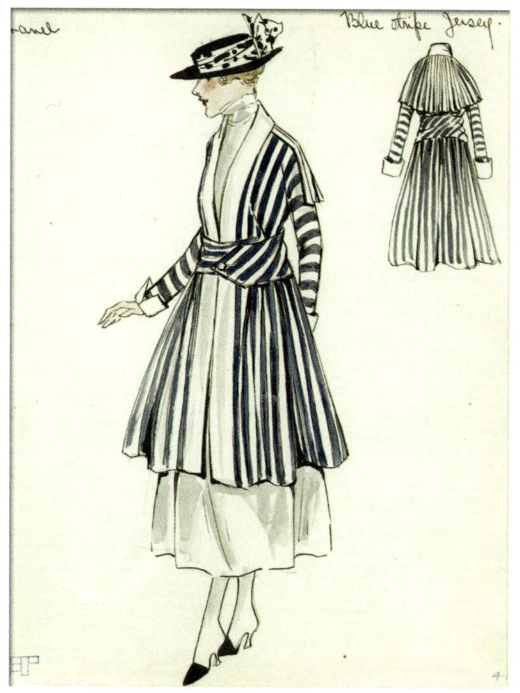
Chanel
Blue stripe Jersey.

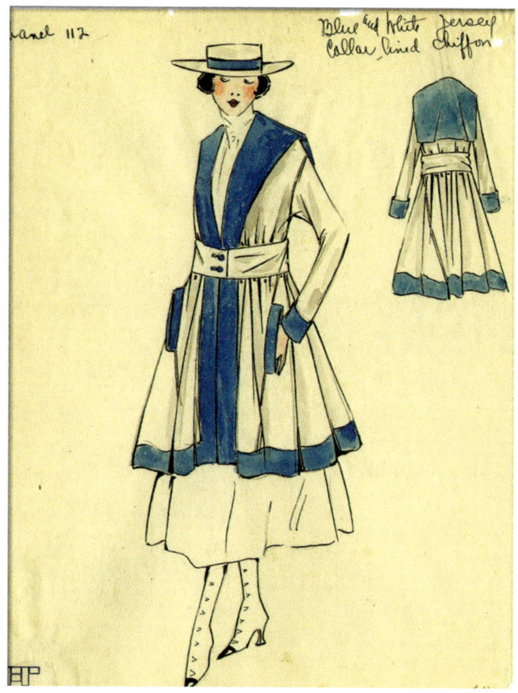
Chanel 112
Blue and White Jersey
Collar lined Chiffon

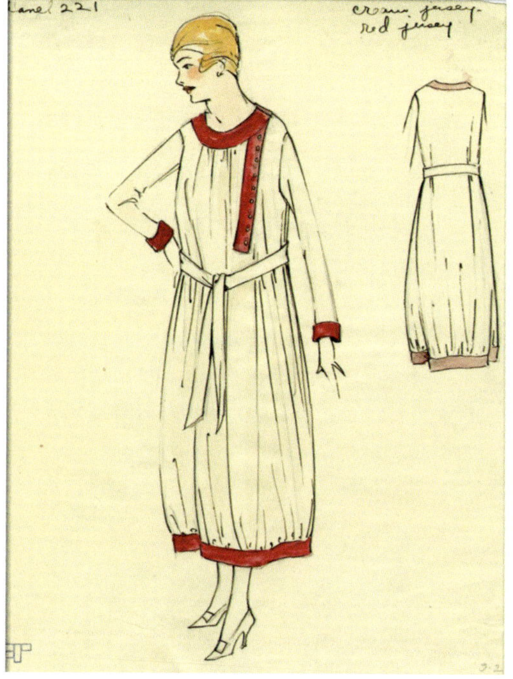
Chanel 221
cream jersey.
red jersey

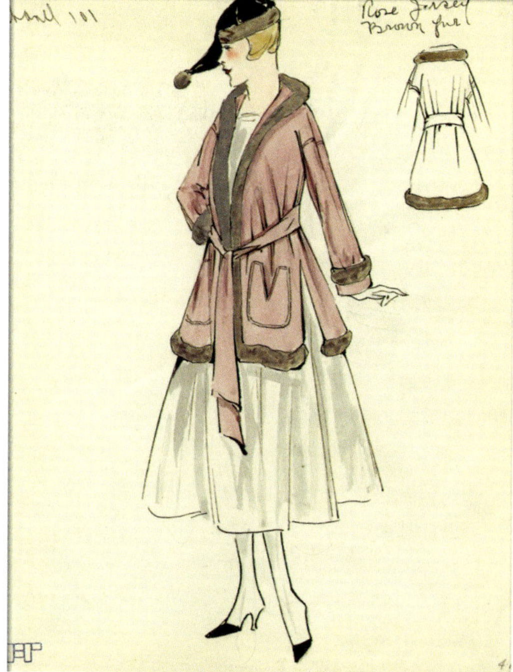
Chanel 101
Rose Jersey
Brown fur

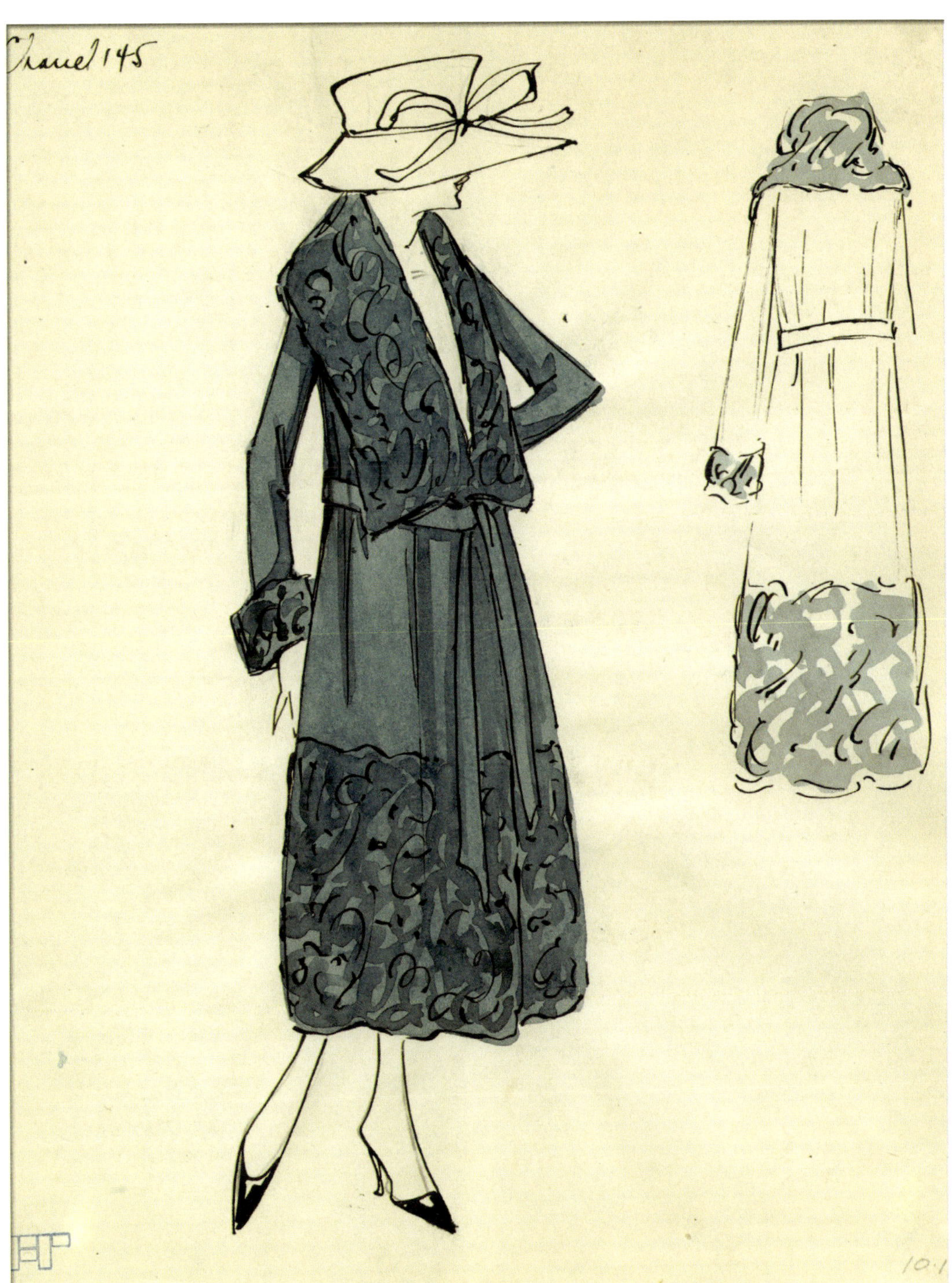

ABOVE & LEFT: Chanel designs, circa 1916-20

ONE MUST ALWAYS BE DIFFERENT 1918-1919

"Scheherazade is easy; a little black dress is difficult."

After the war ended, Coco might reasonably have assumed that life would settle down, whereas in fact she was to undergo some of the greatest shocks of her life.

First came the news that her long term, but errant, lover Boy Capel was to marry a wealthy and beautiful English aristocrat, Diana Wyndham, daughter of Thomas Lister, the 4th Baron Ribblesdale.

While Boy had frequently been unfaithful, Coco always found his other love affairs to be fleeting. For what she had never truly understood was that Boy had two important considerations – his need, as an Englishman, to maintain social etiquette and public reserve, and a desire to climb into the upper echelons of quintessentially English aristocratic society. Marriage to Diana would satisfy both those requirements.

For her part, Diana had been widowed during the

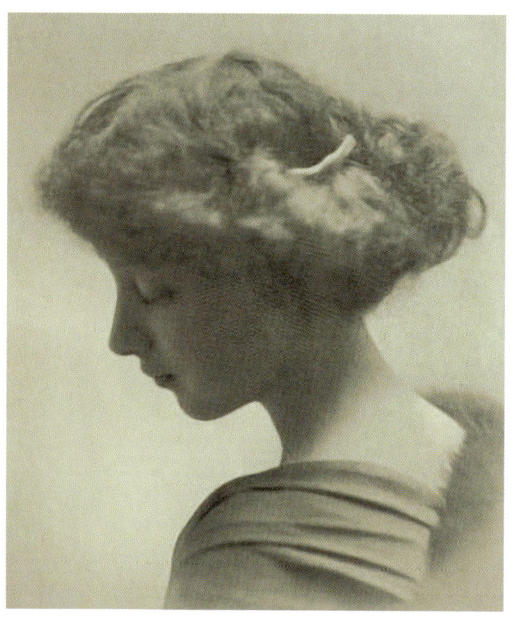

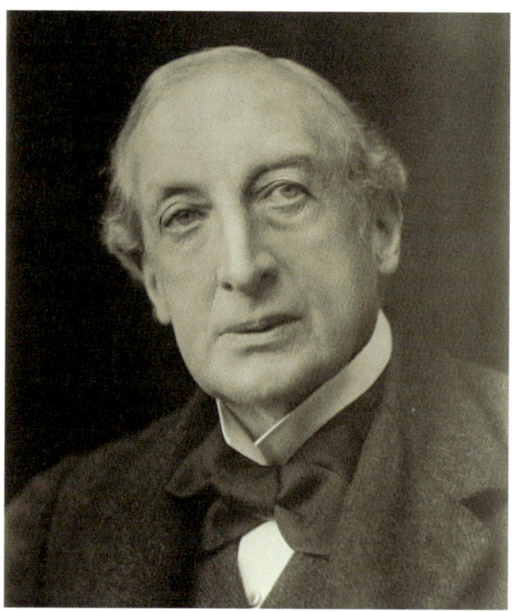

ABOVE LEFT: Diana Wyndham
ABOVE RIGHT: Thomas Lister, the 4th Baron Ribblesdale

war and wished to live the life of luxury that Boy could give her. It was a perfect society match.

The couple had met when Diana was driving Red Cross ambulances in France and Boy was working as a highly regarded French-British liaison officer and political secretary to the Allied War Council. (With the ear of both French premier Georges Clemenceau and Lloyd George.)

Boy's relationship with Diana was cemented by the arrival of a daughter, Ann Diana France Ayesha

'A woman who cuts her hair is about to change her life'

COCO CHANEL

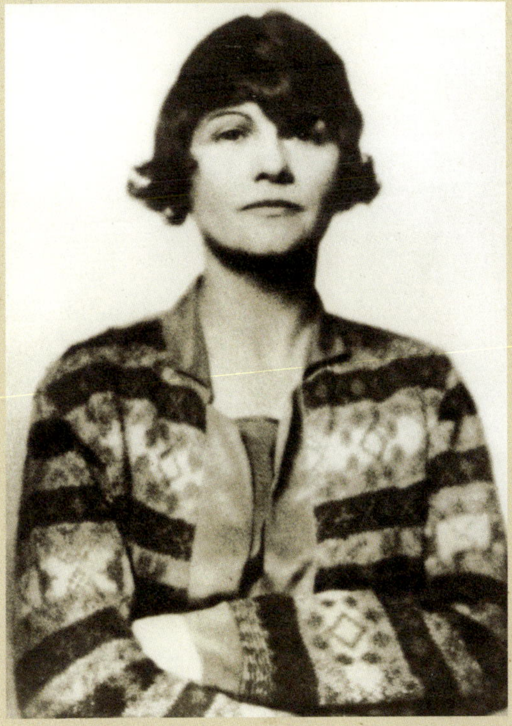

As the war ended Coco made a quite radical change to her appearance, chopping off her waist length hair to produce the classic 'bob' which would characterise her future look. She was highly influential in popularising the new style among 1920s flappers who associated the new look with their new freedoms. Plus it was impossible to dance the Charleston with Edwardian-style coils and chignons.

Of course her explanation of how the new hairstyle came about varied. Her hair shortened gradually, or all at once, depending on which memory she favoured at the time of telling. One story went that she was dressed in white ready to go to the opera when the gas boiler exploded, covering her in soot from head to toe – a fortuitous moment, that led to her snipping off her locks before pulling on a black dress. The impact at the opera was all that she could have wished for, with all eyes trained on this slight, black apparition. She had transformed herself, in her words, into 'the beauty of Paris'.

Serendipity had created a new creature, far removed from the festooned, bourgeois wife; the 'garçonne' had arrived.

From the day her bob made its debut, Coco would harbour a distaste for long hair, often mentioning that her father had hated the smell of hair. This was yet another incidence of her absent father directing her emotions.

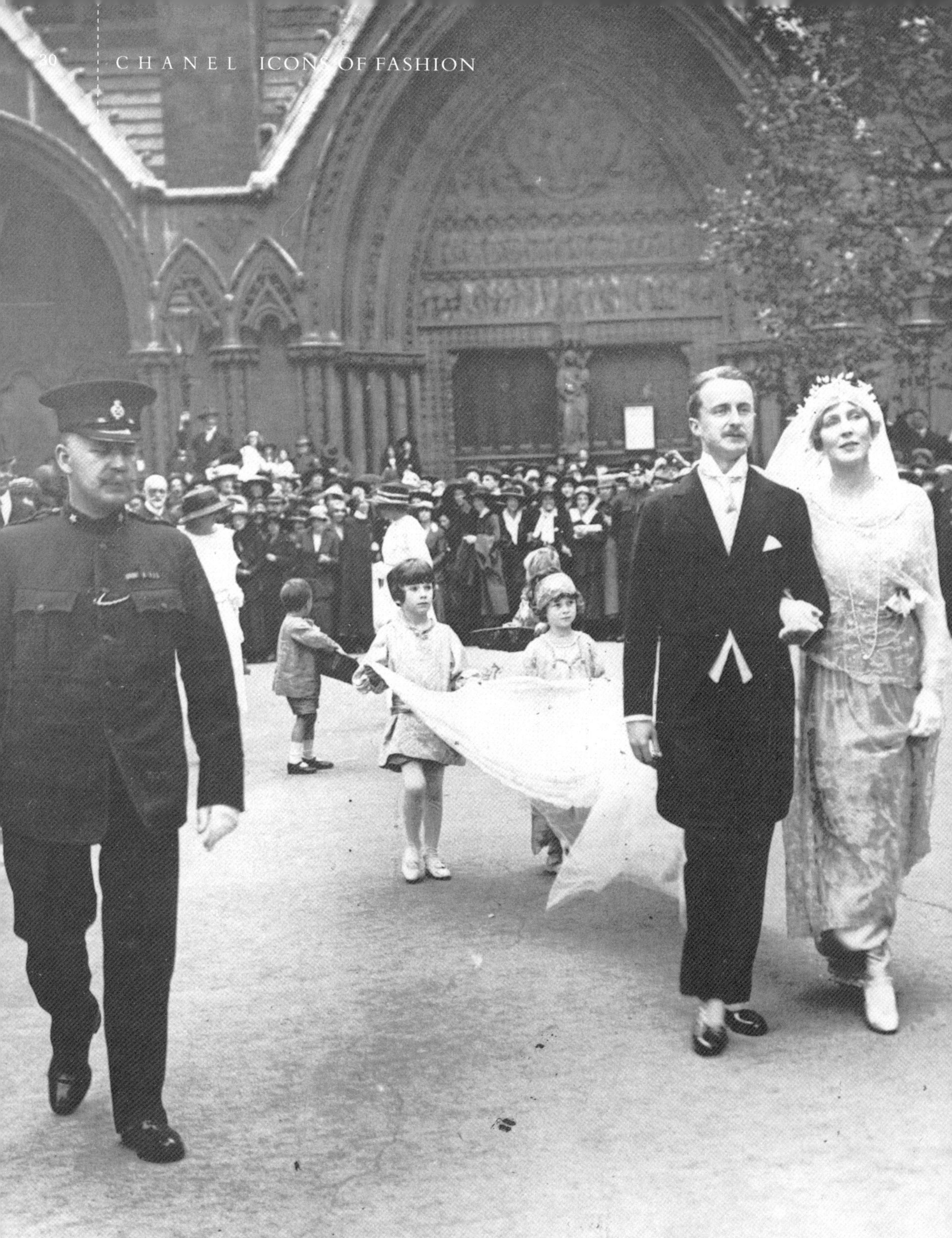

Capel, born in April 1919 and the couple married a few months later, on 3 August.

Confronted with a fait accompli, Coco had no choice but to accept the marriage. She maintained a passionate, unreciprocated desire for his attention and so was not prepared to relinquish the field, carrying on her affair with Boy after his marriage. The couple continued to meet in a rented villa in St. Cloud, just outside the French capital – their lives entwined as before, adding to the emotional entanglements of two people living outside of societal norms.

'Great loves, too, must be endured', Coco mused later in life.

She dealt with the aristocratic treachery in the only way she knew how – by staying silent. She did fire off an occasional broadside in Diana's direction; 'English women are possessive and cold. Men get bored with them,' she intoned.

Playing the long game worked out. Boy's marriage to Diana proved 'impossible', and 'a disaster'. The couple eventually stopped living together, and barely spoke.

Diana had become romantically involved with Alfred Duff Cooper, 1st Viscount Norwich, himself only just married to the actress Diana Manners. Neither of them cared much for the other, apparently; their subterfuge was mere diversion.

Who can say where this tumble of infidelities would have led them all. No one would ever know, for mere months after the marriage, Boy was killed in a car crash on 22 December 1919, whilst driving with his mechanic from Paris to Cannes.

Coco was informed of his death by a friend from her days at Royallieu who saw her face was crushed by pain. She cried without tears, before being driven down to the south of France, where she spent the rest of that appalling night in a chaise longue in the Palace Hotel where Boy's sister lived.

Boy was already in his coffin. Coco could not face the funeral but visited the scene of the accident where the car still lay. Finally, having touched the car, she broke down.

For Coco Chanel, the fact that she had lost the only, albeit inconstant, anchor in her personal life was incomprehensible. She had lost the love of her life and would rarely speak of his death again. What could she say? Her default defence of silence at least shielded her against public curiosity. Her only subsequent comment was that; 'Guilt is perhaps the most painful companion of death'.

In private, she would confess that she had lost everything. Maybe the religious teachings of Theosophy to which Boy had introduced her would help, as she retained the suggestion that 'Nothing dies, not even a grain of sand, so nothing is lost'. The sense that Boy was still a spiritual presence in her life, seemed to be the only way for her to move forward and away from constant, debilitating grief.

'Great loves, too, must be endured'

COCO CHANEL

LEFT: The marriage of British politician Alfred Duff Cooper, 1st Viscount Norwich, to Lady Diana Manners, 1919

ANTOINETTE CHANEL

In November 1919 Coco also lost the services of her younger sister Antoinette who had worked for her since 1910, during the early days of the business at 21 Rue Cambon.

Having married a Canadian airman called Oscar Fleming, Antoinette went to live in his home country, in Windsor, Essex, Ontario.

Sadly Antoinette's happiness did not last long. She is known to have gone to Buenos Aires in Argentina in 1921. There, her life becomes more obscure; she may have died from Spanish flu in 1921, or she committed suicide one year later from a drug overdose.

Coco rarely spoke of her younger sister again.

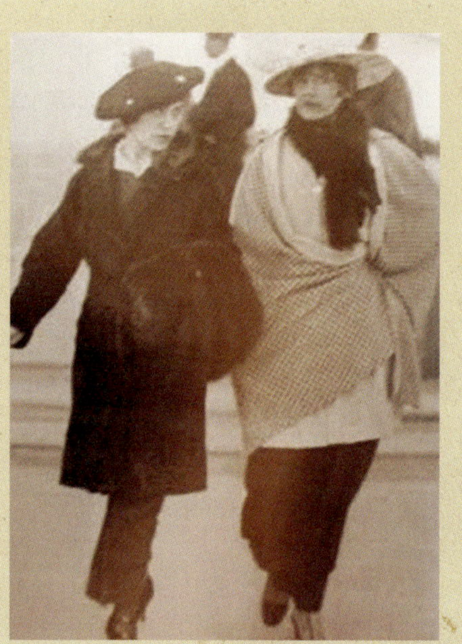

Coco herself would never marry. Perhaps she had been too wounded by the emotional damage visited upon her because of her own humble past, and the shock of Boy's death. Later, with hindsight, she would wisely remark: 'Don't spend time beating on a wall, hoping to transform it into a door'. Boy Capel certainly did not; sadly, passionate Coco could not follow his example.

Boy did prove that Coco was more than just another lover to him by leaving her a £40,000 bequest in his will. It was the last act of affection he could show towards her.

In reality, Coco had not 'lost everything'; except in the sense, perhaps, that she felt drained of any emotional attachment to anyone or anything.

But she was still Coco Chanel, immensely successful couturière. And the bequest from Boy enabled her to expand her growing empire even further and even add a villa for herself in Garche, just to the west of Paris. Her new mansion called Bel Respiro, was repainted in her favourite beige with black shutters. Later, she would lend its name to one of her perfumes.

As for Diana Capel, having remarried to the 14th Earl of Westmorland in 1923, she remained a faithful customer for Chanel's clothing – and, it would seem, retained a tenuous friendship with her former rival – although, true to her nature, Coco never disclosed the inner workings of this odd relationship.

RIGHT: Coco Chanel, circa 1920

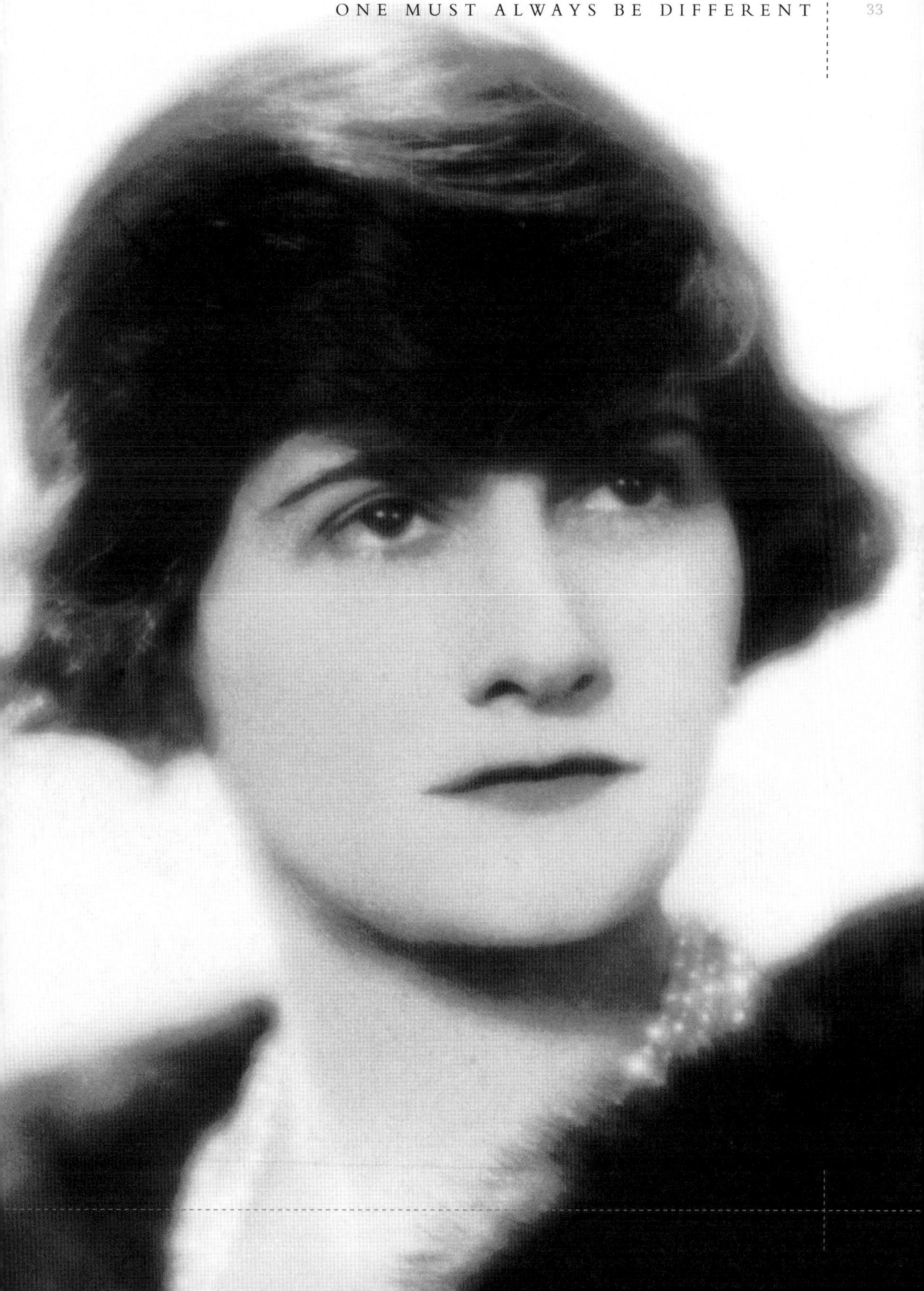

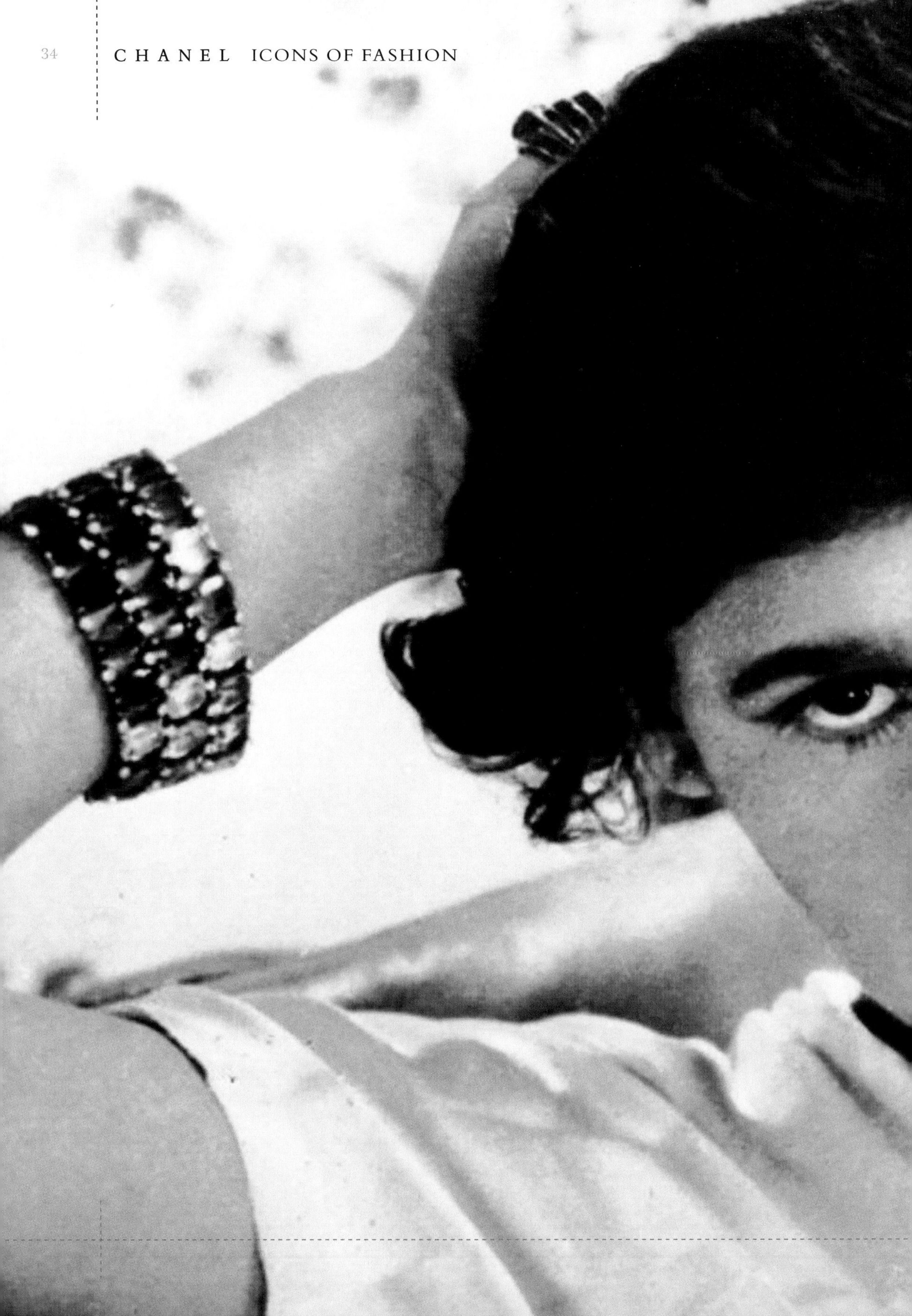

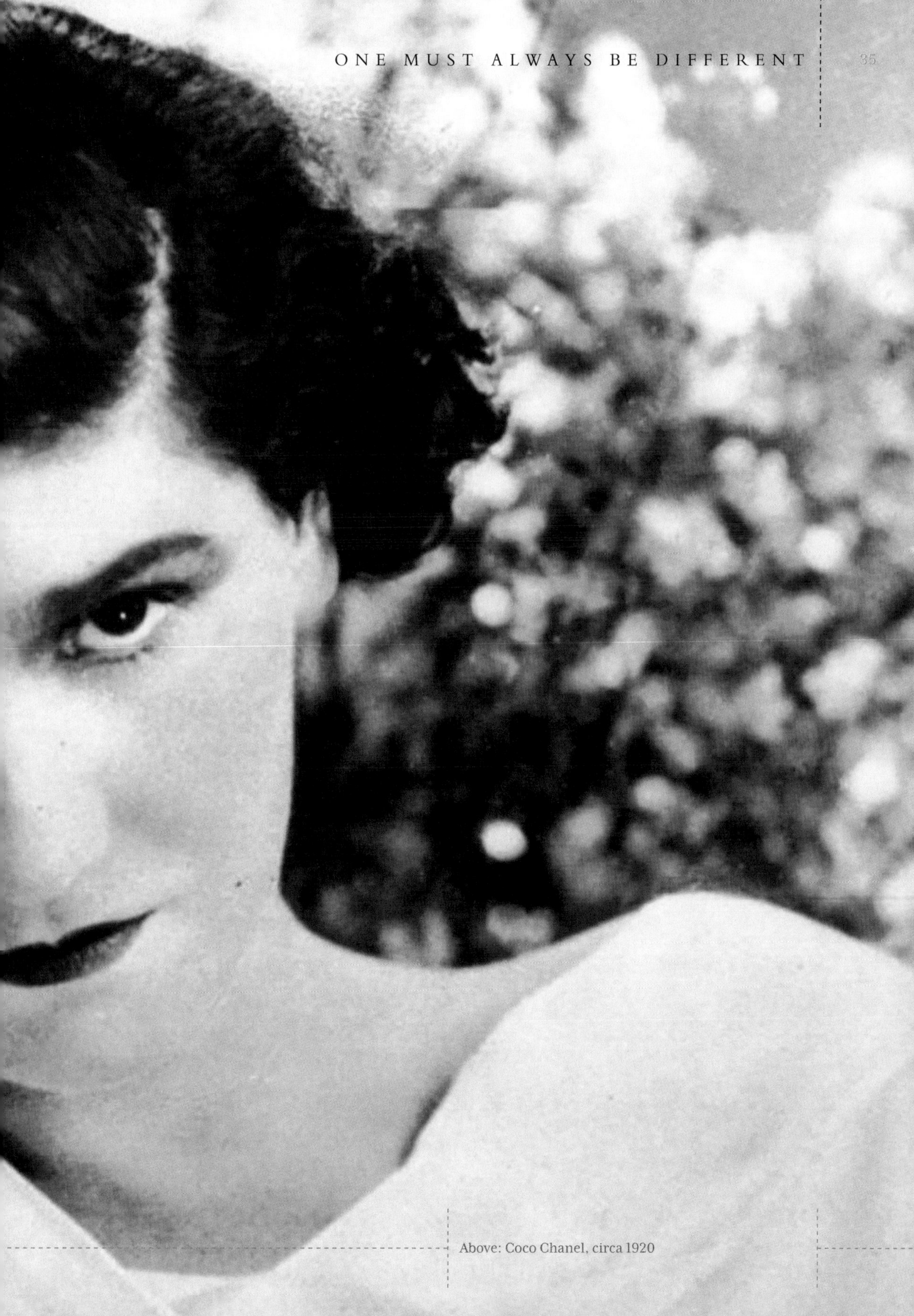

Above: Coco Chanel, circa 1920

THE RUSSIANS ARE COMING 1920

"My friends, there are no friends."

Still grieving the loss of Boy Capel, Coco turned to her friend Misia Sert for support. Misia was a legendary Parisian personality, a patron and friend of numerous artists and intellectual émigrés who had escaped the Russian Revolution.

Cigarette in hand, Coco was drawn into the glorious Slavic vortex of Misia's 1920s Paris salon, little dreaming of the effect that Russian influence would later come to have on her designs.

The two women had first met at a dinner party in 1917 and felt an immediate affinity. 'She seemed to me gifted with infinite grace', Misia said of Coco. 'When I admired her ravishing fur, she put it on my shoulders, saying with charming spontaneity she would be only too happy to give it to me.'

Coco's 'genius, lethal wit, sarcasm and maniacal destructiveness, which intrigued and appalled everyone', seemed to attract Misia, who perhaps recognised a kindred spirit. Both women had passed through emotional suffering and forged their own inimitable paths in life. They remained great friends until Misia's death in 1950.

It was through Misia that Coco met two men who would prove very significant to her, ballet impresario Sergei Diaghilev and composer Igor Stravinsky.

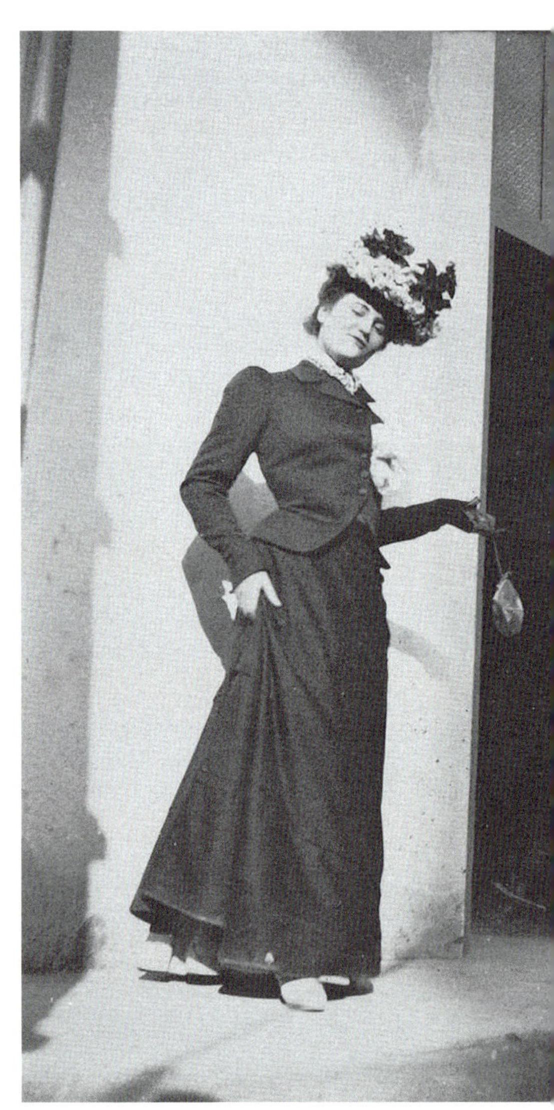

ABOVE: Misia Sert

MISIA SERT

Described as having a 'legendary pair of legs and a bosom that kept strong men awake at night', Misia Sert was married to the Spanish painter Josep Maria Sert i Badia, her third husband, when she hosted her artistic salon in 1920s Paris.

Born Maria Zofia Olga Zenajda Godebska in Russia in 1872, she was the daughter of a Polish sculptor. After attending boarding school in Belgium, where she was taught piano by renowned French composer Gabriel Fauré, she arrived in Paris, where she achieved a central position in the intellectual and artistic world with an adoring entourage at her feet. She was a close friend and financial supporter of the Russian ballet impresario Serge Diaghilev and a muse and model to many of the most famous artists, writers and composers of the time, having been painted by Bonnard, Lautrec and Renoir, and inspired writings from Proust, poetry from Mallarmé and music from Ravel and Debussy.

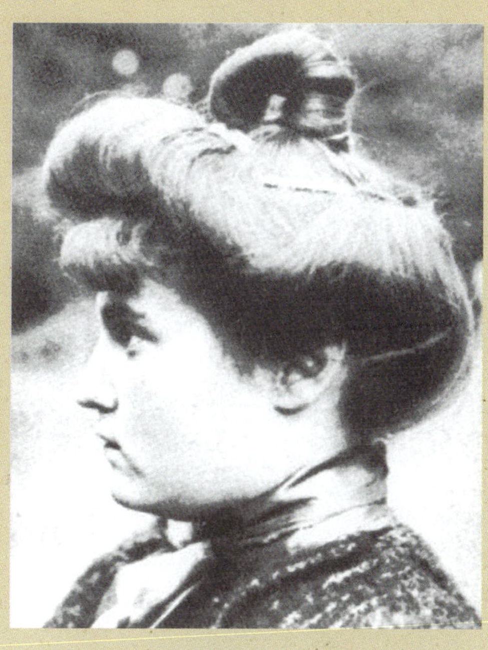

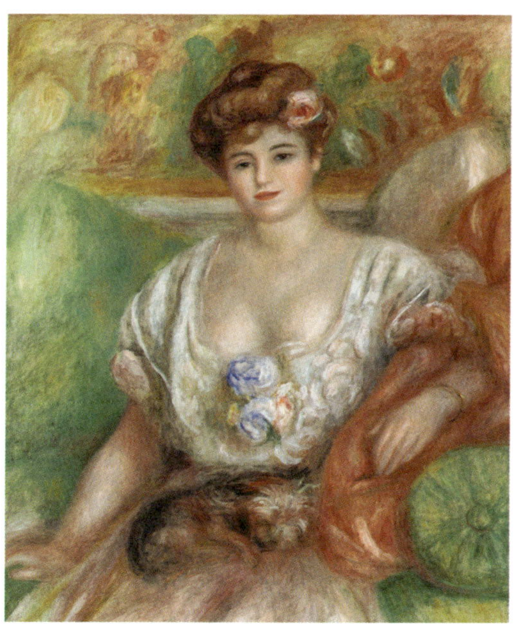

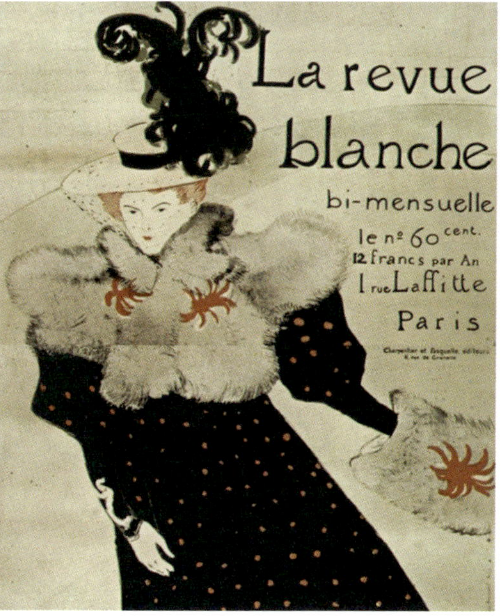

ABOVE LEFT: Misia Sert by Pierre-Auguste Renoir
ABOVE RIGHT: Cover of La Revue Blanche: Misia Sert by Henri Toulouse-Lautrec

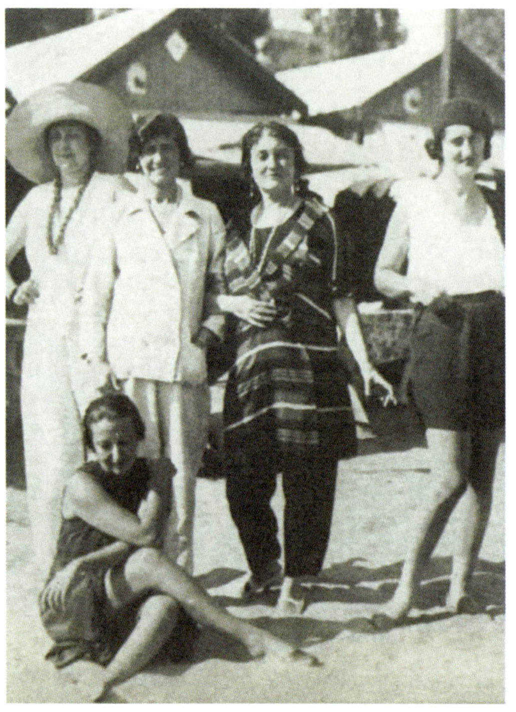

Diaghilev was the creator of the famous Ballet Russes which brought Vaslav Nijinsky and prima ballerinas Tamara Karsavina and Anna Pavlova to international fame. Coco came to share Misia's huge admiration for Diaghilev and joined her in coming to his financial rescue on several occasions.

She is said to have injected 300,000 francs anonymously into Diaghilev's enterprise to ensure the production of The Rite of Spring. This ballet, composed by Igor Stravinsky, the foremost modernist composer of his era, had caused a sensation with the avant-garde nature of its music and choreography at its infamous premiere in Paris in 1913, which Coco had attended.

Stravinsky, another Russian exile, had been living in Switzerland, but arrived in Paris, chronically short of money, to resume his partnership with Diaghilev as

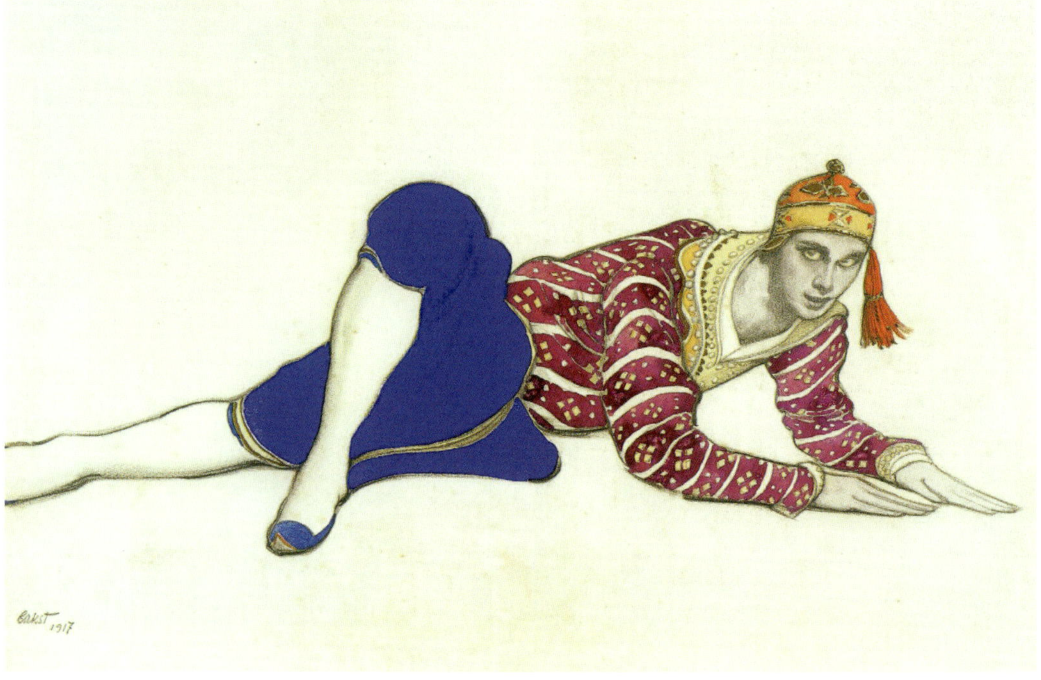

TOP: Coco with Misia Sert in Venice, 1923
ABOVE: Vaslav Nijinsky as the Chinese Dancer in Les Orientales. 1917

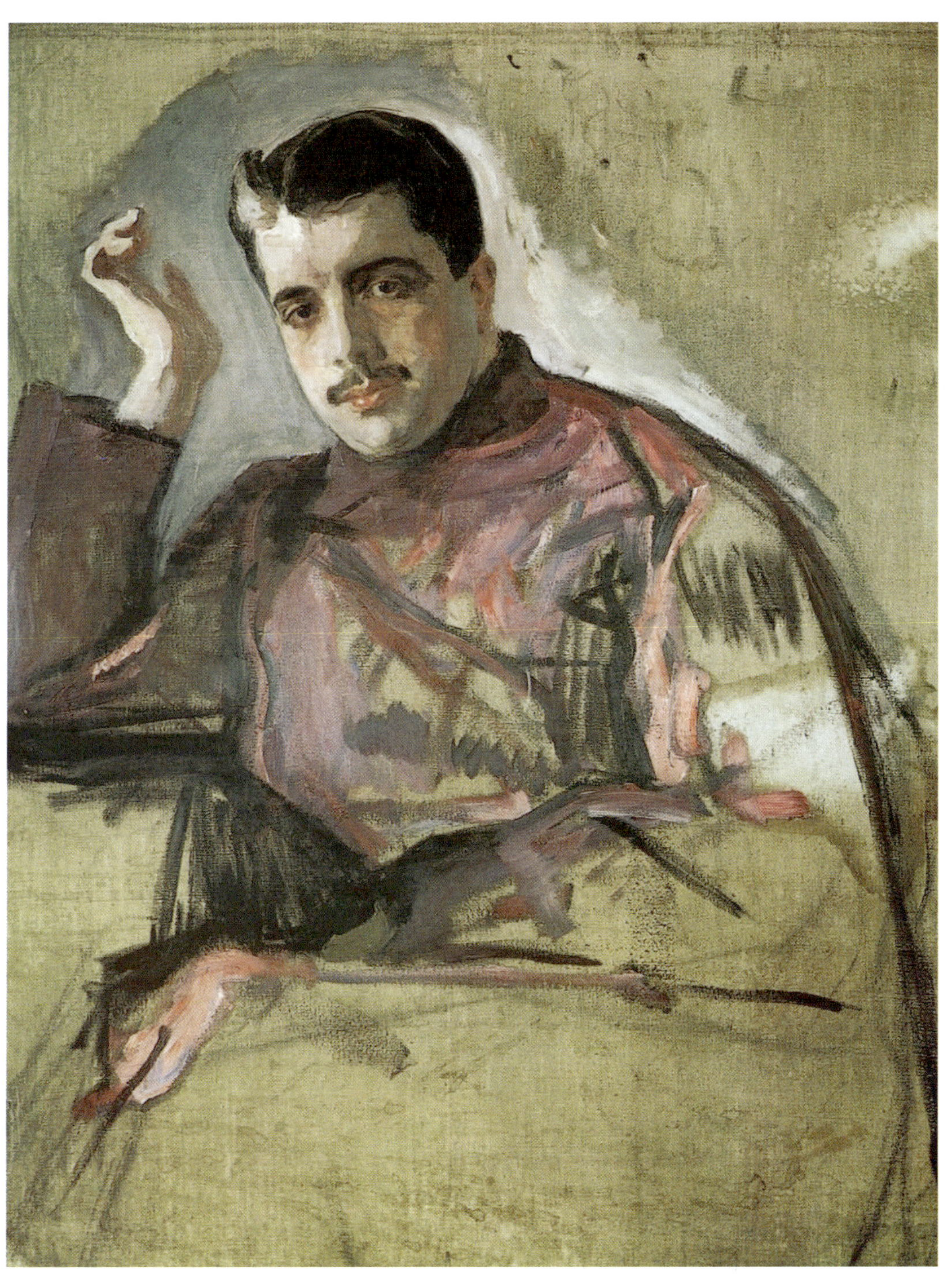

ABOVE: Portrait of Sergei Diaghilev

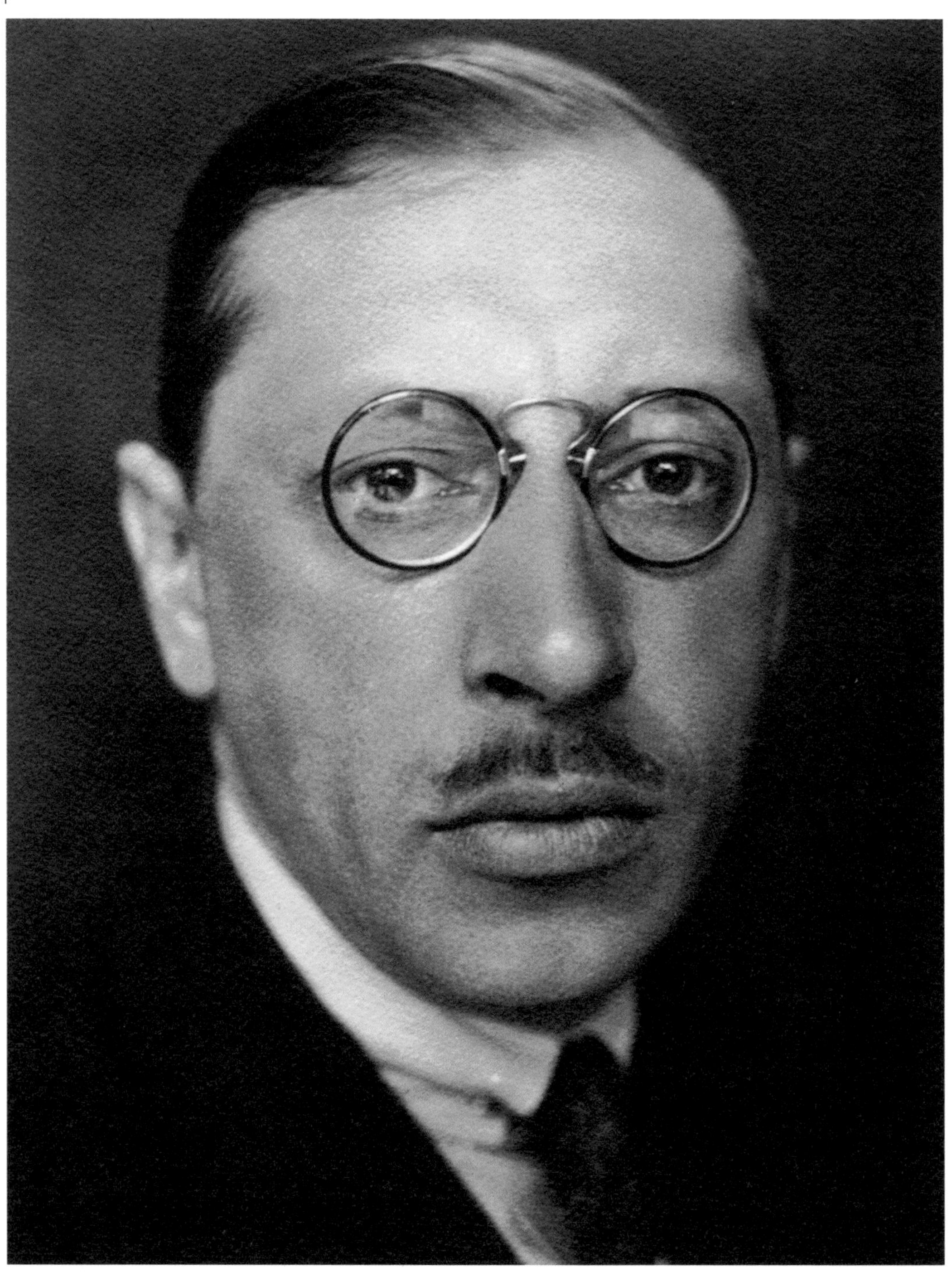

ABOVE: Igor Stravinsky, 1920

they attempted to mount another production of their ballet. Diaghilev had introduced Stravinsky to Coco in the spring of 1920, and when she learned that the composer and his family needed somewhere to live she offered them her Bel Respiro apartment until they found a suitable home of their own.

So it was that a mentally strained Stravinsky, his wife Katherina and their four children arrived in Paris in September 1920. His time in the French capital proved musically fruitful. Despite his ongoing mental stress, he completed the modernist masterpiece Symphonies pour instruments à vent, and also Les cinq doigt, a piano piece whose title imbued it with symbolic significance. The number cinq (five) set tongues wagging, because Stravinsky was now rumoured to be having an affair with Coco who had famously chosen 'five' as her lucky number, believing it to signify the pure embodiment of a thing, its spirit, its mystic meaning. She would often present her dress collections on 5 May, the fifth day of the fifth month. The number would of course go on to make her very wealthy when she chose it as the name for her perfume.

The evidence for an affair with Stravinsky is circumstantial. Katherina Stravinsky was suffering from consumption during her stay at Bel Respiro, leaving her husband free to roam with Coco in the large estate. But for what followed next, if anything, there is only Coco's account, which hints that they indulged their urges. In her retelling, she said that Stravinsky found her attractive and initiated the affair. For her part, she found him, '… very Russian in his ways, with the look of a clerk in a Chekhov short story. A small moustache beneath a large rat-like nose. He was young and shy…' This coming together of two of the most radical creatives in their individual fields seemed likely, especially when coupled with the knowledge that Stravinsky had a reputation as a philanderer and Coco was never averse to a little romance.

However, Stravinsky's second wife, the Russian-American dancer Vera de Bosset whom he married in 1940, maintained ever afterwards that no such love triangle as Stravinsky, Coco and Katherina had ever existed. Whatever form the 'dalliance' had taken there was evidently no lasting upset as Stravinsky would continue to benefit from Coco's largesse in the future.

'One must not let oneself be forgotten, one must stay on the toboggan. The toboggan is what people who are talked about ride on. One must get a front seat and not let oneself be put out of it'

COCO CHANEL

MEDUSA RISING
1920-1924

"A women who doesn't wear perfume has no future."

The inter-war years were good for Coco, personally and professionally.

The early 1920s was a time of prosperity and decadence, when young women, known as flappers, were charging the barriers and gaining economic, political and sexual freedoms as never before. It was the decade of the jazz age and came to be known as the Roaring Twenties as women got into top gear, with Coco to the fore.

Her new creations proved incredibly popular with customers keen to adopt her style and propelled her to international fame and enormous wealth.

And she had found a new lover; an expatriate aristocrat, the Grand Duke Dmitri Pavlovich, a first cousin to Prince Philip, Duke of Edinburgh, husband of the Queen of England and also to Tsar Nicholas II of Russia. Although their affair would be brief, it would have a lasting influence on her future designs.

She had become fleetingly acquainted with Dmitri back in 1916 when she opened a shop in Biarritz, and now met him again in Paris where he had lived since escaping the Russian Revolution. He was lucky to get away due to his being a co-conspirator in the plot to assassinate Rasputin, as well as being so closely related to the Tsar.

Although he was now impoverished, he was sufficiently imbued with an air of scandal to pique Coco's interest and the couple spent a happy summer together visiting Monte Carlo and then Arcachon on the west coast of France.

The passion was evidently burnt out by the end of season, with Coco commenting; 'Tall, handsome, superb these Russians are. And behind that is nothing: hollowness and vodka'.

Nonetheless, the connection with Dmitri had two major impacts on Coco's life. The first was that Coco became aware of the rich seam of motifs and designs embedded in the Slavic and Byzantine culture of Russia. Dmitri had managed to bring a bag of jewels from Russia, and presented Coco with many of the pieces, so that she was often seen out and about wearing 'a mass of pearls'. She was evidently inspired by their Byzantine origins which came to infuse the design of some of her own jewellery later and could also be seen in her clothing collections.

The second legacy of Coco's relationship with the Duke Dimitri was the introduction of a new product

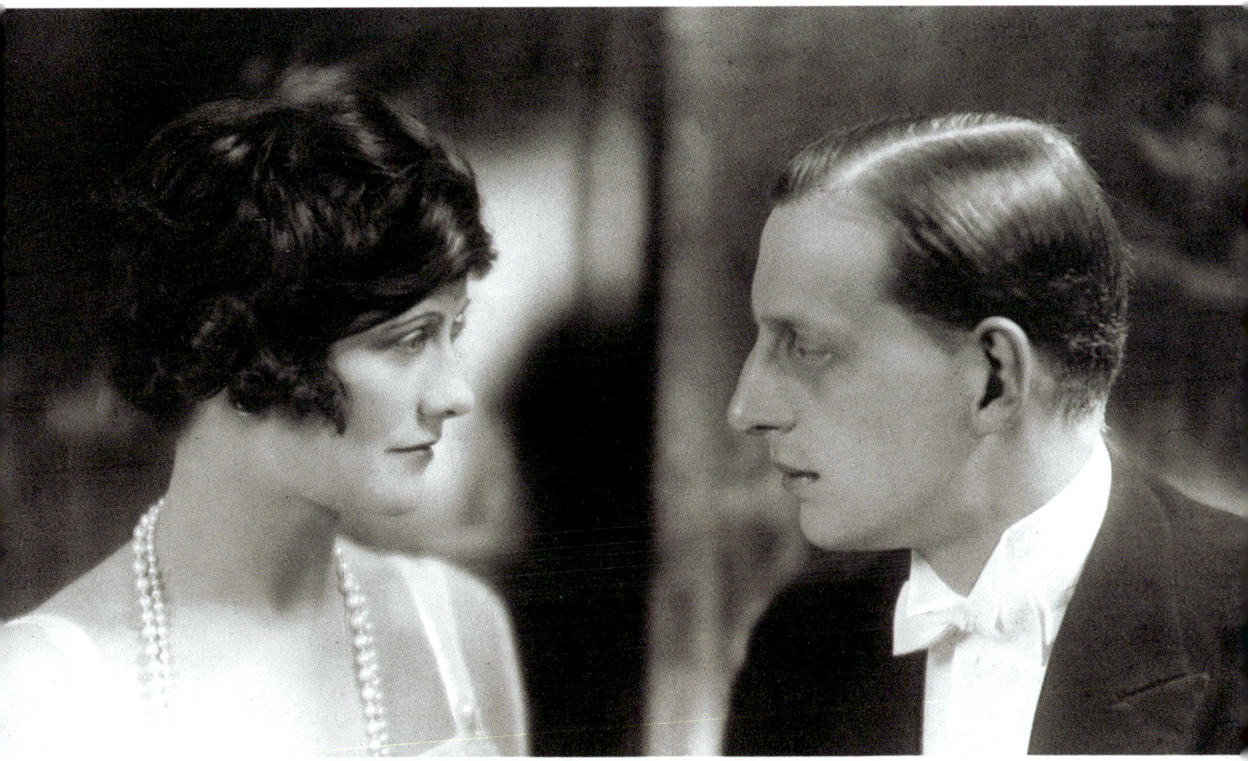

A MODEL CHOICE

Coco usually chose a particular type of girl to model her Byzantine-influenced clothing collections. Generally slim and ethereal, with a Slavic look and high cheekbones, the girls would usually be well-connected – none more so than Mary Eristavi who became one of Coco's most famous models.

A former favourite of the Russian Imperial Court, Mary was famed for her beauty and was reputed to have entranced Tsar Nicholas II who said to her: 'It is a sin, princess, to be so beautiful'.

It pleased Coco to have a 'princess' working for her.

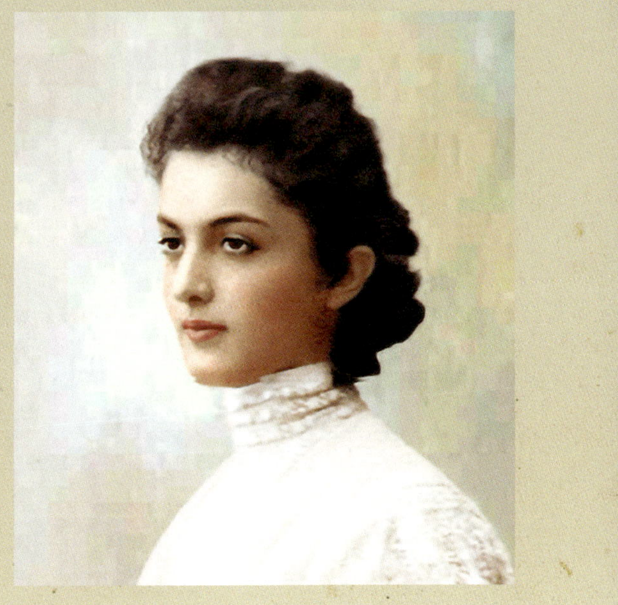

ABOVE: Mary Eristavi
TOP: Coco with Dmitri Pavlovich, 1920s

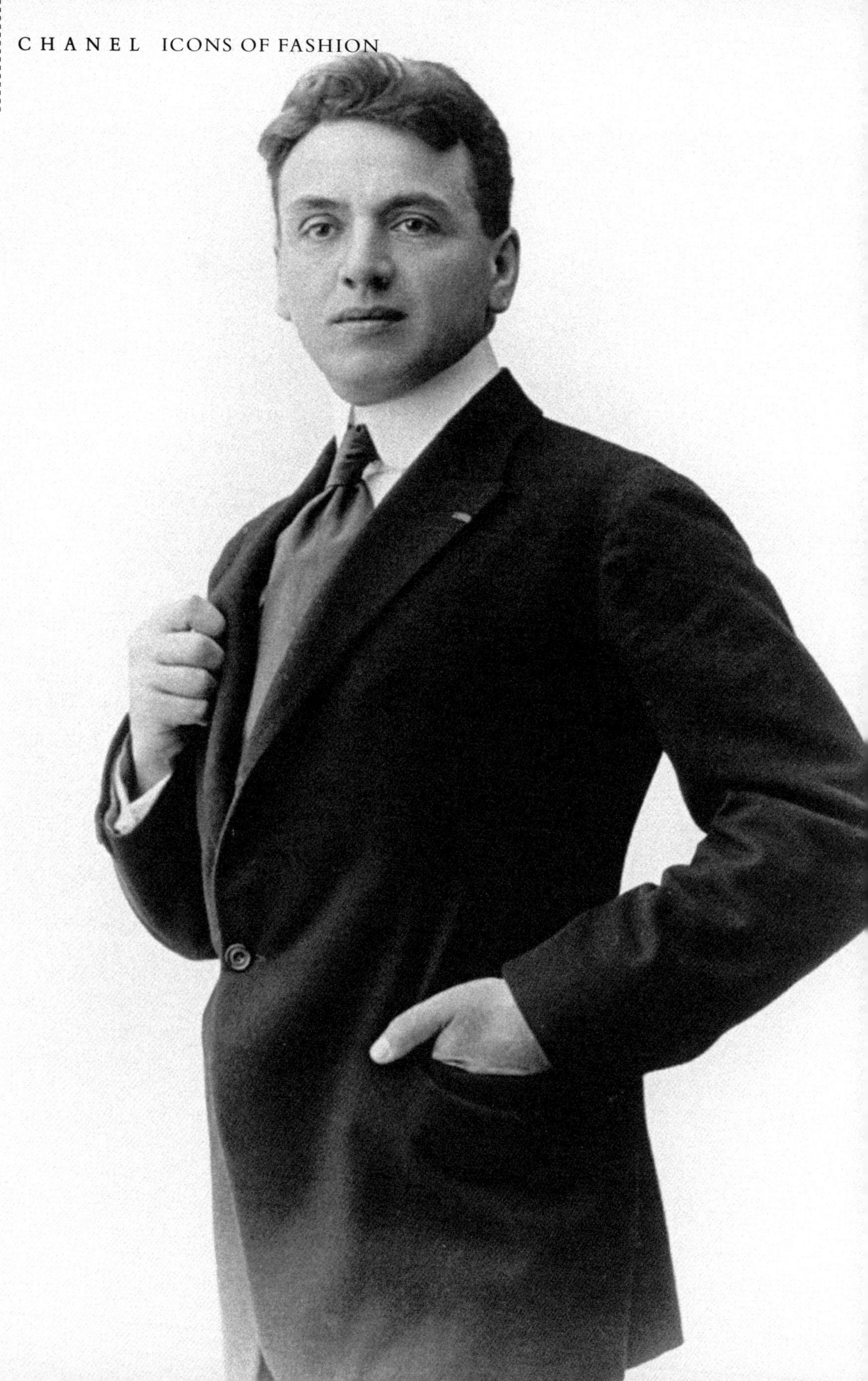

for Coco's Chanel brand which would prove iconic – perfume.

Several other fashion houses had begun to promote scent and Coco was keen to follow suit. Fastidiously clean, Coco was allergic to the stinking musk and body odour that she claimed was attached to the mistresses of the wealthy. During the summer of 1920 which she spent with Dmitri, he introduced her to Ernest Beaux, another Russian exile who was a former parfumier to the Tsars, who was at that time living and working in Grasse in southern France.

According to Beaux, he had started experimenting with a new fragrance in 1920 and created the perfume from his memory of his time '... above the Arctic Circle, during the midnight sun, where the lakes and rivers exuded a perfume of extreme freshness'. He achieved this with innovative use of synthetic and natural ingredients combined with Jasmine and, as rumour has it, a strong percentage of aldehydes which were added by mistake, but

ADORNMENT WINS THE DAY

The Russian influences on Coco's work became greater than it might have been, thanks to Dmitri's older sister, Grand Duchess Maria Pavlovna. As penniless as her brother after the revolution, Maria was keen to improve her fortunes and opened an embroidery and sewing shop called Kitmir. On hearing that Coco was having a problem with her normal supplier of embroidery and beadwork, Maria offered to take on the job for the cut price of 450 francs per blouse.

Her quality work brilliantly complimented Coco's designs at that time, which included a reinvention of traditional Russian tunics and coats such as the short fur-trimmed jackets usually worn hanging loose over the left shoulder of Russian hussars, and the traditional blouse, the 'roubachka'.

Featuring Maria's elaborate trimmings and edgings, including pearls and strings of sparkling bugle beads, Coco's 1922 Russian-influenced spring collection launched on 5 February was a huge success. On the back of this, Coco expanded her range to include collections with patterns copied from of Indian jewellery, Chinese vases, Coptic weaves, Persian miniatures and Oriental rugs.

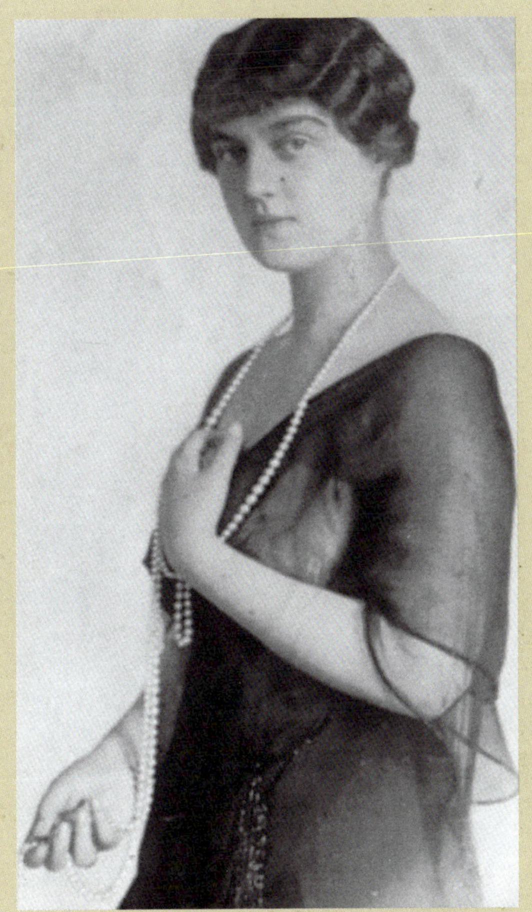

LEFT: Ernest Beaux

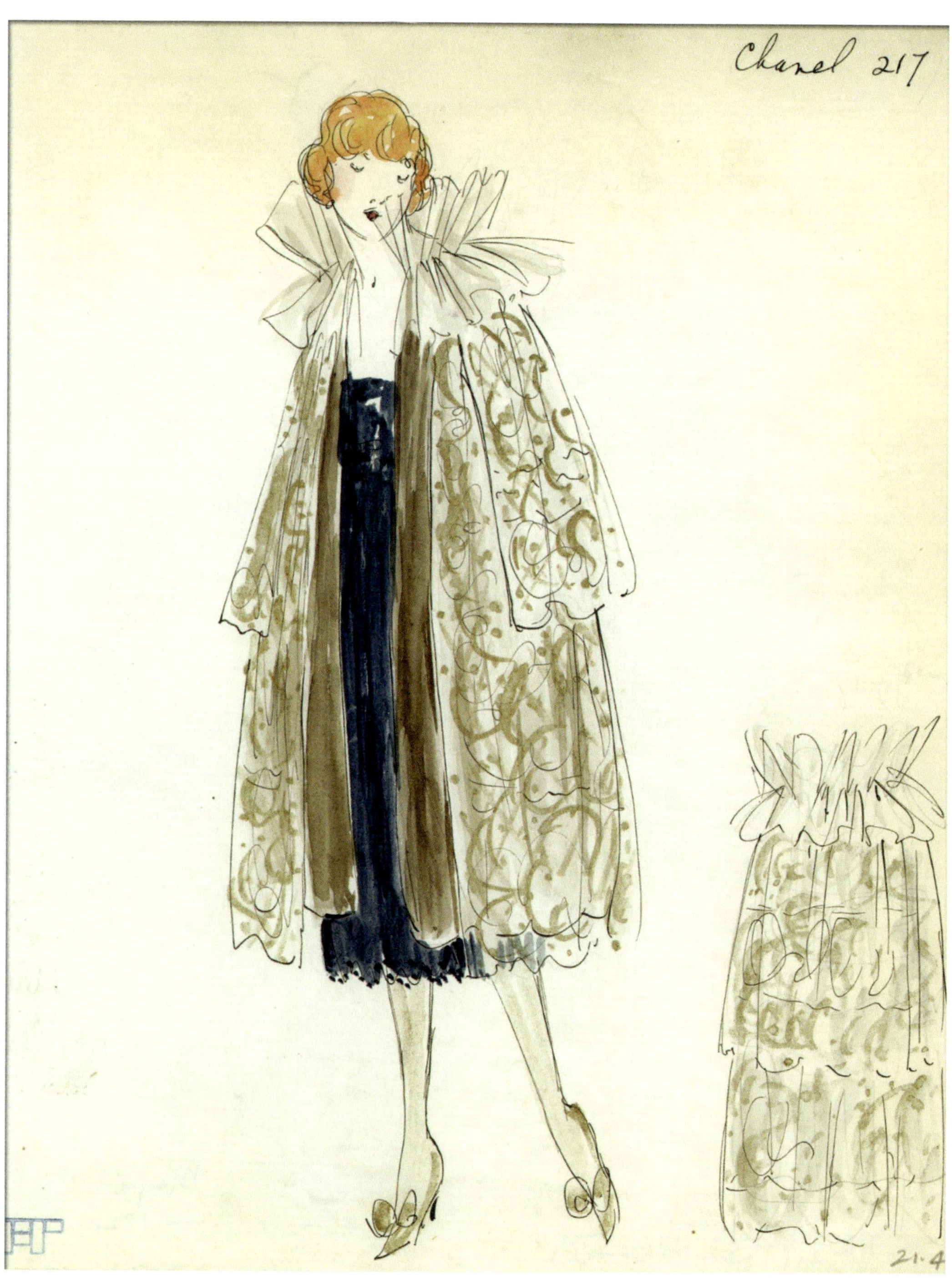

ABOVE: Chanel design, circa 1920
RIGHT: Chanel design, circa 1923

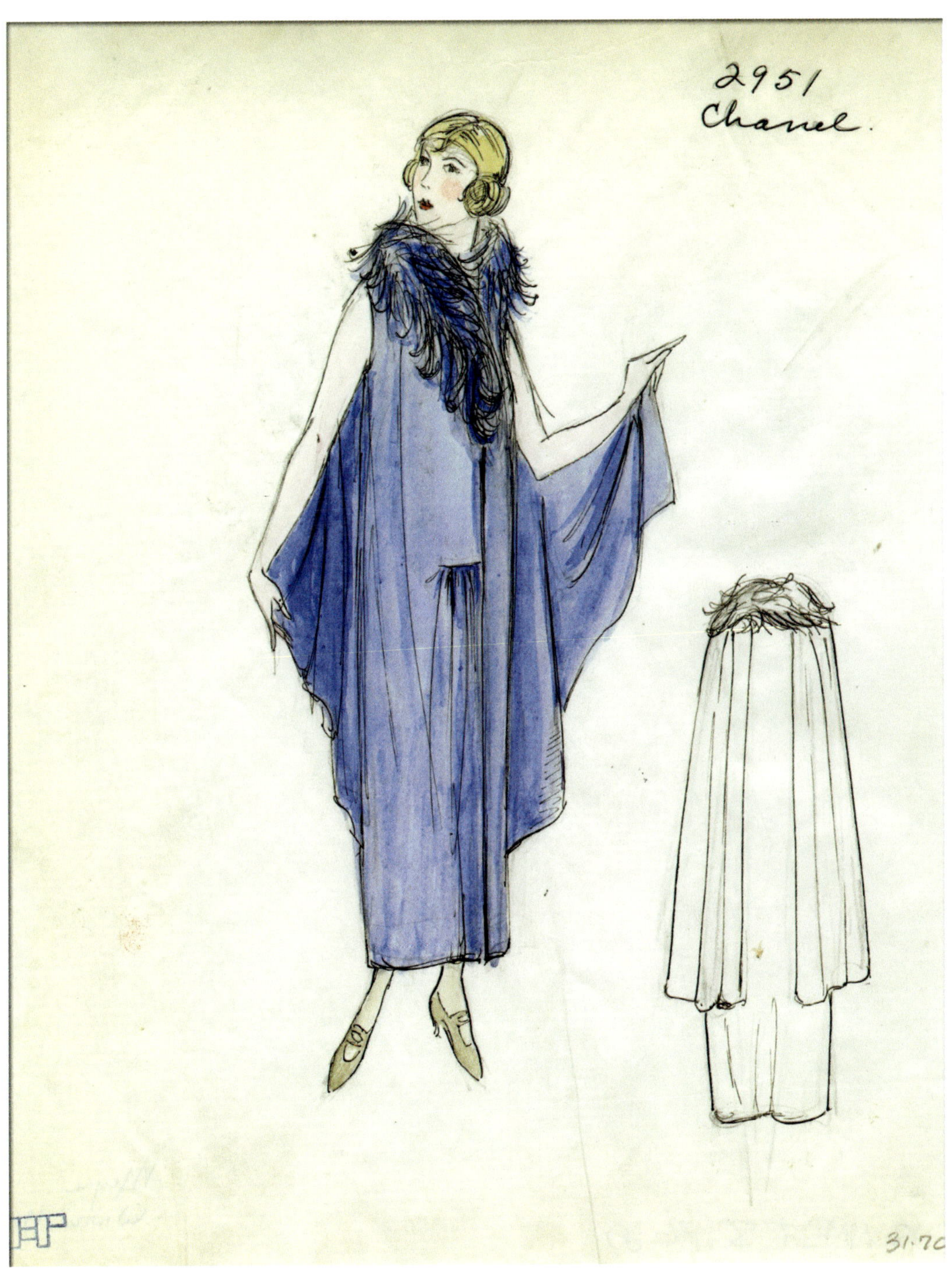
2951
Chanel.
31.7C

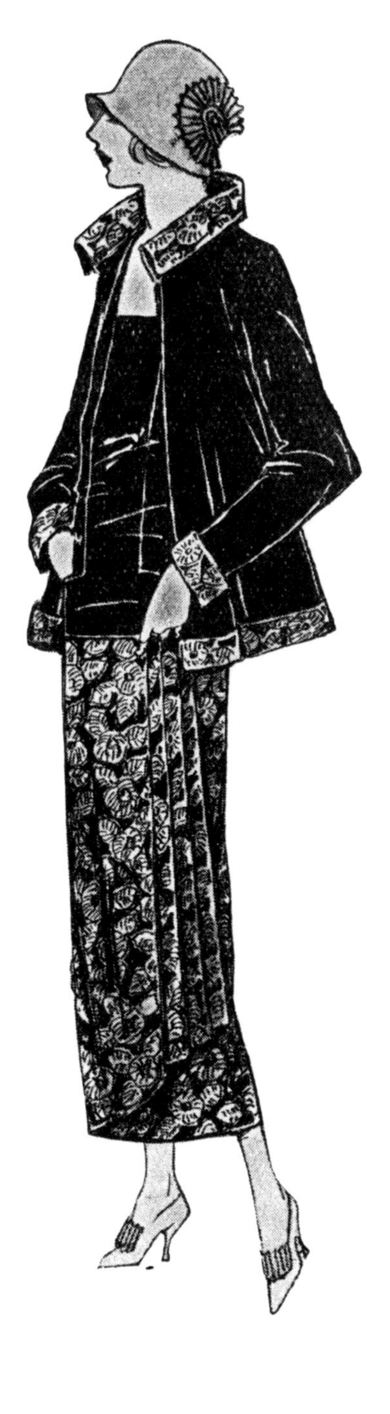

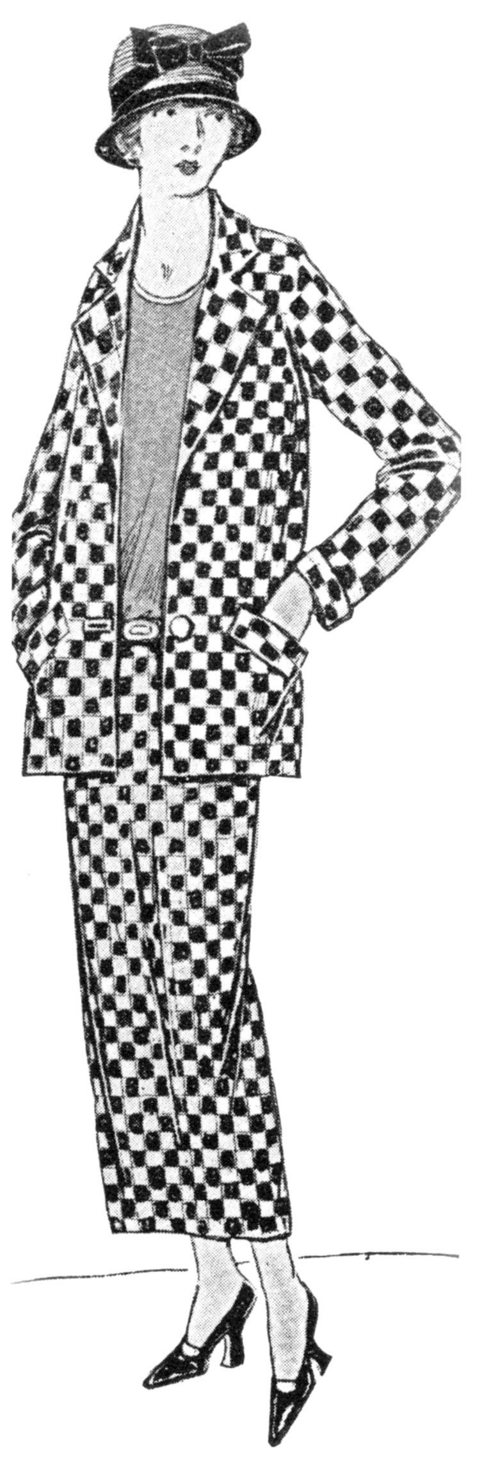

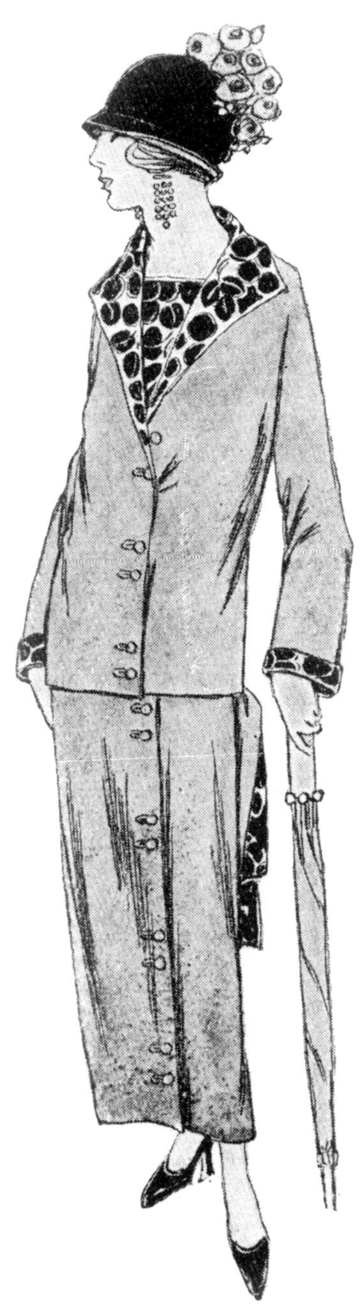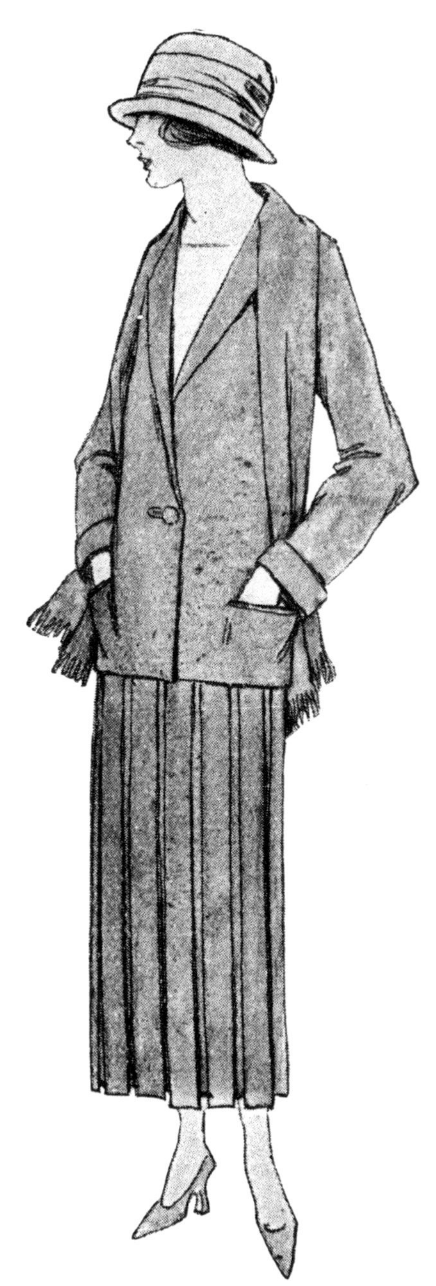

ABOVE: Various Chanel designs, circa 1923

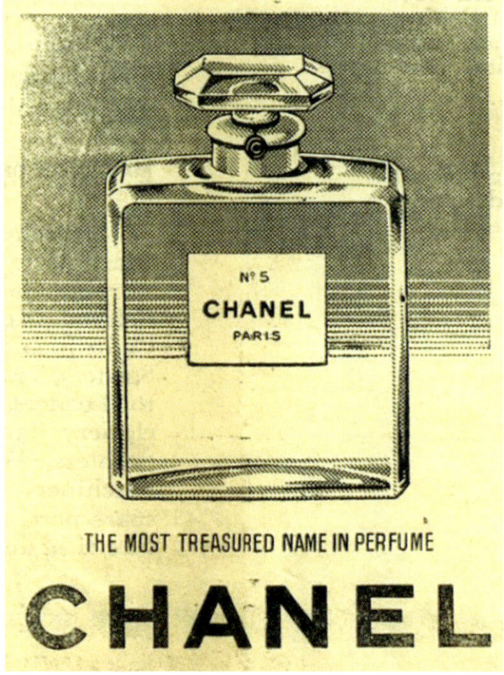

which had the benefit of causing the scent to linger for longer on the skin.

Coco loved the scent, saying, 'It was what I was waiting for. A perfume like nothing else. A woman's perfume with the scent of a woman'. She snapped it up and named it No 5. As well as being her

preferred number, the fragrance was coincidentally the fifth in a series of adaptions by Beaux.

In later years, Coco would cut Ernest Beaux out of the story of the Chanel Nº5 formulation, preferring to say that the scent was her creation alone, using her childhood memories of the linen cupboard her 'aunts' freshened with herbs, their polished furniture and the smell of soap. This tale was rather undermined by the fact that Beaux would go on to produce four other Chanel perfumes, Chanel Bois des Iles, Cuir de Russie and Gardénia.

For now, having revolutionised fashion, Coco was about to do the same for women's scent. She designed a bottle for her new perfume loosely based on the whiskey decanters that Boy had favoured, with a diamond stopper which resembled the outline of the Place Vendôme. Its fragile form was slightly adapted later to make the glass more robust.

In 1921, the iconic Chanel Nº5 bottle began to adorn her shop windows, for sale to selected clients, before going into mass production in 1924 after Coco made a deal with the perfume house Bourjois owned by brothers Pierre and Paul Wertheimer.

THE CC LOGO

The mass production of Nº5 began in 1924, also the year in which she launched her first red lipstick and when Coco's iconic logo of interlocking 'Cs' first made an appearance. It has always been assumed that the double 'C' was intended as a homage to man who meant so much to her; Boy Capel.

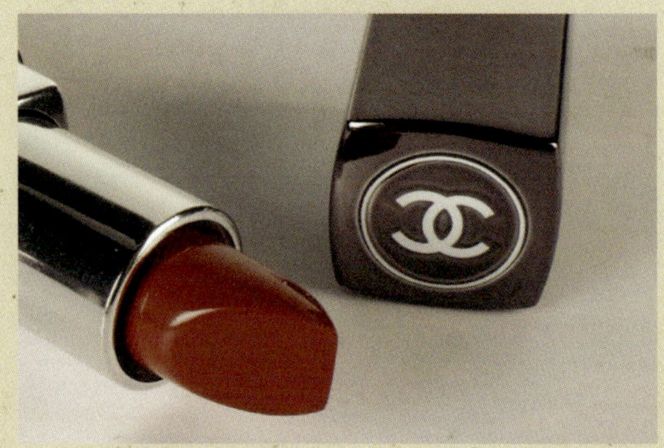

ABOVE: Early Chanel N°5 advert, 1920s

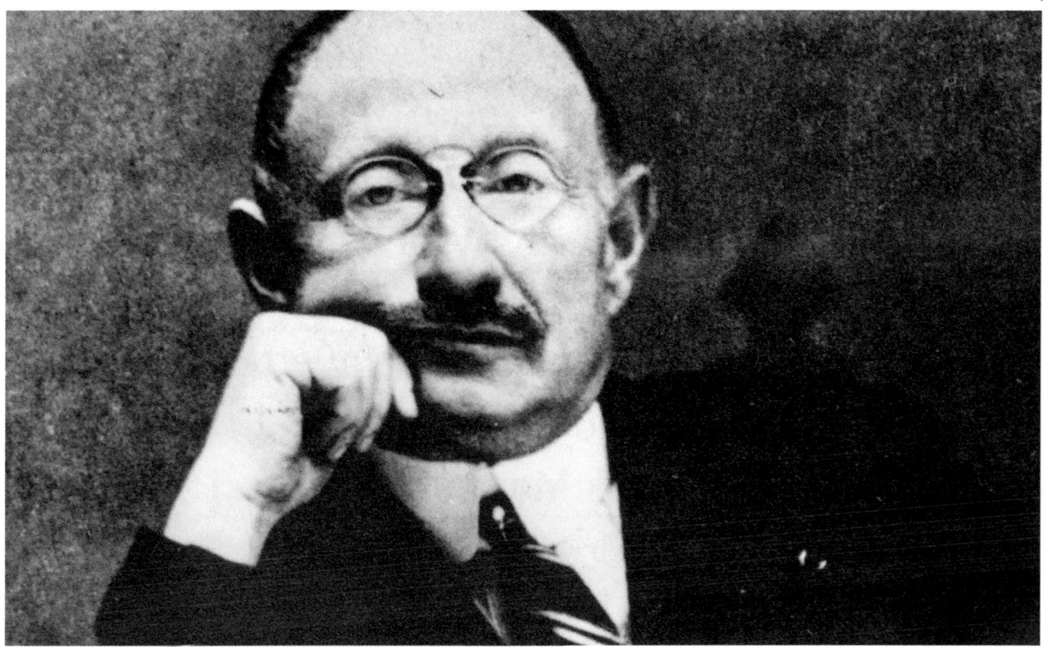

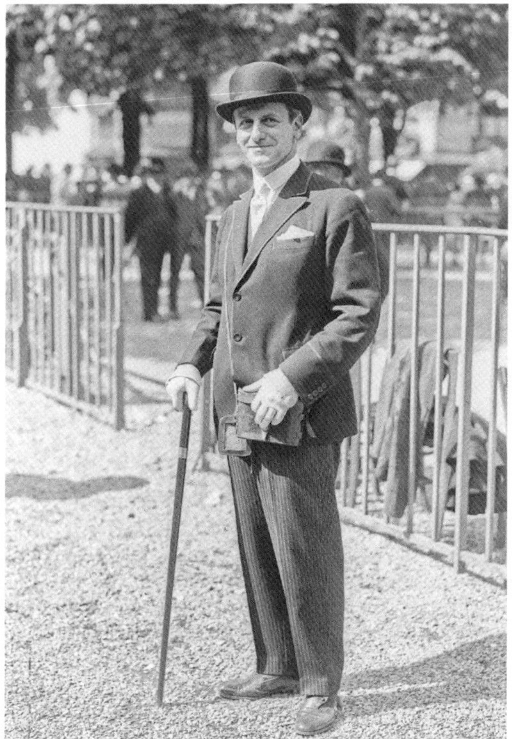

Théophile Bader, proprietor of the famous Galeries Lafayette had first introduced Coco to Pierre and was keen to be in on the deal. So it was that the trio set up a new 'Parfums Chanel' company, with ownership split between them all – 10% for Coco, 20% for Bader and 70% for the Wertheimers.

Despite her consequently smaller share of the eventually vast profits causing Coco constant ire – she even took legal action at one point – it was a good deal which helped the brand survive into the modern age with its independence intact. Coco and Pierre were bound for life by their partnership, Pierre proving more loyal than any lover. Coco came to understand, however reluctantly, that it was Pierre who had given her wealth and with it the freedom to live the secure and independent life she had always wanted.

TOP: Théophile Bader
ABOVE LEFT: Pierre Wertheimer

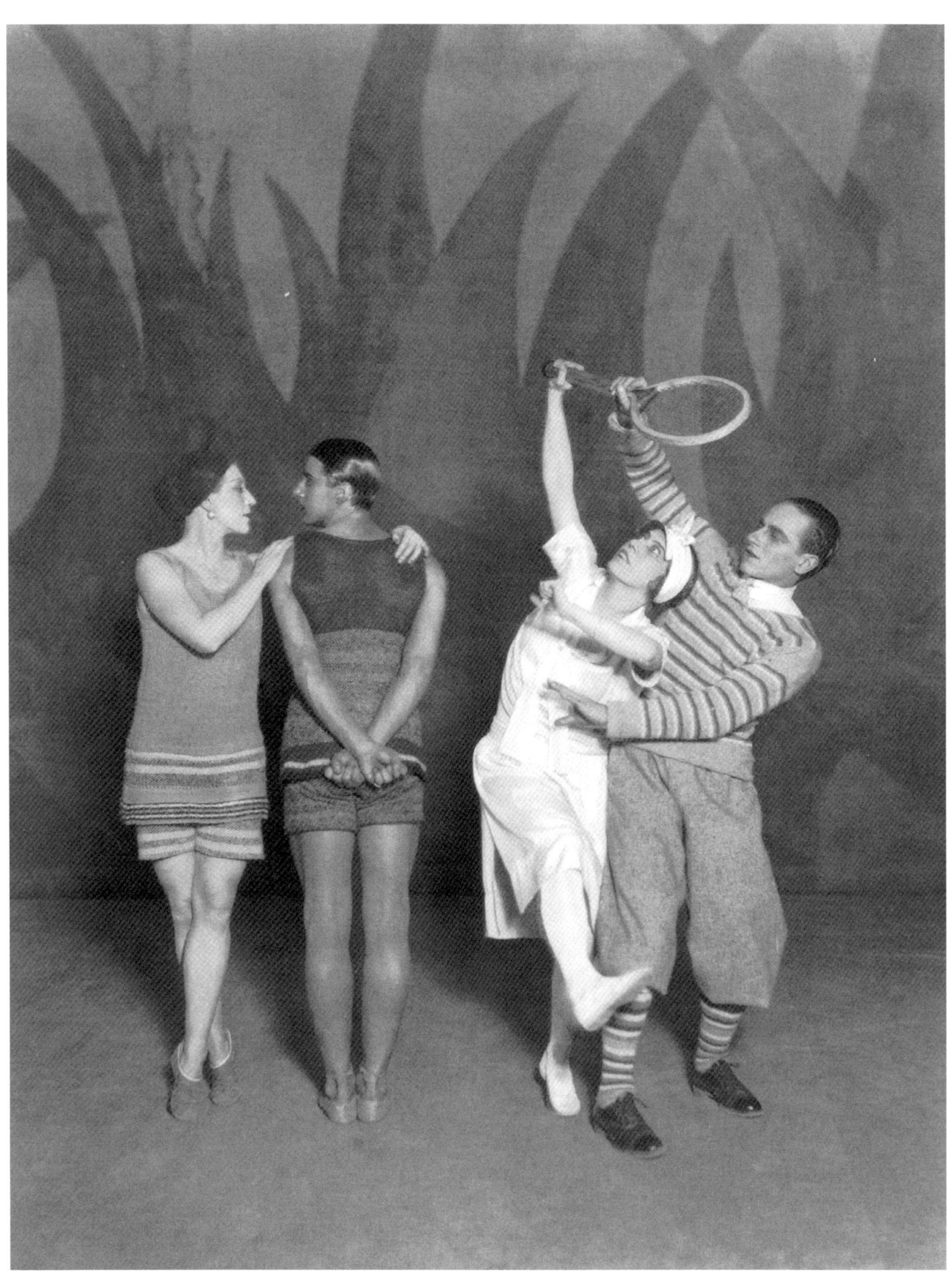

ABOVE: Ballet dancers perform in the
Diaghilev Ballets Russes production of 'Le
Train Bleu'. Costumes by Coco Chanel, 1924

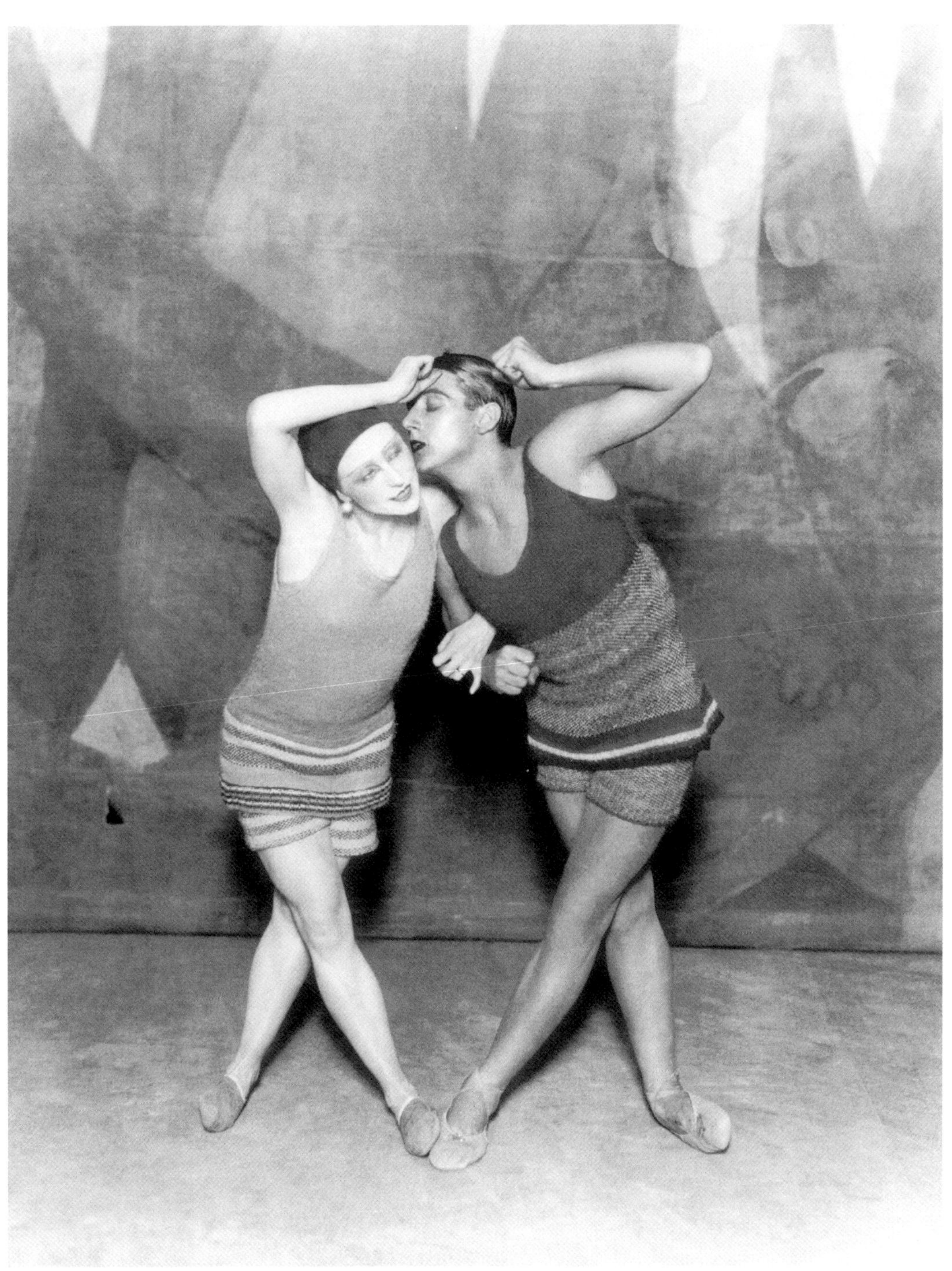

ABOVE: Dancers Lydia Sokolova and Anton Dolin in the Diaghilev Ballets Russes production of 'Le Train Bleu'. Costumes by Coco Chanel, 1924

THE DUKE OF WESTMINSTER 1923-1927

"I have employed society people, not to indulge my vanity or to humiliate them (I would take other forms of revenge, supposing I were seeking them), but ... because they were useful to me."

Bouncing from one high-profile affair to the next, Coco met the Duke of Westminster, the richest man in Britain, at a dinner in 1923 in Monte Carlo.

They were introduced by their mutual friend Vera Bate Lombardi, a socialite who Coco felt was useful for networking purposes and therefore used unabashedly as go-between to establish wealthy connections.

And they didn't come much wealthier than the 44-year-old playboy Hugh Richard Arthur Grosvenor, 2nd Duke of Westminster – known to his friends as 'Bendor'.

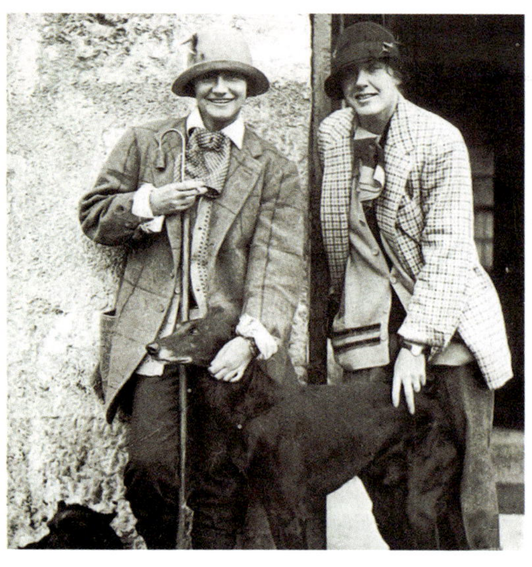

His vast riches left him free to indulge his love of the fast life and passion for yachts, fast cars and raucous company. At over 6ft tall, handsome and said to be likeable and kindly, his good looks and charm proved as effective on Coco as they had on many other women and the two began an affair which would last 10 years.

The fact that his wealth was on another scale, even from Coco's own, must have appealed, particularly in comparison to the impoverished Dmitri. But apparently Coco also saw beyond the Duke's hedonistic lifestyle, believing him to be isolated by his wealth and circumstance and describing him as 'the shyest person I've ever met'.

However it was several months before she persuaded

ABOVE RIGHT: Coco with Vera Bate
RIGHT: Hugh Grosvenor, 2nd Duke of
Westminster at Chester Races with Coco
Chanel, May 1924

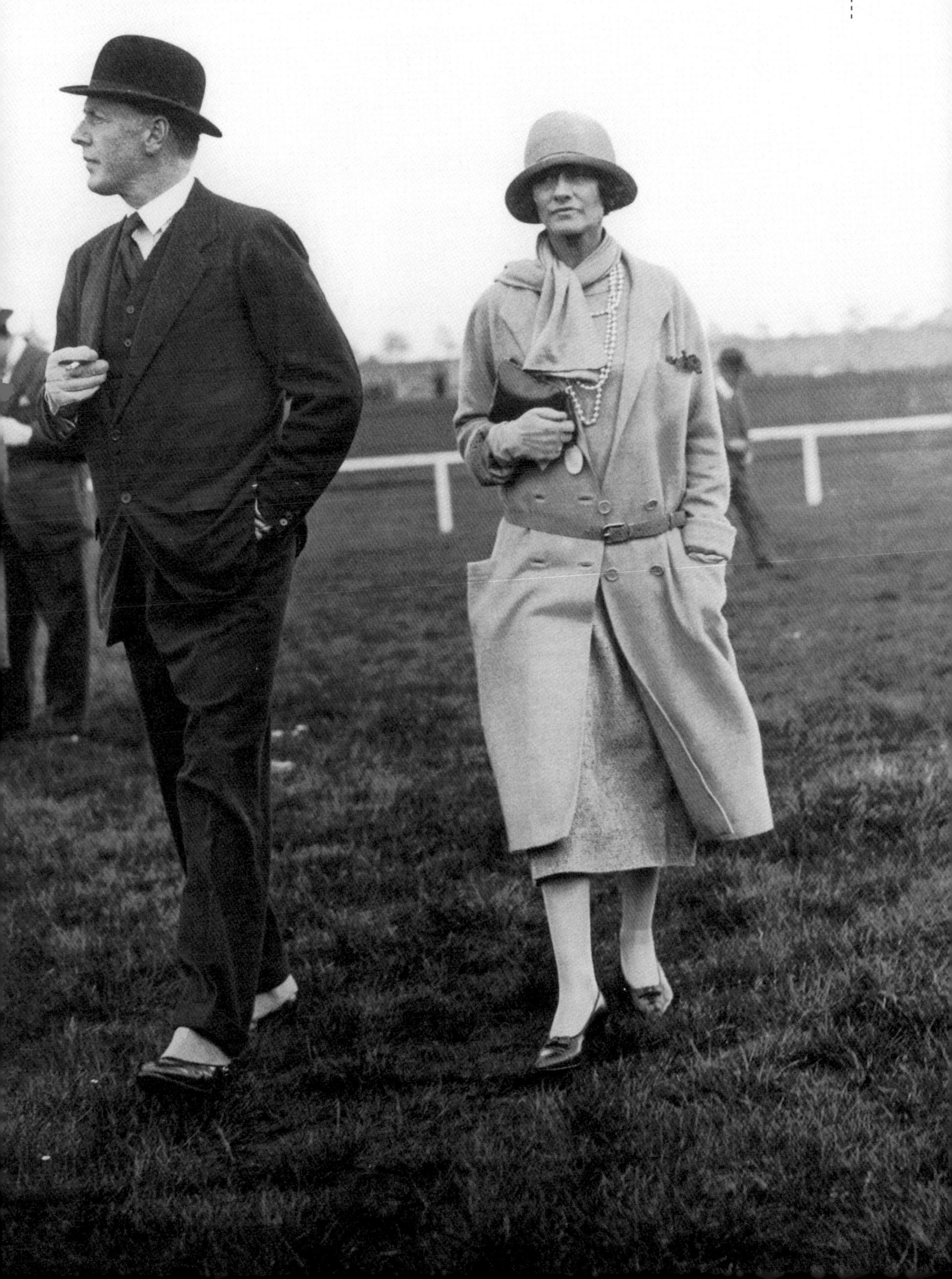

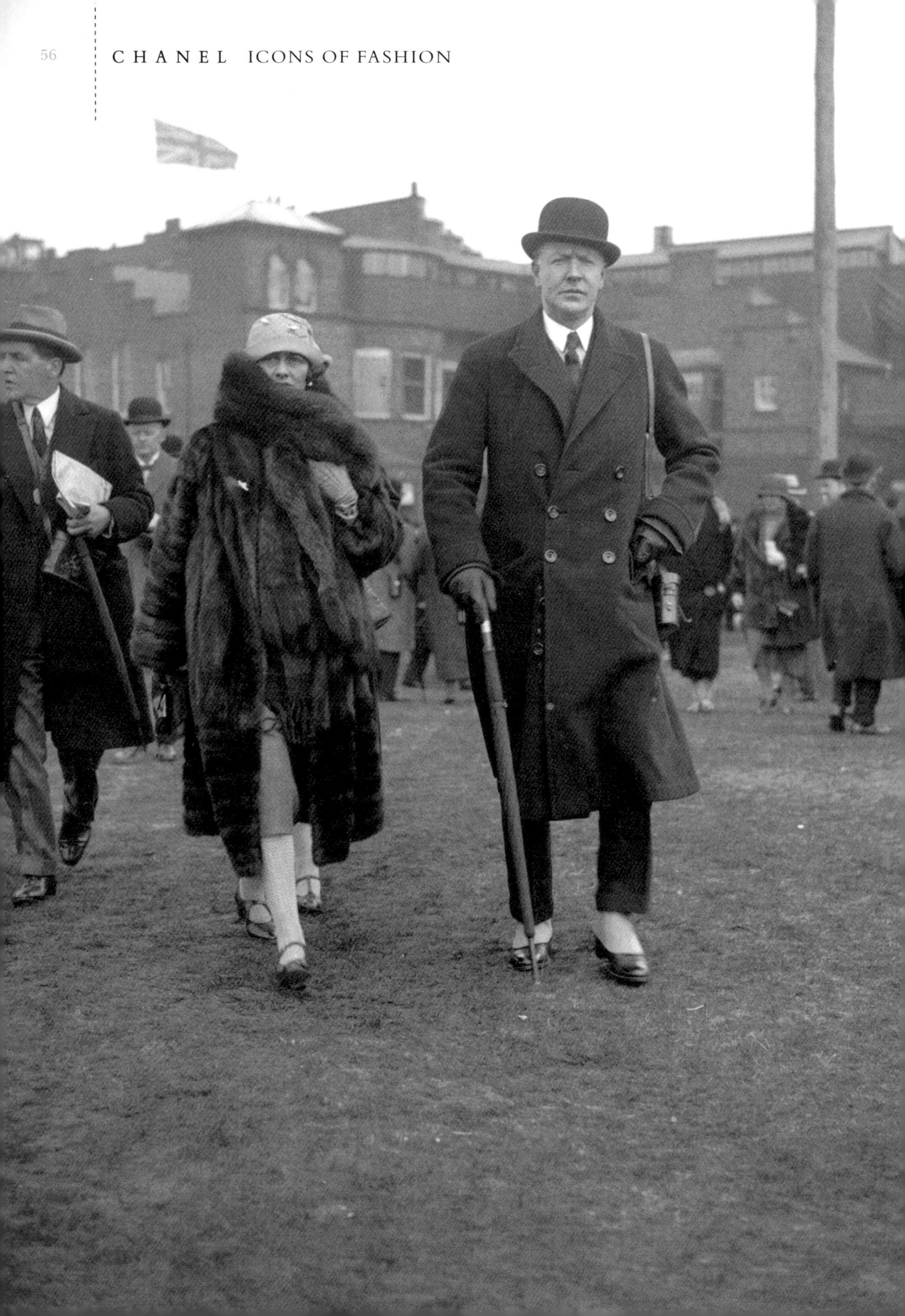

herself to enter the liaison. Bendor was married to his second wife, Violet Nelson, when he met Coco, and perhaps she had pause for thought realising that no wealthy man was ever going to be a faithful companion; she had known many womanisers after all. But wealth of that magnitude was an aphrodisiac for someone as keen to mingle with movers and shakers as Coco. She would have known that Bendor could introduce her into a strata of society that was not available to normal mortals of the world. So eventually Coco accepted an invitation to come aboard his beloved yacht Flying Cloud, and their affair began.

Despite saying '… I loved him, or I thought I loved him, which amounts to the same thing', Coco seemed to need a justification for the fact that she had yielded to male power and wealth once again. So she

THE 2ND DUKE OF WESTMINSTER

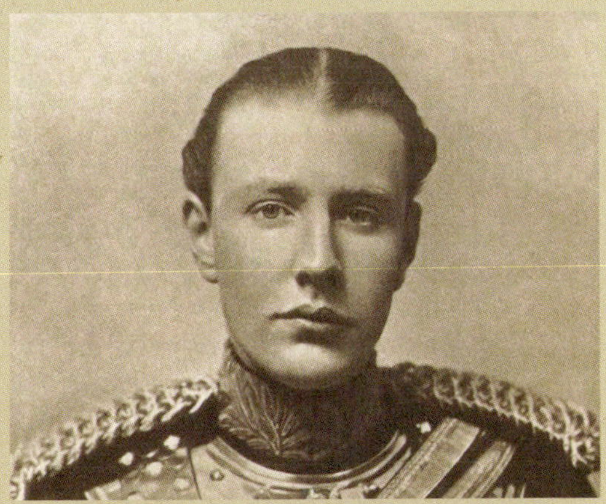

Born on 19 March 1879, the 2nd Duke of Westminster came to be nicknamed Bendor after his grandfather's racehorse Bend Or, won The Derby Stakes in 1880.

Having served during the Second Boer war, Bendor succeeded his grandfather as Duke in 1899 when he was 20 and married Shelagh Cornwallis-West two years later on 16 February 1901.

The couple had three children, but lost their four-year-old son, Edward George Hugh, to appendicitis in February 1909, leaving them with two daughters: Ursula Mary Olivia and Mary Constance. The Westminsters were legally separated just before the First World War.

Having volunteered for front-line combat, Bendor came through the war with a DSO medal for distinguished service and a promotion to Colonel. He was famous for undertaking a successful mission to rescue British prisoners at Bir Hakeim, Libya, which involved a 120 mile race through the desert for which he commandeered 37 cars, nine of them armoured.

He famously loved cars and is said to have owned 17 Rolls Royces. He also had two yachts and was an Olympic standard motorboat racer.

After the war he went to work for his good friend Winston Churchill at the Ministry of Munitions.

Alongside numerous love affairs, Bendor remarried three times after divorcing his first wife, but had no more children:

- In 1920, to Violet Nelson, daughter of the wealthy Sir William Nelson. Divorced 1926.
- In 1930 to Loelia Ponsonby. Divorced 1947.
- In 1947 to Anne Sullivan who outlived him by 50 years.

Bendor died on 19 July 1953, from coronary thrombosis at his Scottish estate, aged 74.

LEFT: Duke of Westminster and Coco Chanel at the Grand National, March 1925

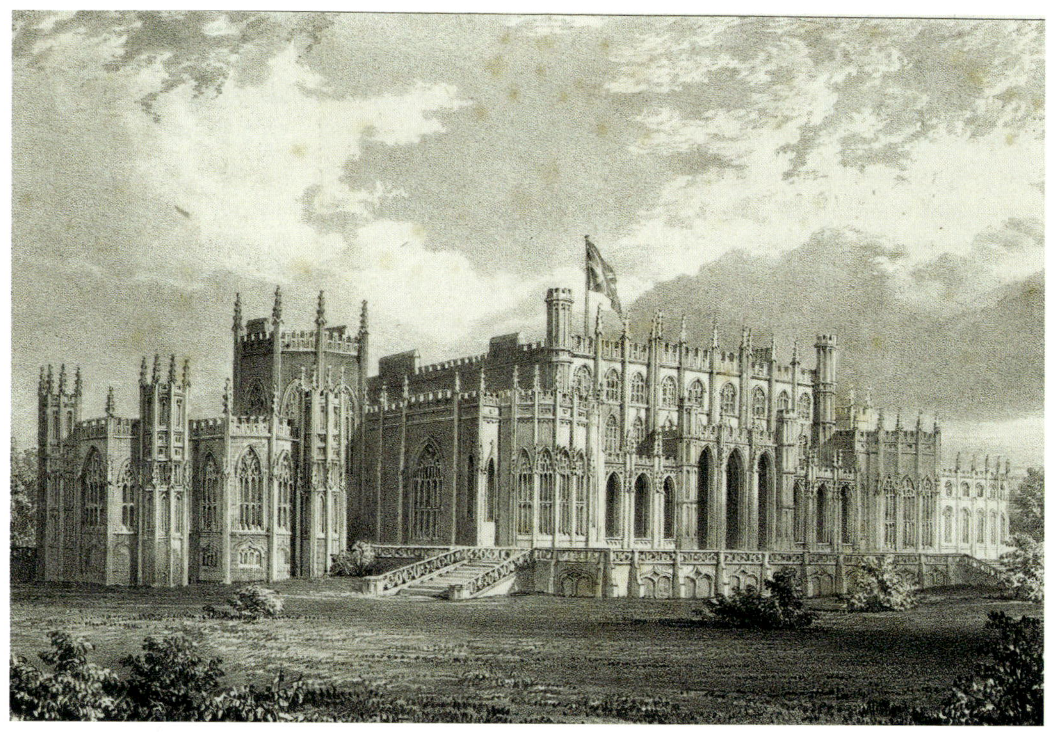

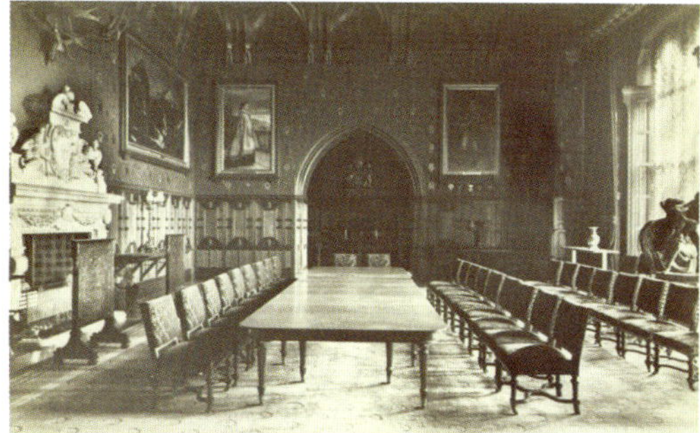

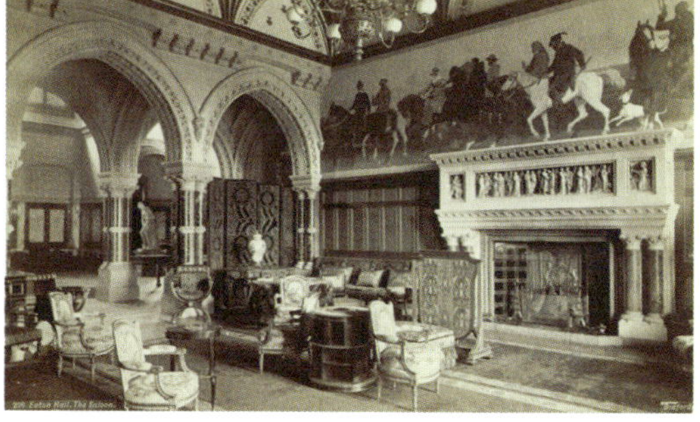

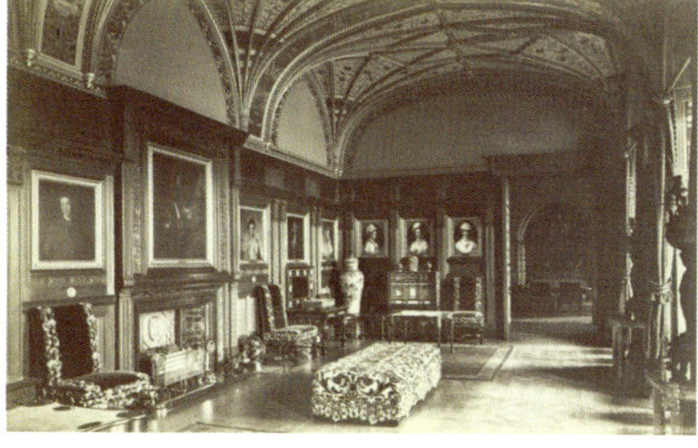

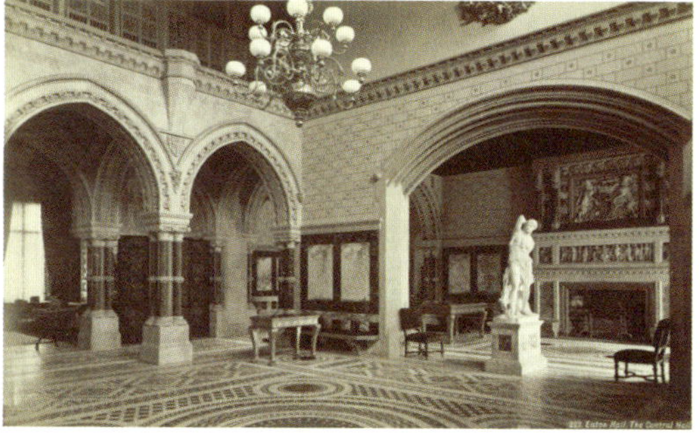

TOP: Eaton Hall
ABOVE: Interior of Eaton Hall

explained it away by promoting the idea that wealth of such magnitude was no longer vulgar. In fact, it was '… located well beyond envy, and it assumes catastrophic proportions'.

Prone to making lavish gifts, Bendor showered Coco with exotic flowers and priceless jewels throughout their time together.

Despite his evident adoration of her, she never seemed to hold him, or men generally, in particularly high esteem. 'As long as you know men are like children you know everything,' was one of her more derogatory utterances. To that she added that she didn't know why women wanted what men had, anyway, '…when one of the things women have is men'. But maybe these witty asides were to deflect from the almost savage desire that she herself had personal and financial freedoms that were largely the privilege of men in her era.

She was not generally enamoured of life aboard yachts either. 'As soon as you set foot on a yacht, you belong to some man and not yourself and you die of boredom' she complained. However, there was inspiration for new design ideas everywhere, including on the Flying Cloud. Yachting also provided another avenue to fame and fortune when, after returning from a trip to the Mediterranean with a bronzed face she was complimented sufficiently to realise that tanning lotions might prove popular. She was right, again.

Back on dry land, Coco became well acquainted with Bendor's ancestral country seat, Eaton Hall, a 54-bedroom mansion set in 11,000 acres of land in Cheshire, England which boasted works of art by Rembrandt, Raphael, Goya and Rubens, amongst

others. Scotland also become familiar to her as she and the Duke spent time at his 100,000-acres Reay Forest estate, where Coco learned salmon fishing.

This new outdoor life continued at Mimizan in Aquitaine on France's south-western coast, where Bendor liked to hunt boar. His guests there at Château Woolsack – built for him in 1911 as a royal reward for his courageous actions as a front-line soldier in the Boer War – included Winston Churchill, Charlie Chaplin and Salvador Dalí. Coco also brought friends and employees to relax at this 'Royal Shrine at the Edge of the Lake'.

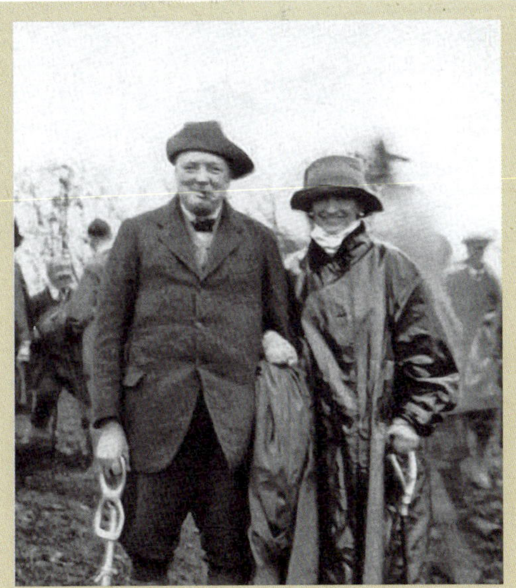

WINSTON CHURCHILL

Coco made a very favourable impression on Winston Churchill, who wrote of her; 'The famous Coco turned up & I took a gt (sic) fancy to her. A most capable and agreeable woman – much the strongest personality Benni (Bendor) has yet been up against.'

And so Coco's life became a whirlwind as she raced from England to Paris, where she was involved in every aspect of preparing her fashion designs, from pinning to cutting and altering.

Her collections were again influenced by her high-flying lover, as they had been by Boy. For example, she began using colours and motifs from the sailing world and even the livery of Bendor's footmen fed her imagination and was reflected in her new designs.

But all this success was overshadowed by another iconic Coco design that featured in *Vogue* magazine in 1926, the little black dress. It became, and remains, a fashion staple.

Tired of the gaudy fashionable colours that 'made her feel ill', she was determined to eradicate them from the streets. The colour gave rise to more maxims; 'When I find a colour darker than black, I'll wear it. But until then, I'm wearing black!' she said. At that time the idea of wearing black day and night, when not in mourning, was revolutionary.

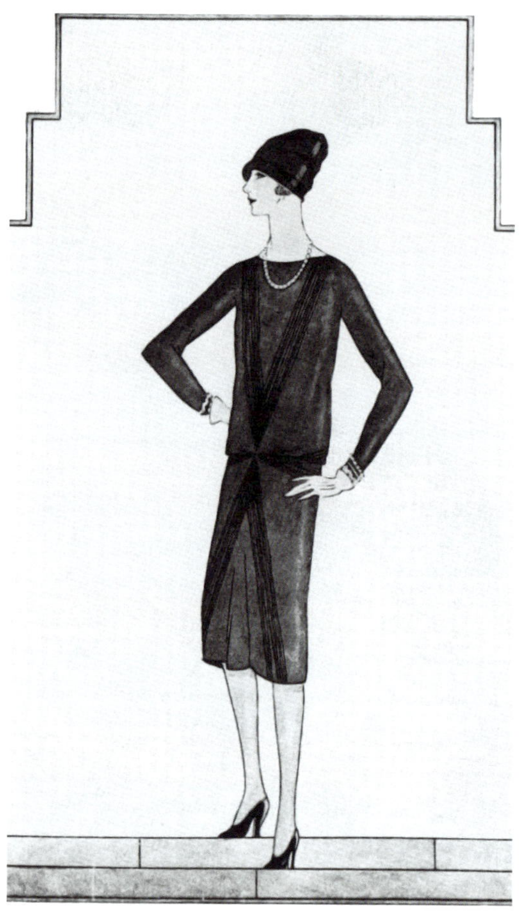

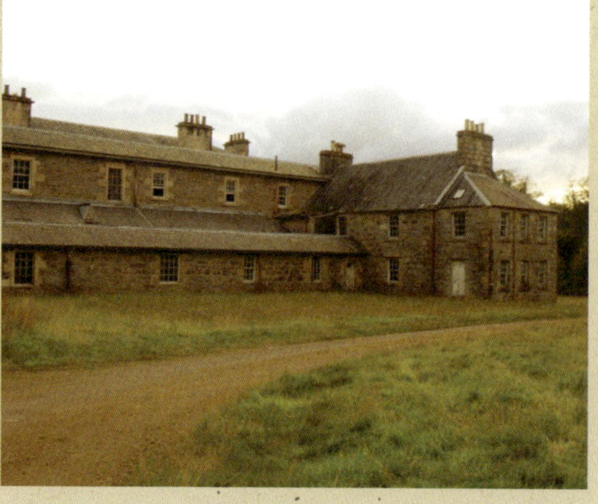

ROSEHALL

In 1926, Bendor bought Rosehall, a Scottish estate and fishing lodge, which Coco re-decorated and furnished. As far as anyone knows, Rosehall was the only property in Britain that she decorated. Her designs were simple, but chic, incorporating beige walls and timber, and painted chimney pieces, a highly unusual sight for that era.

ABOVE RIGHT: 1926 *Vogue* 'Little Black Dress' illustration
MAIN IMAGE: Coco Chanel photographed by Man Ray

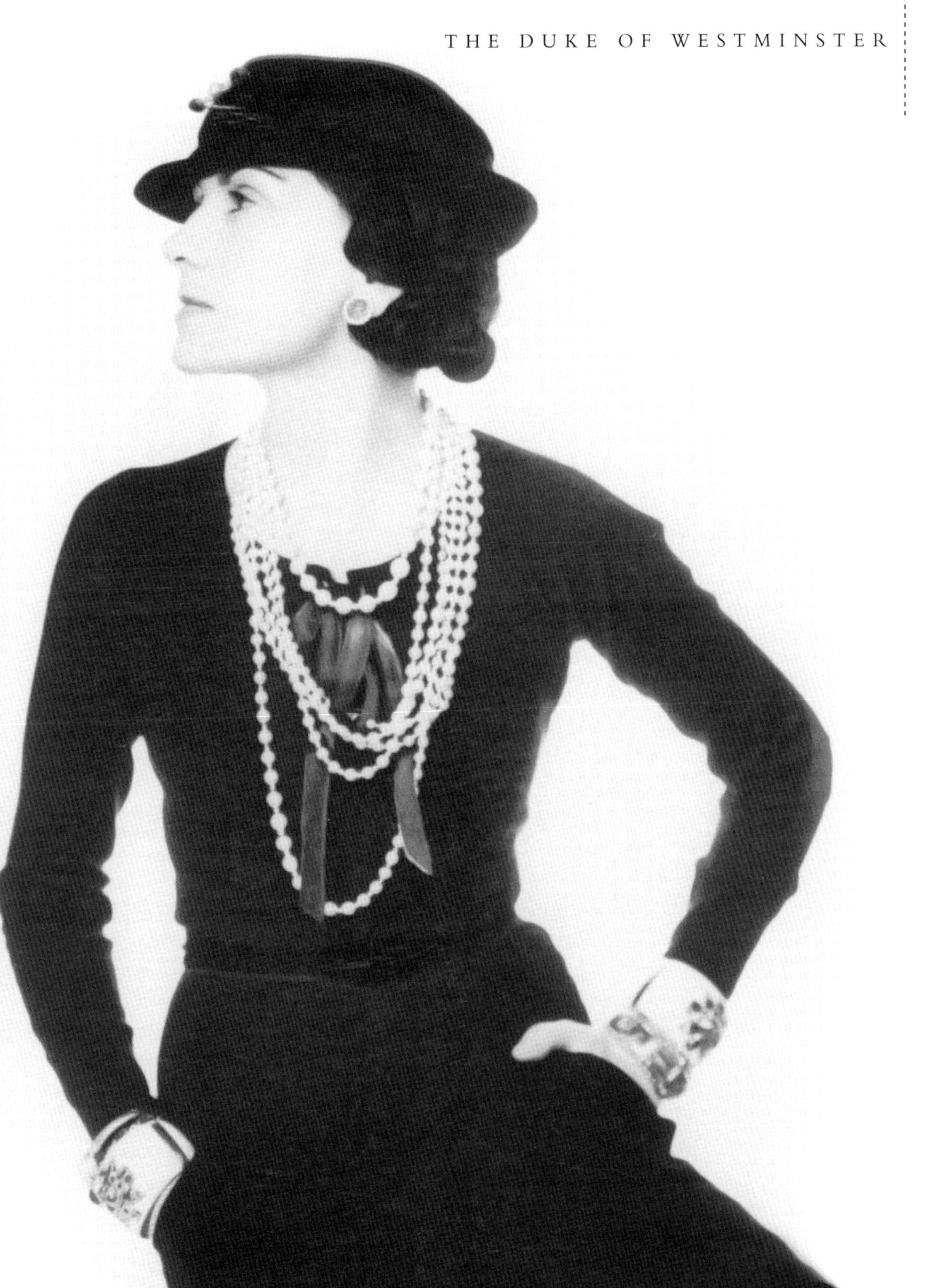

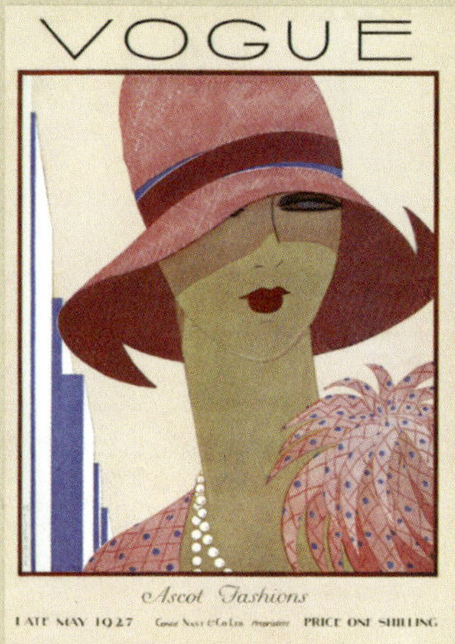

CHANEL'S ENGLISH LOOK

As she came to spend more time in England, Coco opened a Chanel branch in London in June 1927 in a beautiful Queen Anne house, with panelled walls and parquet floors.

Vogue's announcement of the news tantalised readers with its accompanying sketches of Coco's new line, dubbed 'Chanel's English Look' including a little black lace dress, a blue silk dress with polka dots designed for Ascot, and taffeta court gowns in brilliant white.

Simplicity was the watchword as ever, but Coco had also clearly absorbed the lessons learned from Bendor that the English season required certain customs to be observed.

Her latest collection, targeted at the London elite, was modelled by '... mannequins graceful and slender as lilies', and with the Duke's reflected kudos shining on her, Coco would conquer the snobbery of the British aristocrat. No mean feat.

Part of the 'English Look' was influenced by Bendor's Scottish tweeds which influenced Coco's clothing style in a different way. Having started out by wearing Bendor's clothes herself, she began incorporating the tweed fabric into her own designs.

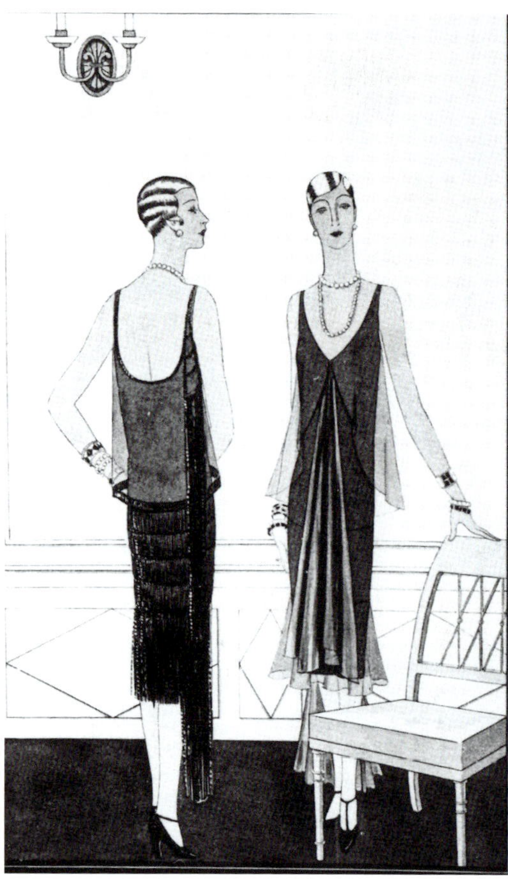

Her other work at that time included making costumes for dancers in Diaghilev's one-act ballet Le Train Bleu in 1924, drawing on the clothing styles of the Côte d'Azur to fit out the dancers in a range of costumes that mimicked the sportswear that she had made fashionable. The dancer's comfort was a priority, so she used light materials to create bathing suits in striking stripes, tricots, tennis attire, sandals, and golfing shoes.

As her successful career continued, she was able to expand her premises at 21 Rue Cambon in Paris so that by the end of 1927, she also owned numbers 23, 25, 27 and 29.

ABOVE: Illustration from *Vogue* magazine of two robes designed by Coco Chanel, April 1926

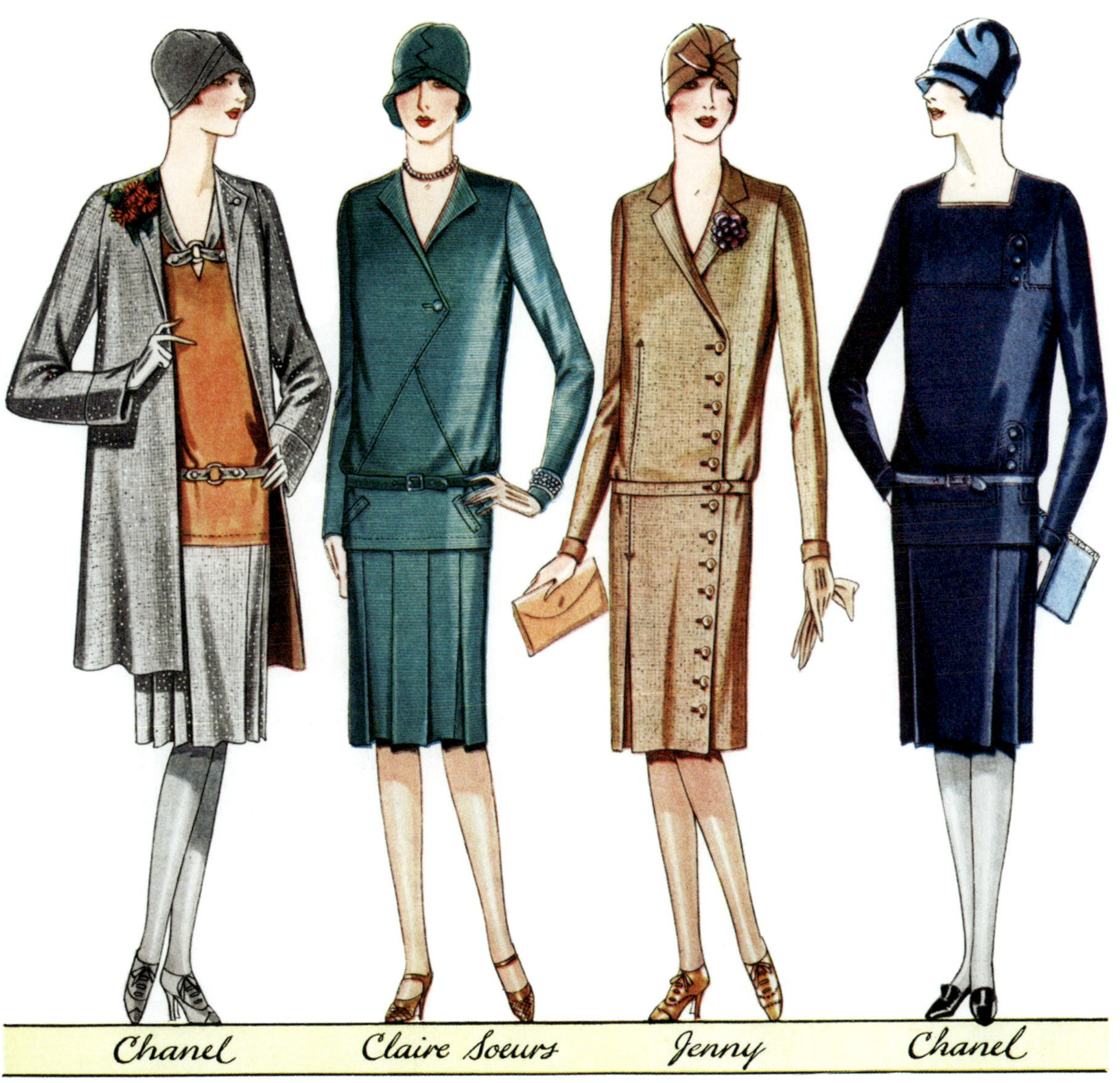

But the hectic pace of combining her professional commitments with life with Bendor took its toll privately. He wanted her by his side as he travelled between his various properties in Europe where he enjoyed sailing, hunting, fishing, shooting, and entertaining. Coco tried to work more in Britain so as to meet Bendor's demands on her time, but the schedule was punishing. In 1927 she even expanded the Chanel portfolio by launching a range of 15 skincare products which were the talk of the town in London.

At some point something would have to give – though it was never likely to be her business.

ABOVE: 1928 American magazine illustration of the Paris Spring fashions from Chanel and others

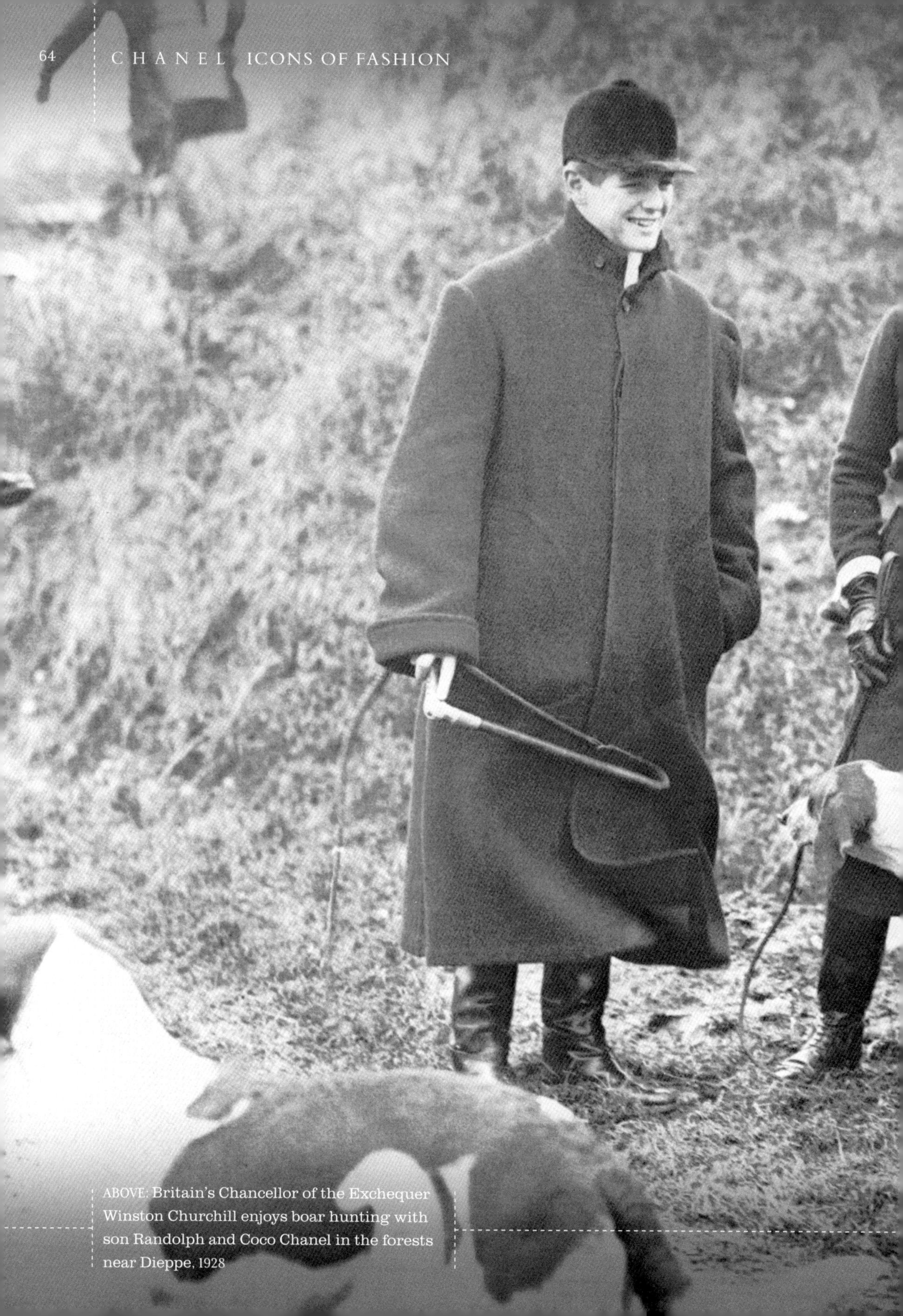

ABOVE: Britain's Chancellor of the Exchequer
Winston Churchill enjoys boar hunting with
son Randolph and Coco Chanel in the forests
near Dieppe, 1928

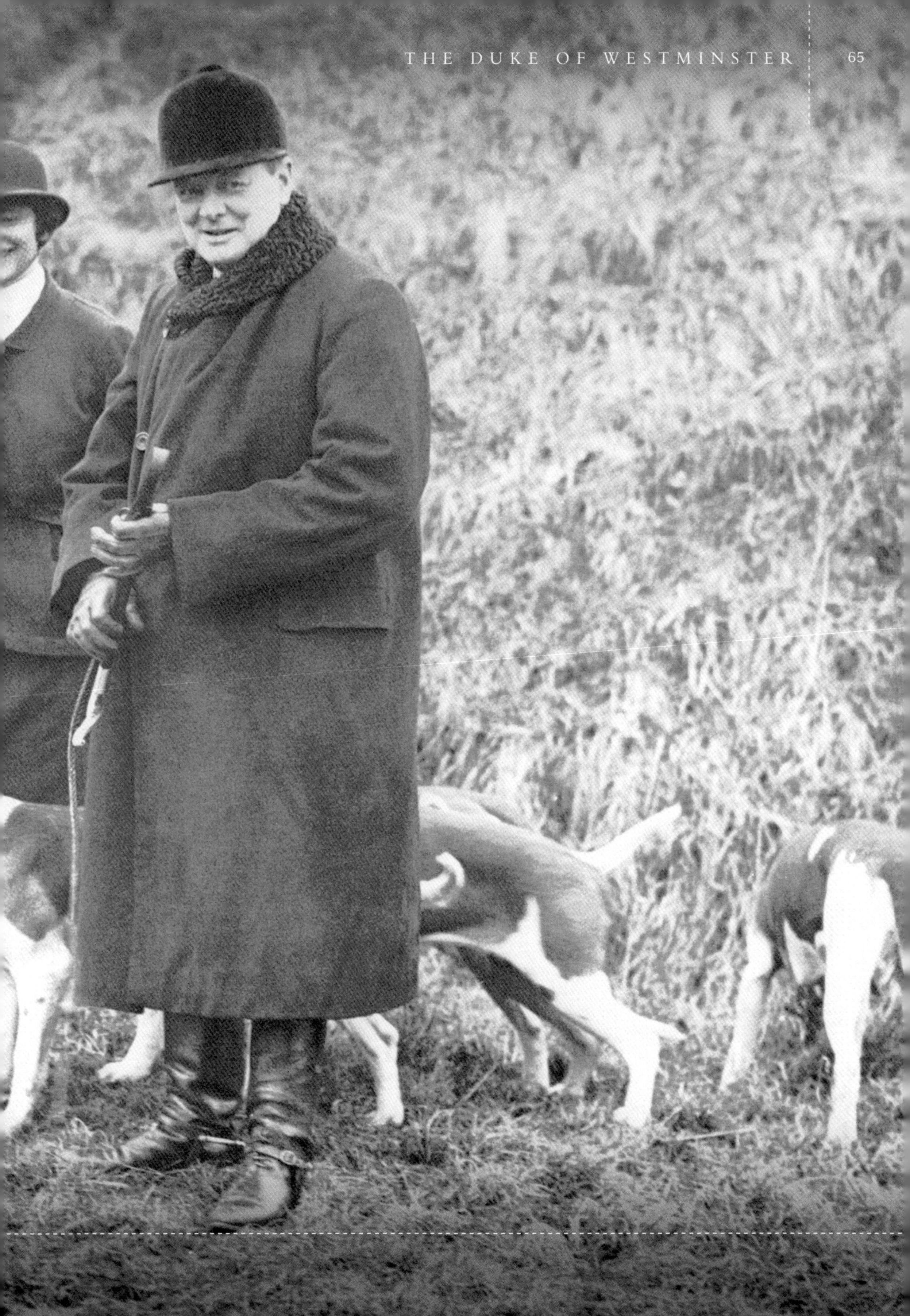

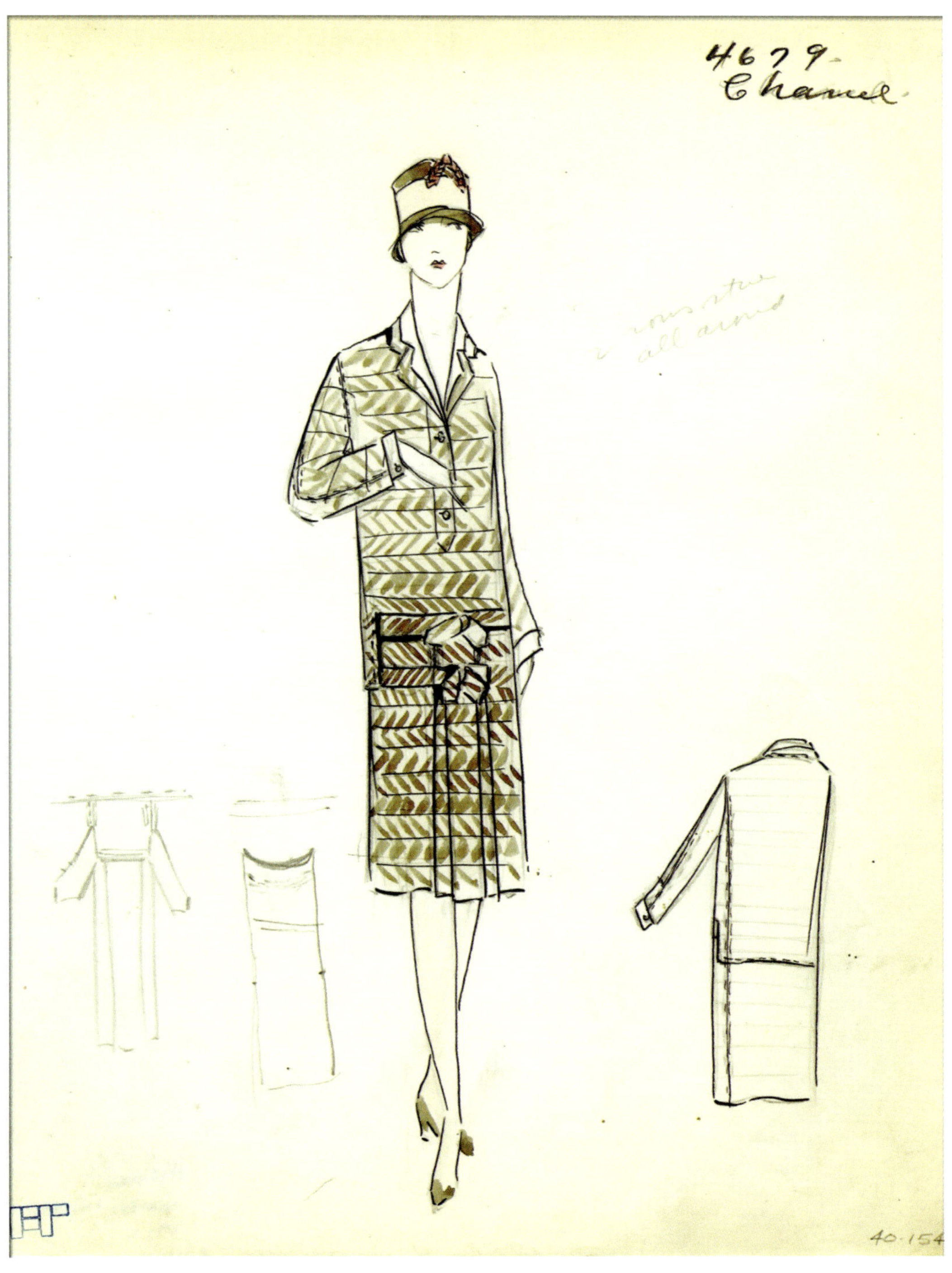

ABOVE: Original sketch from A. Beller & Co. of
a Chanel suit, winter 1926

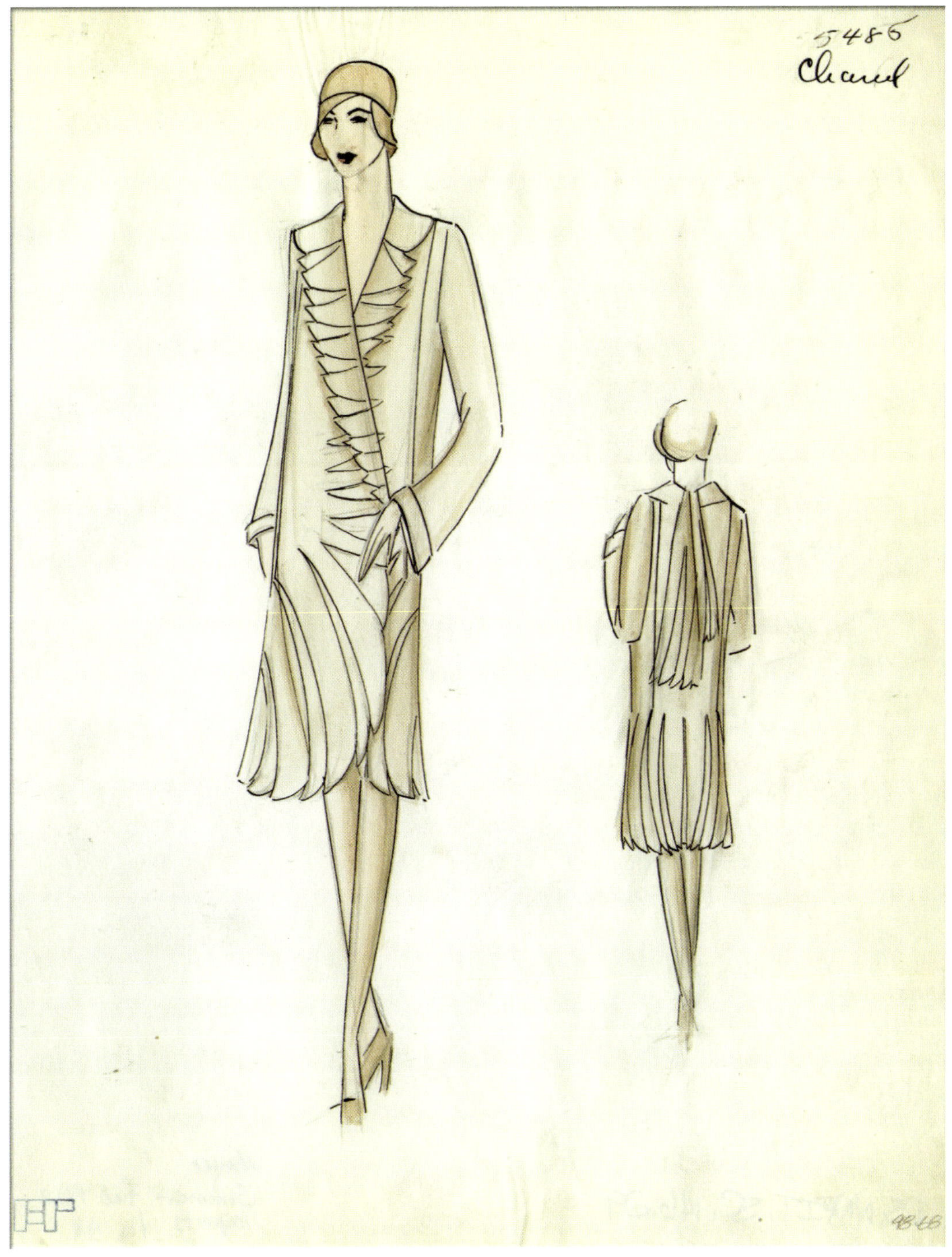

ABOVE: Original sketch from A. Beller & Co. of a Chanel design, February 1929

LA PAUSA; HEAVEN AND HELL 1928

"There have been many Duchesses of Westminster, but only one Coco Chanel."

In the event, it was Bendor who brought about the end of their relationship.

He evidently valued Coco's friendship, but, now in her mid-40s there was one thing she could not provide – the son and heir he needed. It would prove fatal to their relationship, as it had done years before with Boy Capel.

The shattering blow came in 1929; the woman who dealt it was Loelia Ponsonby, daughter of Sir Frederick Ponsonby, later Baron Sysonby. Bendor had met her in a London nightclub, proposed not quite one month later and married her on 20 February 1930. Ironically, it became a union of 'unadulterated hell' which produced no children either.

Coco was not best pleased – despite her struggle to combine the relationship with her professional commitments and the heated arguments between the pair over Bendor's continued dalliances with other women, she did not appreciate being permanently cast aside.

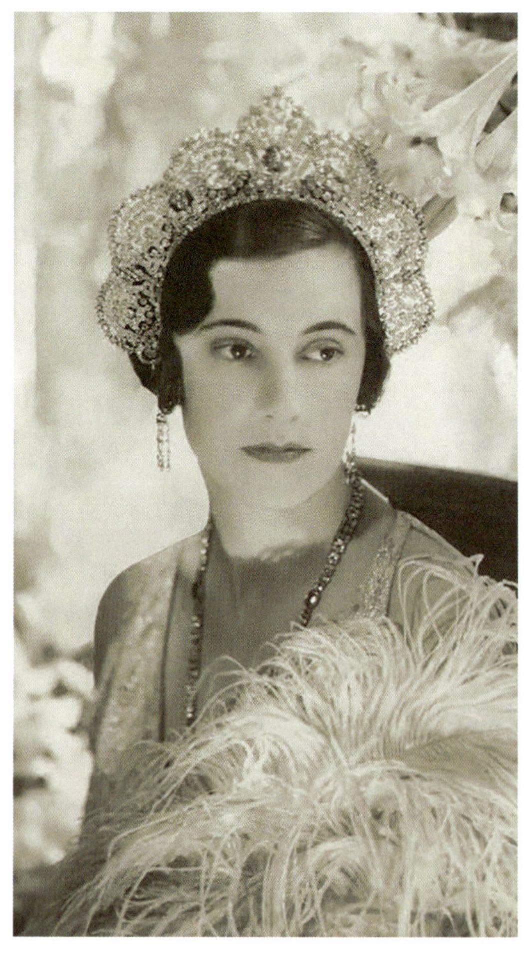

RIGHT: Coco in Biarritz, France, circa 1928
ABOVE RIGHT: Loelia Ponsonby

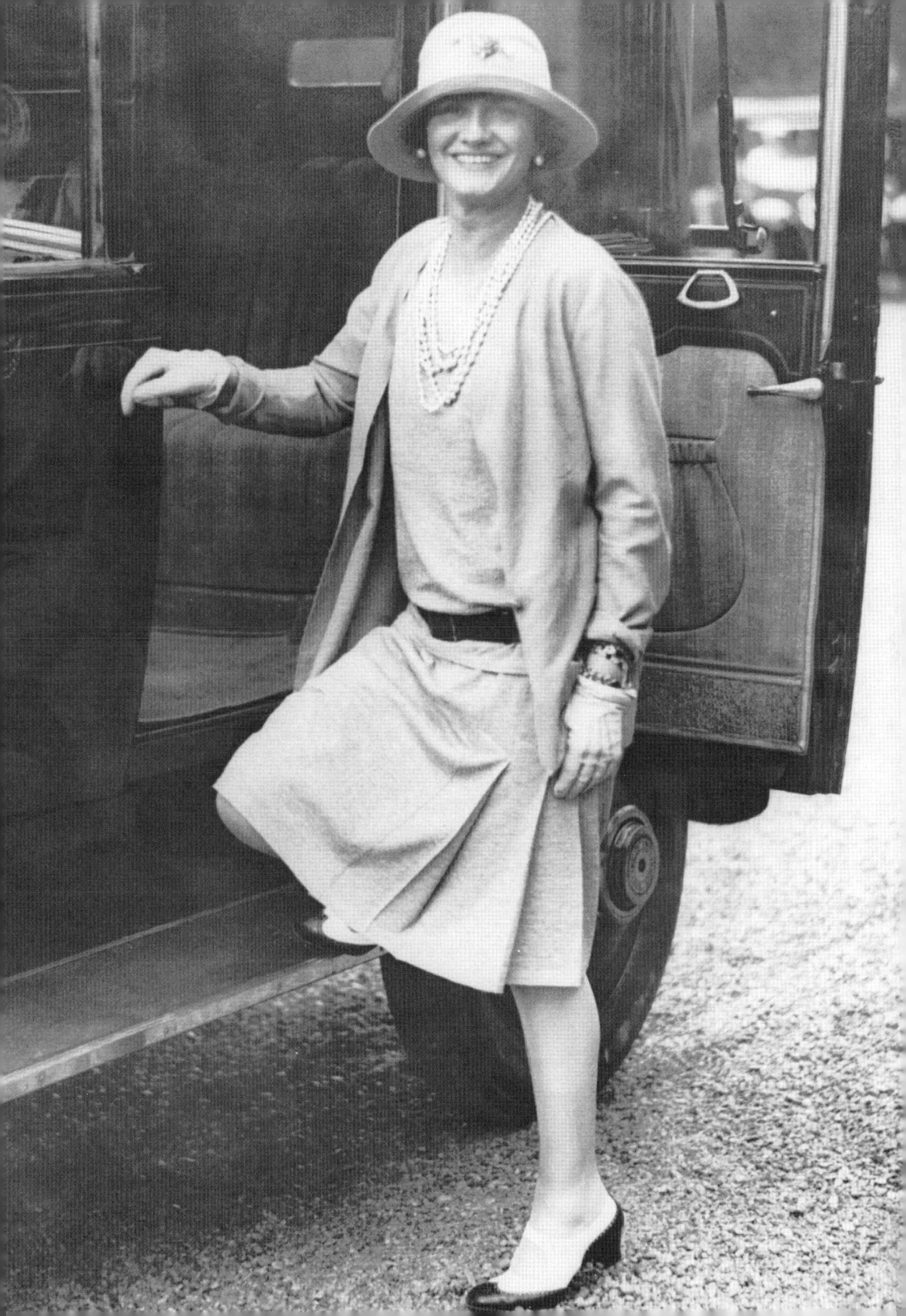

"If you are sad, if you are heartbroken, make yourself up, dress up, add more lipstick and attack. Men hate women who weep."

COCO CHANEL

Once again her emotional life had been upset by a woman born into privilege, unlike her, and in circumstances beyond her control, a situation that she could least abide.

Her way of coping was again to re-write the situation. She retrospectively relegated her 10-year relationship with Bendor into insignificance, declaring that she was 'bored with the excessive, careless way of life', adding 'For ten years, I did everything he wanted. But fishing for salmon is not life.'

She emerged from the relationship with an enviable property portfolio which must have been of some comfort.

Until 1934 she retained the use of Bendor's house in South Audley Street, London, rent-free. And also she now had her house La Pausa, built on five acres of land in Roquebrune-Cap-Martin in the Alpes-Maritime in southern France, surrounded by orange groves and wild olives and overlooking the Mediterranean.

It's unclear whether the land was bought with her own money or that of Bendor, but one or both of them made the purchase of the land for six million francs, in 1928. La Pausa was built in record time and was ready by 1930 – the only house that Coco designed from first to last.

Displaying design elements that floated up from

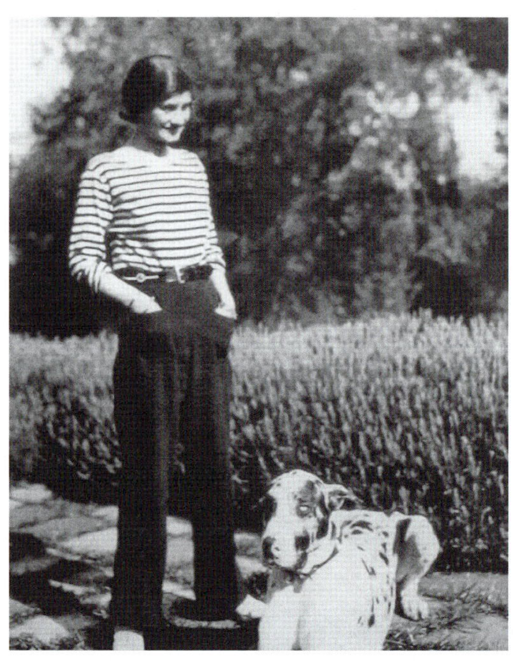

her past at Aubazine – the large staircase was replicated, for example, and there were cloisters on three sides around a courtyard – La Pausa was stylish, elegant, with white walls and lush carpets, but devoid of superfluity.

Windows were arranged in groups of five, recognition of Coco's lucky number and the Chanel N°5 perfume that made such luxury possible. The roof was adorned with over 20,000 hand-made tiles.

For the next 20 years, this retreat would be a peaceful harbour for Coco and her illustrious friends including Salvador Dalí, Jean Cocteau and Misia Sert.

RIGHT: Coco Chanel, circa 1928
ABOVE RIGHT: Coco at Villa La Pausa in Roquebrune, in the French Riviera, with her dog, Gigot

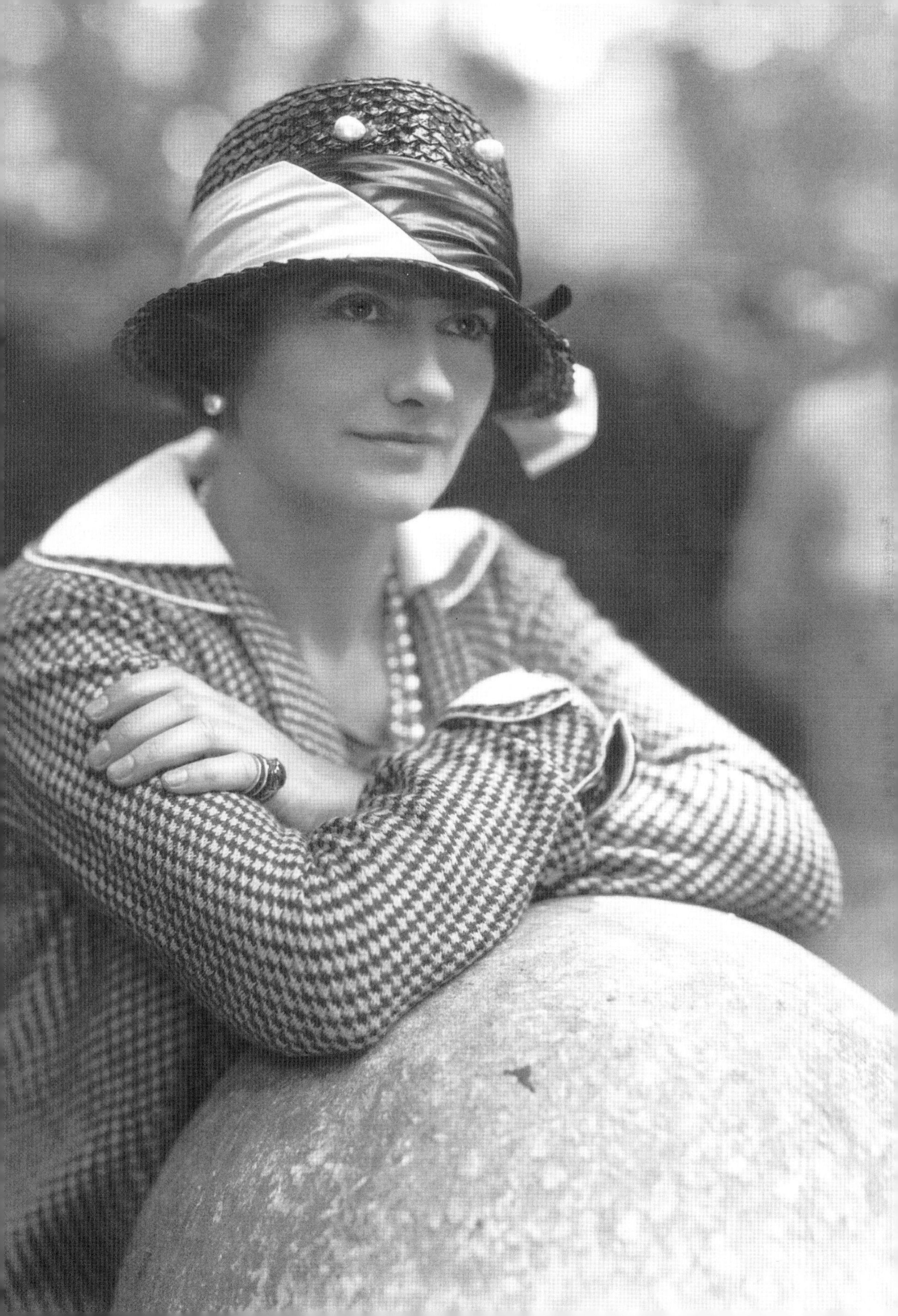

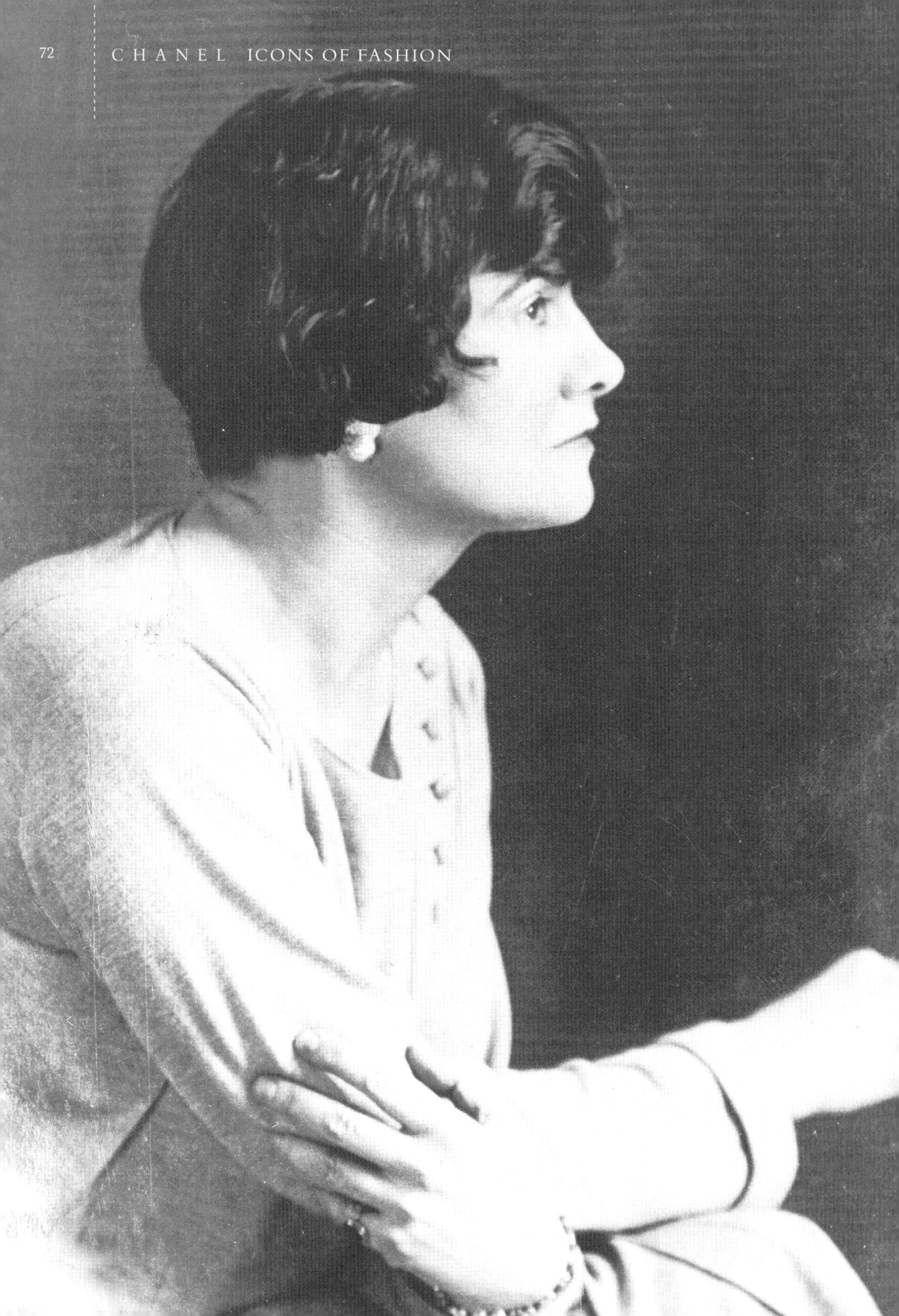

GOODBYE TO DIAGHILEV

Coco Chanel required all her considerable mental strength to negotiate the emotional turbulence of 1929. The year had brought its share of new creative impulses such as the Ballets Russes production of 'Apollon musagète', choreographed by George Balanchine with music composed by Stravinsky.

But the first shock of the year arrived unexpectedly in August when Coco and Bendor, together with Misia Sert, now single having been abandoned by her husband for a Russian beauty Roussy Mdivani, were cruising in the Mediterranean on Flying Cloud.

It was Misia who was handed a telegram from Diaghilev: 'Am sick; come quickly. Sergei'.

The relaxing cruise was immediately ended and Flying Cloud turned for Venice, where Diaghilev, who had been suffering from diabetes, was lying in his bedroom in the Grand Hotel des Bains. When the trio entered, they found the dying impresario in great pain, sweating profusely, with Boris Kochno, his secretary and Serge Lifar, one of the foremost ballet dancers of his generation, at his side.

Sergei is said to have whispered how happy he was to see them both, saying 'I love you in white. Promise me you will always wear white'.

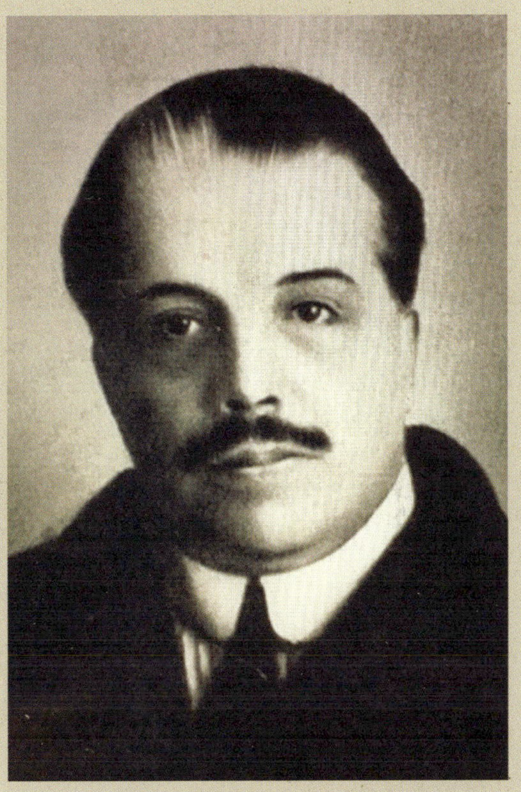

Flying Cloud had arrived in Italy on 17 August and Diaghilev died two days later on Coco's 46th birthday.

Even after his demise, the ever loyal Misia tried to raise money for the Russian's debts by pawning her jewellery. Coco then paid for everything and the two women sat by Sergei on the day of his funeral, wearing white as he had wanted, before he was taken by gondola to his final resting place, the Isola di San Michele, the Venetian Isle of the Dead.

'Of all the wonders that the world had to offer, only art promised immortality.'

SERGEI DIAGHILEV

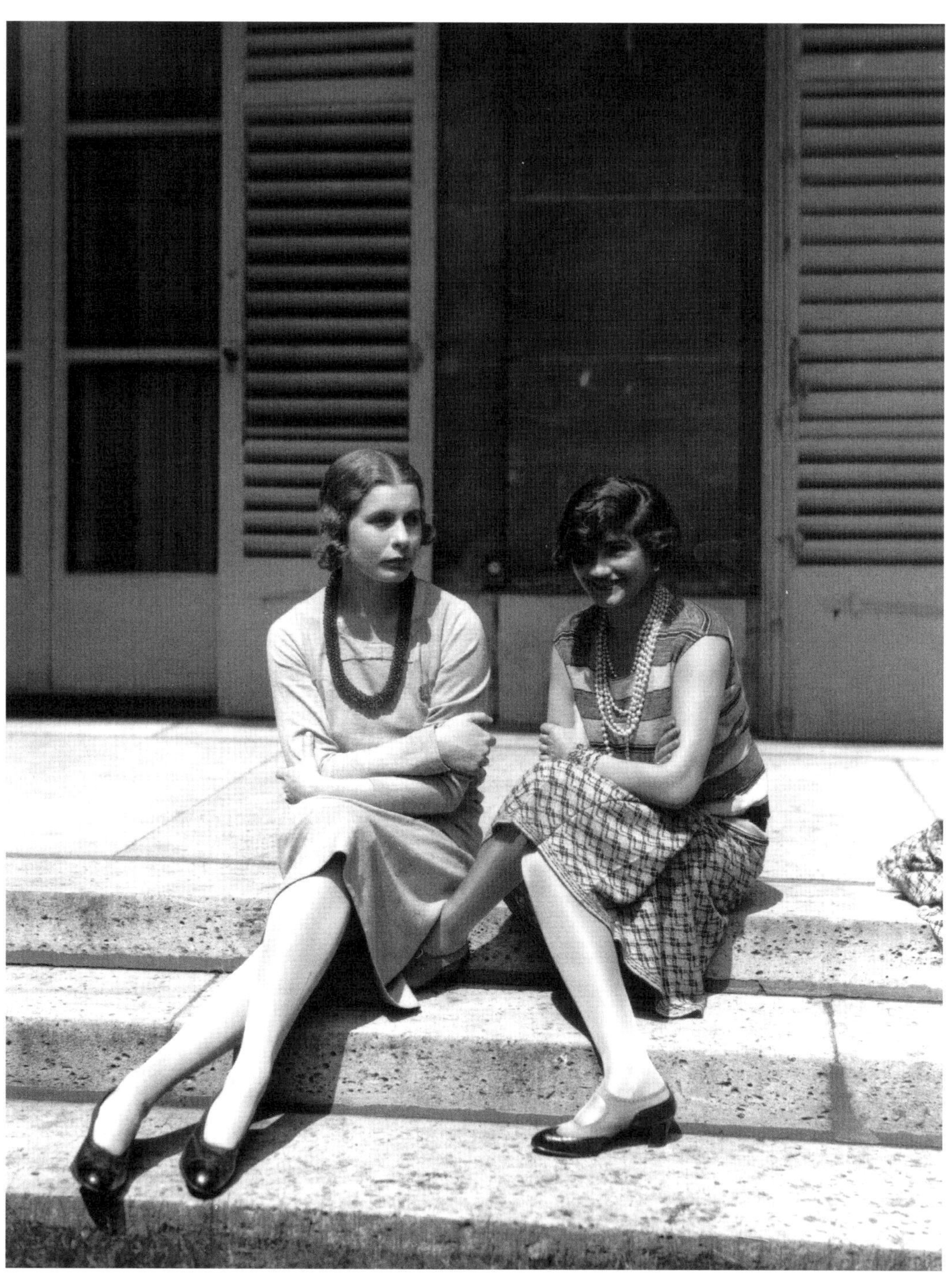

ABOVE: Coco Chanel with Lady Abdy at Faubourg
St Honoré in France, 30 May 1929

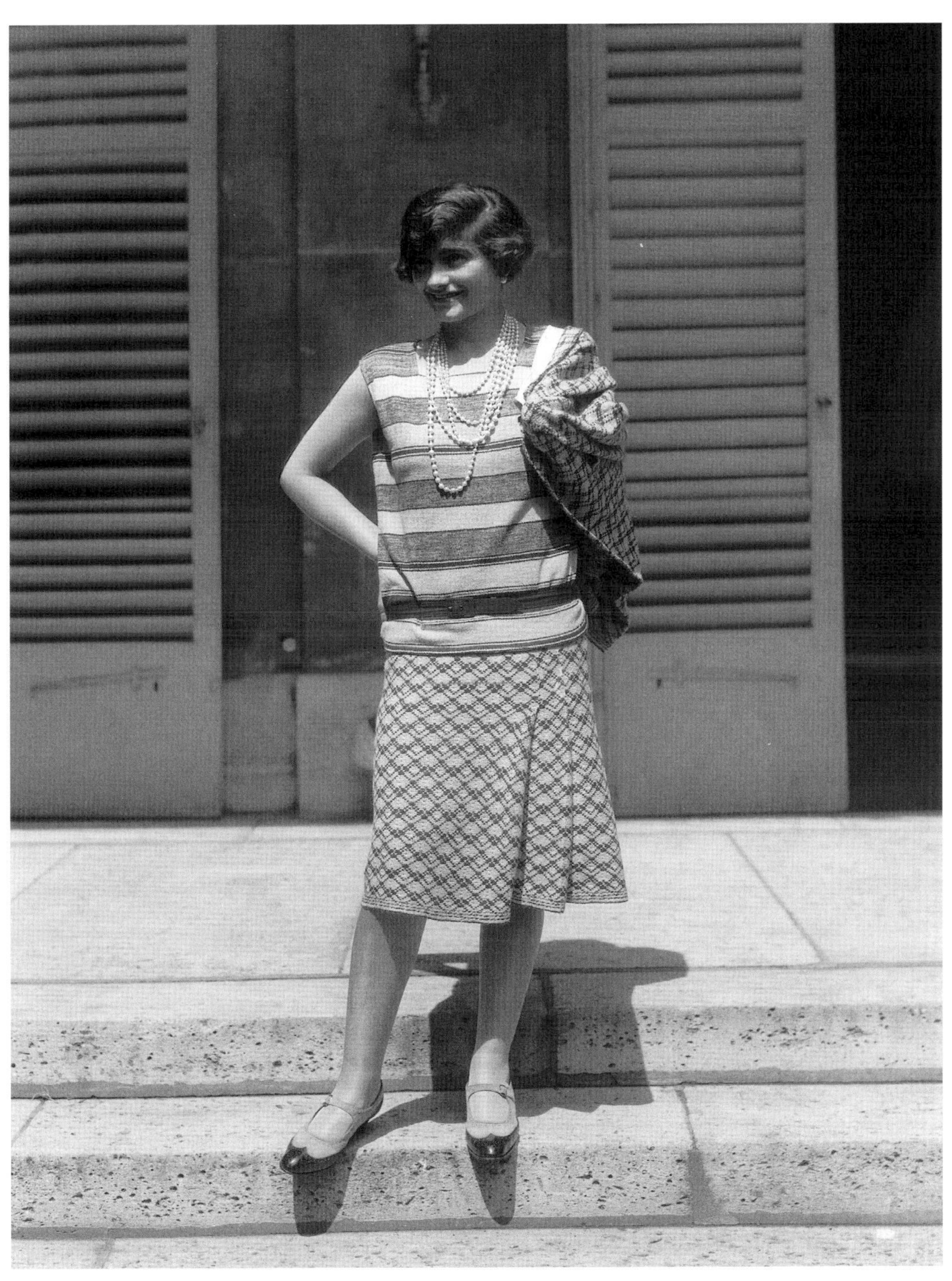

ABOVE: Coco Chanel at Faubourg St Honoré in France, 30 May 1929

WHEN THE WORLD COLLAPSES, DANCE 1929-1931

"Those who create are rare; those who cannot are numerous. Therefore, the latter are stronger."

Despite being famous for having invented 'the little black dress', by 1929 Coco began making the colour white fashionable, too – possibly influenced by Diaghilev's dying words.

Frequently photographed clad in white – traditionally the colour of purity and innocence – Coco was a vision on the Lido in Venice, sporting her jewelled bracelets to set off white beach pyjamas. She would also appear at La Pausa looking cool and elegant in tennis whites, replete with shoes and hat. And aboard the yachts of the great and wealthy she might bring out a white dress and jacket for the hosts' and photographers' delight. Her clients began appearing glamorous parties and balls draped in white satin evening gowns, pearls gleaming.

Coco was so busy that at first she failed to notice the turmoil in the American financial world which finally culminated in the Wall Street Crash of 29 October 1929; Black Tuesday.

NEVER THE BRIDE

Even in the midst of her 'white' period, Coco would rarely design a wedding gown, preparing just a few in the 1930s.

Perhaps because she had never been a bride herself, Coco was not a big fan of weddings and even made a point of breaking with tradition by eschewing the tradition of showing wedding trousseaux as the finale of a Paris collection; no such 'circus' would demean her shows, she announced.

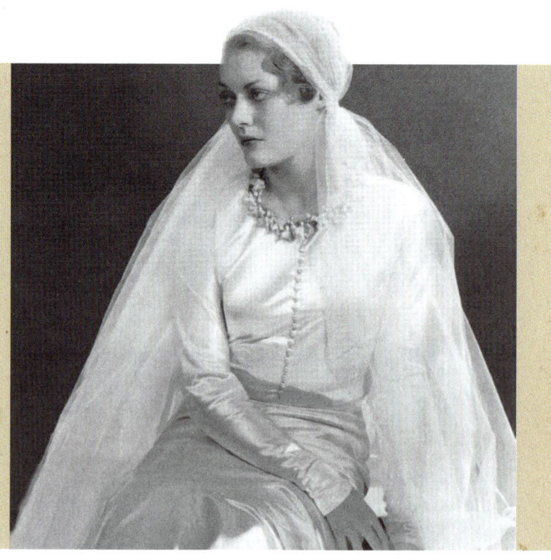

RIGHT: Coco Chanel posing in her suite at the Hotel Pierre during her first visit to New York City. She wears a white silk jacket and pants with pearls, 1931

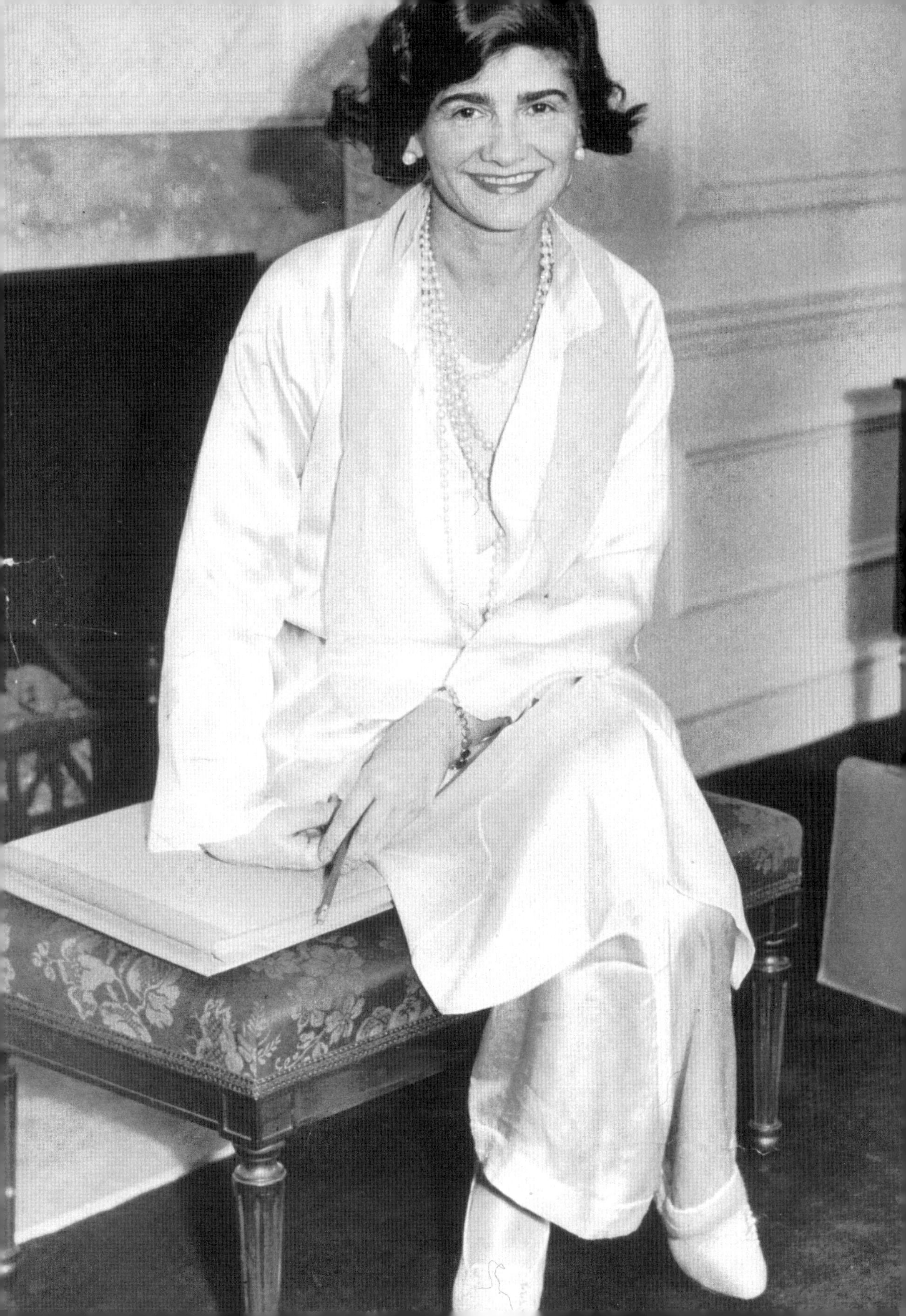

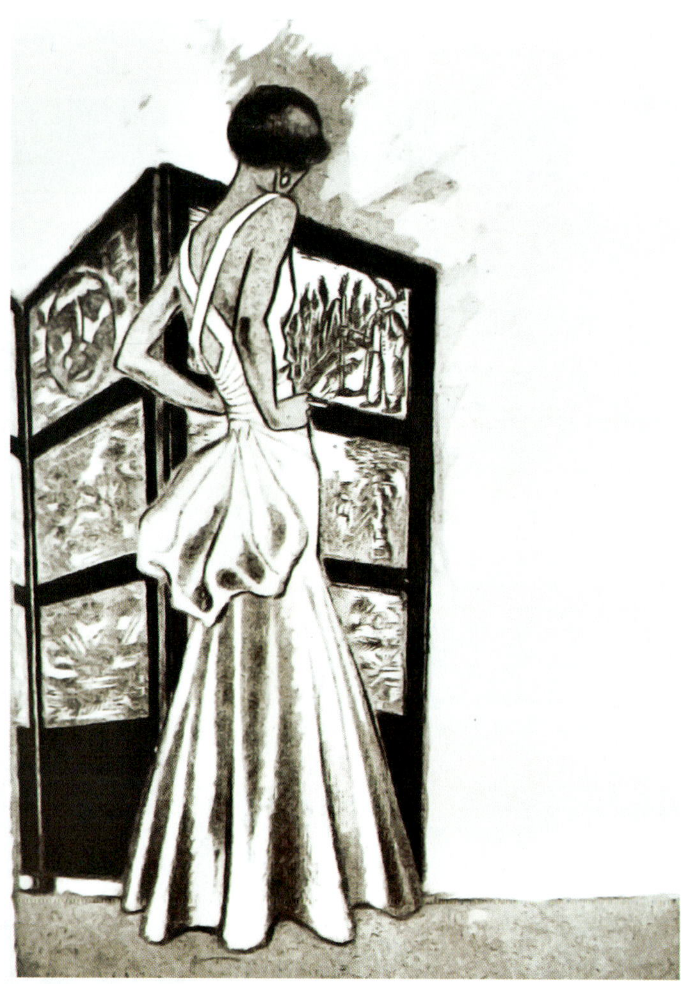

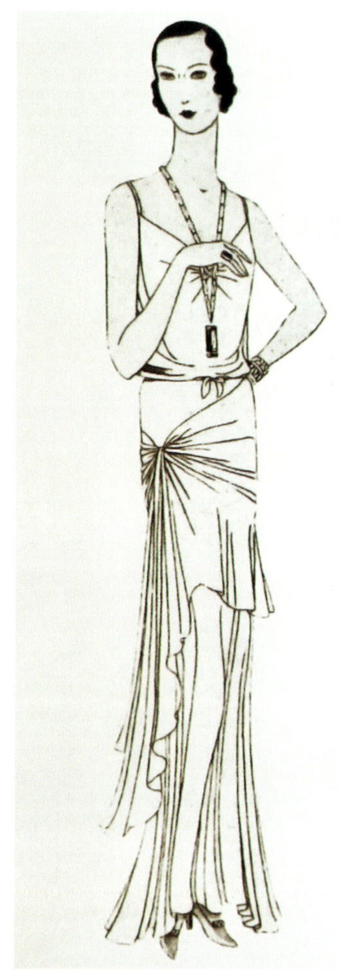

The Great Depression that followed saw hemlines drop back down to full length. Amongst those with less money to burn, the fun and daring of the 1920s faded and modesty, in keeping with the all-pervading sobriety of the mood, made a timid return. The mood became sombre and some designers were bankrupted by the unpaid bills of clothes their customers had paid for by credit.

But in the upper strata of society where Coco moved, the well-to-do socialites whose wealth had survived the crash began to engage in frenetic rounds of balls in the summer of 1930.

One spectacular example of the gay abandon on display in those desperate years was the famous 'White Ball', where Coco's white gowns could be admired en masse, amongst Jean Cocteau's white-plaster mask and wig creations. In Paris, parties were reported to be frequent, fantastic and remarkable, and for the fortunate few, held in the 'true spirit of their time'.

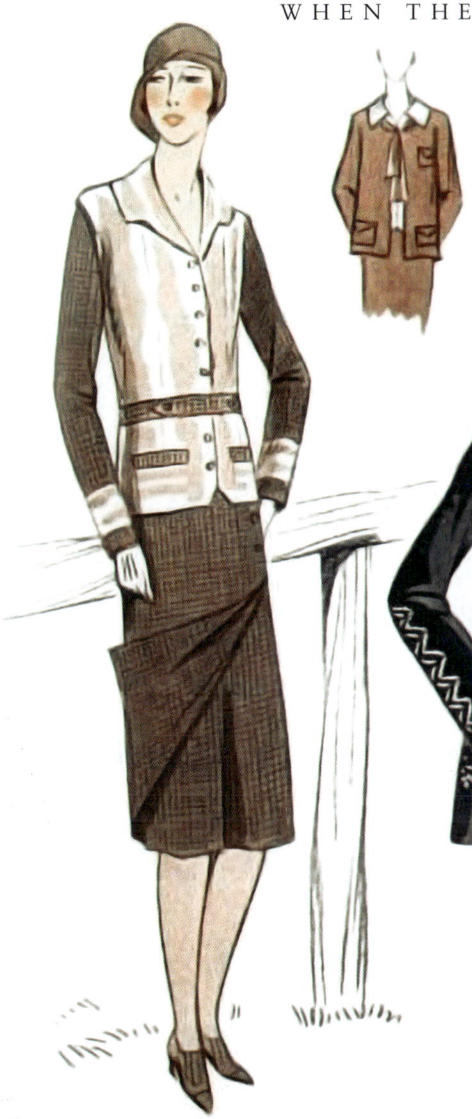

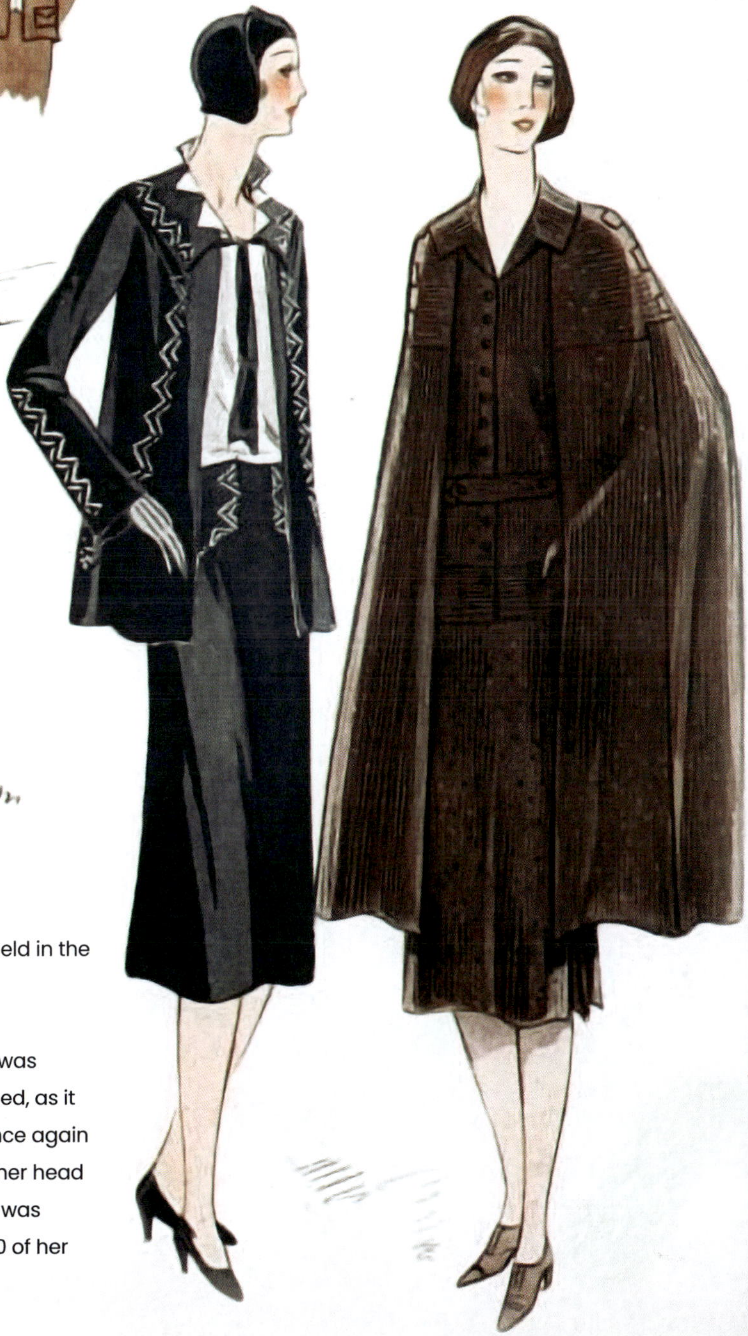

For Coco this outbreak of fearful gaiety was profitable news and her business boomed, as it had done throughout the Great War. Once again Coco emerged from a world crisis with her head above water. As 1931 approached Coco was employing 2,400 workers to prepare 400 of her designs to be shown in two shows.

ABOVE: Chanel designs, circa 1930
LEFT: Chanel designs featured in *Vogue*, 1930s

COCO GOES TO HOLLYWOOD 1931

"I don't care what you think of me. I don't think of you at all."

As the recession gripped America and hit cinema box offices, Hollywood producer Sam Goldwyn had the idea of attracting more customers by incorporating Coco Chanel's famous fashions into his movies.

He figured that adding some Chanel sparkle and elegance to the actors' costumes would make the ladies eager to come to the cinema. His brief to Coco was to create fashionable clothing ahead of its time so that it would still be cutting-edge by the time the films were shown many months after shooting. She was also required to visit the US twice a year and dress the stars on and off screen, so lending them some all-important 'class'.

Coco wasn't exactly bowled over by the offer, despite it involving a million-dollar contract, but she accepted because by now the recession was affecting her business too – Americans of reduced circumstances were cancelling orders and

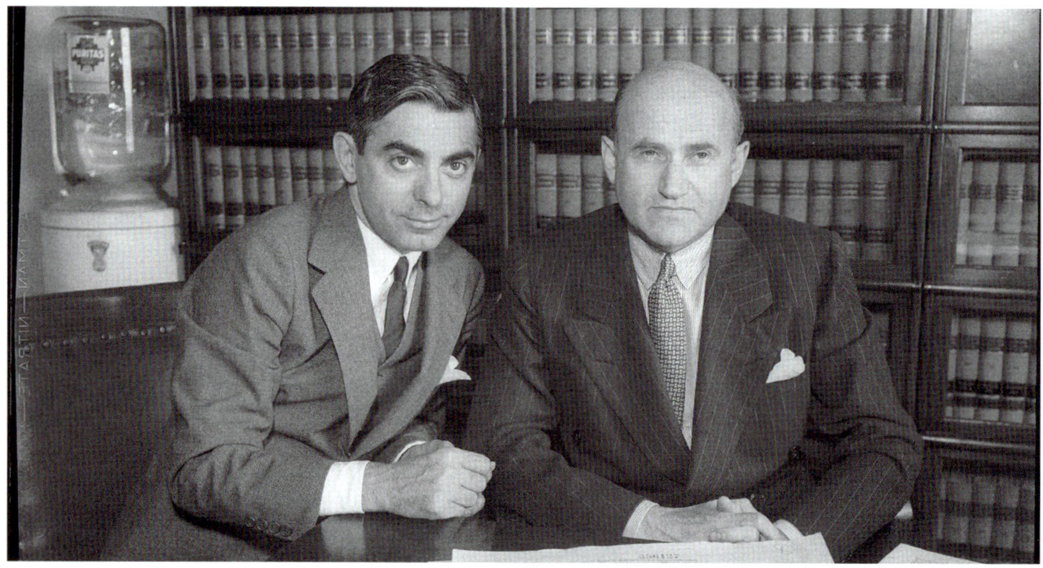

ABOVE: Eddie Cantor (L) and Samuel Goldwyn (R)
TOP RIGHT: Coco Chanel with actress Ina Claire, 1931

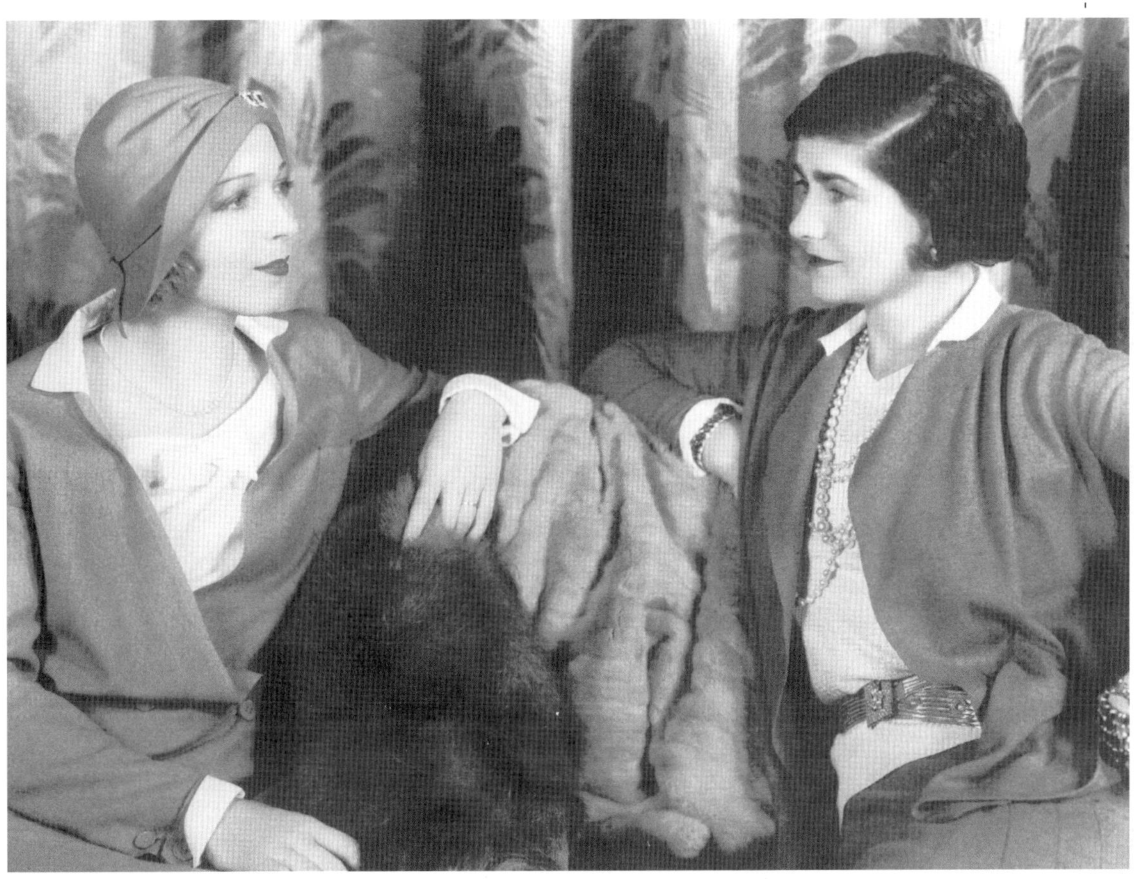

departing France, so she had to reduce her prices. She made it crystal clear that she was not a costume designer, declaring on her arrival in California that she had '... not brought my scissors with me', intending her designs to be completed back in Paris.

Could the world-renowned fashion queen satisfy the pampered darlings of the silver screen? As 47-year-old Coco set sail for America on 25 February 1931, many journalists wrote indignant columns about 'Europe' supposedly coming to rescue American women.

She was accompanied by her friend Misia Sert and Maurice Sachs, a young writer and secretary to Jean Cocteau. After a short stay in New York, where Coco fronted a press conference wearing a rose-red jersey and a white knit blouse adorned with a long string of pearls, the party travelled to Los Angeles on a white train, pampered with champagne and caviar.

Waiting in Hollywood to welcome Coco was the famous actress Greta Garbo who accompanied Coco to a reception at Sam Goldwyn's house where the glitterati were gathered, including director Eric von Stroheim and actors Frederic

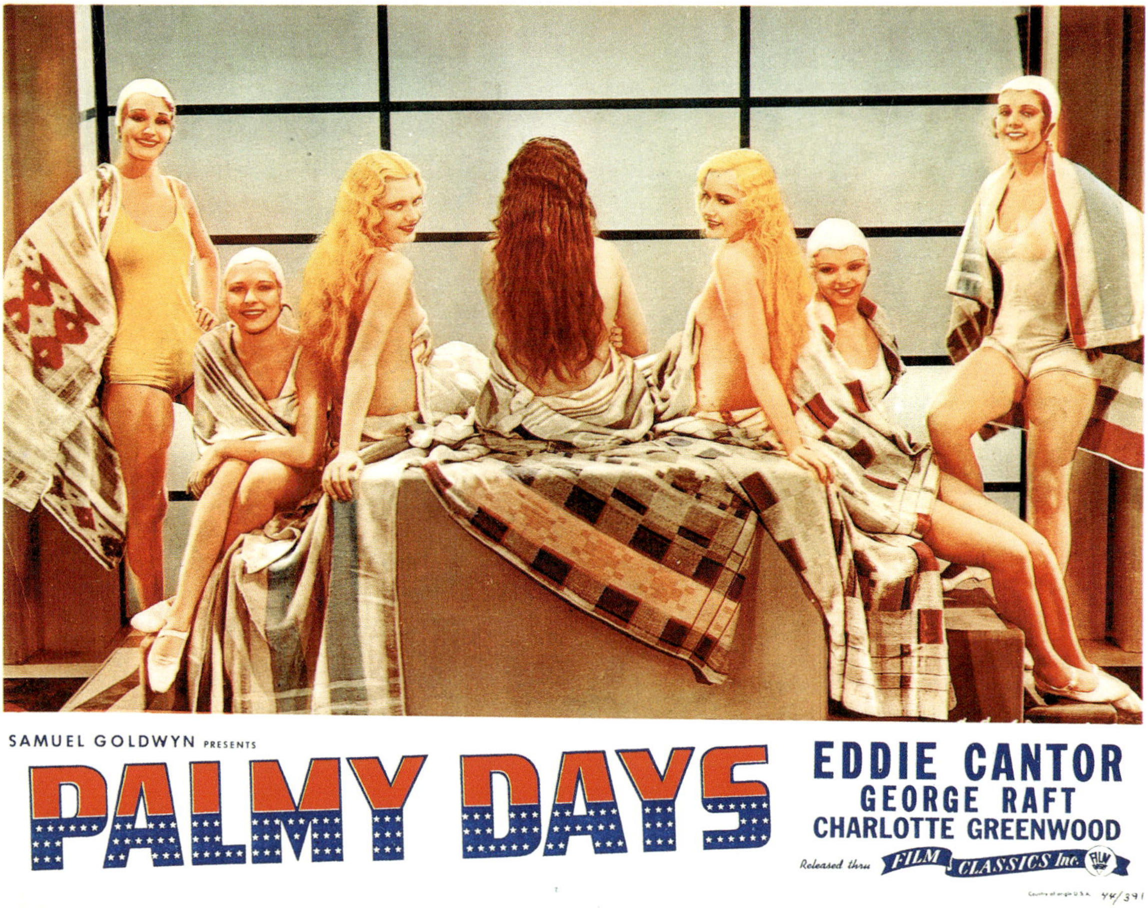

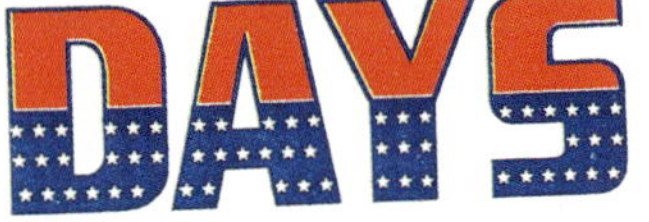

March, Marlene Dietrich and Claudette Colbert.

Coco once said of Greta Garbo '… the greatest actress the screen has given us, was the worst dressed woman in the world'.

Knowing that moviegoers sought to escape the gloom of their everyday lives, Goldwyn had chosen a bubbly Eddie Cantor/Busby Berkeley musical called 'Palmy Days' as Coco's first film. Coco was to dress its leading lady Charlotte Greenwood, with the help of two assistants. One of them, Adrian Adolph Greenberg, had the unenviable task of explaining to Coco the requirements that distinguished movie costumes from real-life clothing. The wardrobes had to be photogenic – subtlety would be lost on the screen – and the designs should show off and embellish the actresses. Coco's contribution to the movie's success was minimal.

The second film, 'The Greeks had a Word for Them'

ABOVE & RIGHT: Movie posters for films featuring costumes designed by Coco Chanel

which premiered in February 1932, involved Coco designing some 30 dresses for the three leading actresses Joan Blondell, Ina Claire, and Madge Evans.

Then in what would be her third and final Hollywood project, Coco dressed Hollywood diva Gloria Swanson in 'Tonight Or Never'. This was the most daunting project of them all as Gloria was already cited as one of the 'Top Ten Best-Dressed Women in the World' and, favouring the designs of her preferred couturier René Hubert, she did not take kindly to being contractually forced into Chanel creations.

Despite the resulting tension, Coco's costumes for Swanson were beautiful and understated. Even Swanson herself conceded that one black satin gown which draped to the floor, was, '… a great work of art in the eyes of both of us'.

An added challenge for Coco was that Swanson became pregnant in the weeks between fittings and had to wear a girdle to make the gowns fit. Swanson was pleased that as a result of Coco's skill, even in those extreme circumstances, it was impossible to detect the pregnancy on screen.

Despite the beautiful dresses, the film, however, failed to ignite the box office and after that Coco packed up shop and returned to Paris, Hollywood having failed spectacularly to work its charms on her. Afterwards she said disdainfully, 'Once it is agreed that the girls were beautiful in their feathers there is not much to add'.

The feeling was more or less mutual, it seemed.

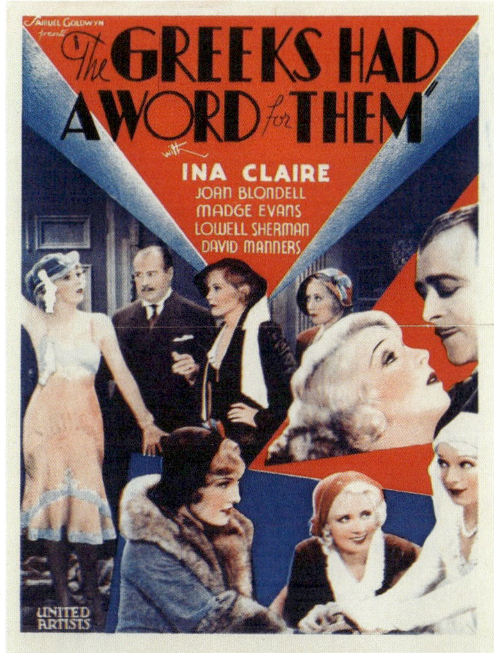

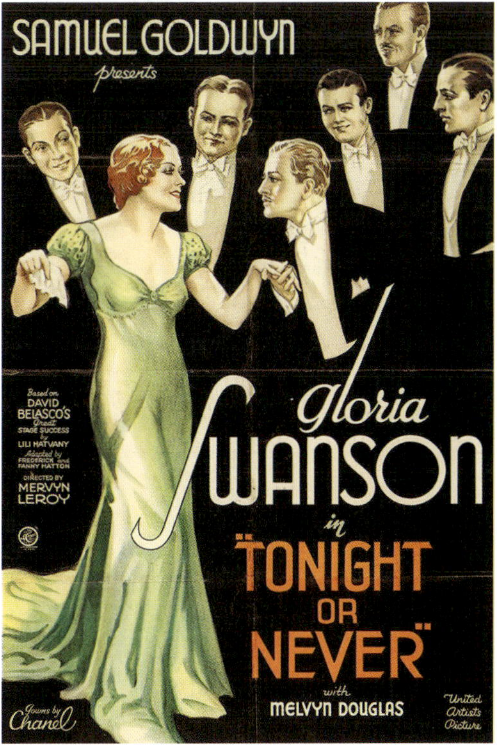

ROARING THROUGH THE THIRTIES 1932-1935

"Jump out the window if you are the object of passion. Flee it if you feel it. Passion goes, boredom remains."

Coco's ability to maintain deep friendships with those she had taken as lovers, sustained two important relationships in her life: one with the poet Pierre Reverdy, and the other with Paul Iribe, illustrator and designer of decorative arts.

Romance with Reverdy, with whom she begun a liaison in 1921, foundered in 1926 when he retreated to the Pays de la Loire with his wife. Nevertheless their subsequent friendship endured for 40 years. Those oft-quoted Chanel maxims are thought to have been partly crafted by Reverdy because Coco's private letters show little of the flourish that inhabit her enduring 'proverbs for a modern life'.

Paul Iribe and Coco became lovers in 1931 when he was still married to Maybelle Hogan, an American heiress by whom he had two children and who funded his Parisian shop on the chic Faubourg Saint-Honoré, where Coco also lived. However, when he questioned Coco's need to be surrounded with so much luxury, she abandoned Faubourg Saint-Honoré and took up residence in two modest rooms. They eventually both ended up in the Ritz Hotel.

It was Paul who worked with her to design pieces for the glittering exhibition of diamonds Coco staged in 1932. Called the 'Bijoux de diamants' collection, it included jewellery of magnificent beauty and worth millions; necklaces without clasps, wrap-around rings, a 'fringe' necklace, ear-drops, brooches, tiaras and bracelets.

It was a huge success, visited by over 30,000 people. Yet Coco was under pressure for ignoring the moral considerations of the contrast between a show of such giddy wealth and the everyday lives of ordinary citizens struggling as the depression continued to cut deep.

As 1933 came around Coco felt obliged to defend in public, in a magazine article, her displays of sumptuous fashion in times of bitter hardship and distress. The main thrust of her defence was that she provided employment to those who would otherwise, perhaps, be destitute. She was providing money to keep the economic wheels rolling at least a little.

Paul and Coco's relationship became so intense that by 1933, many thought that marriage was

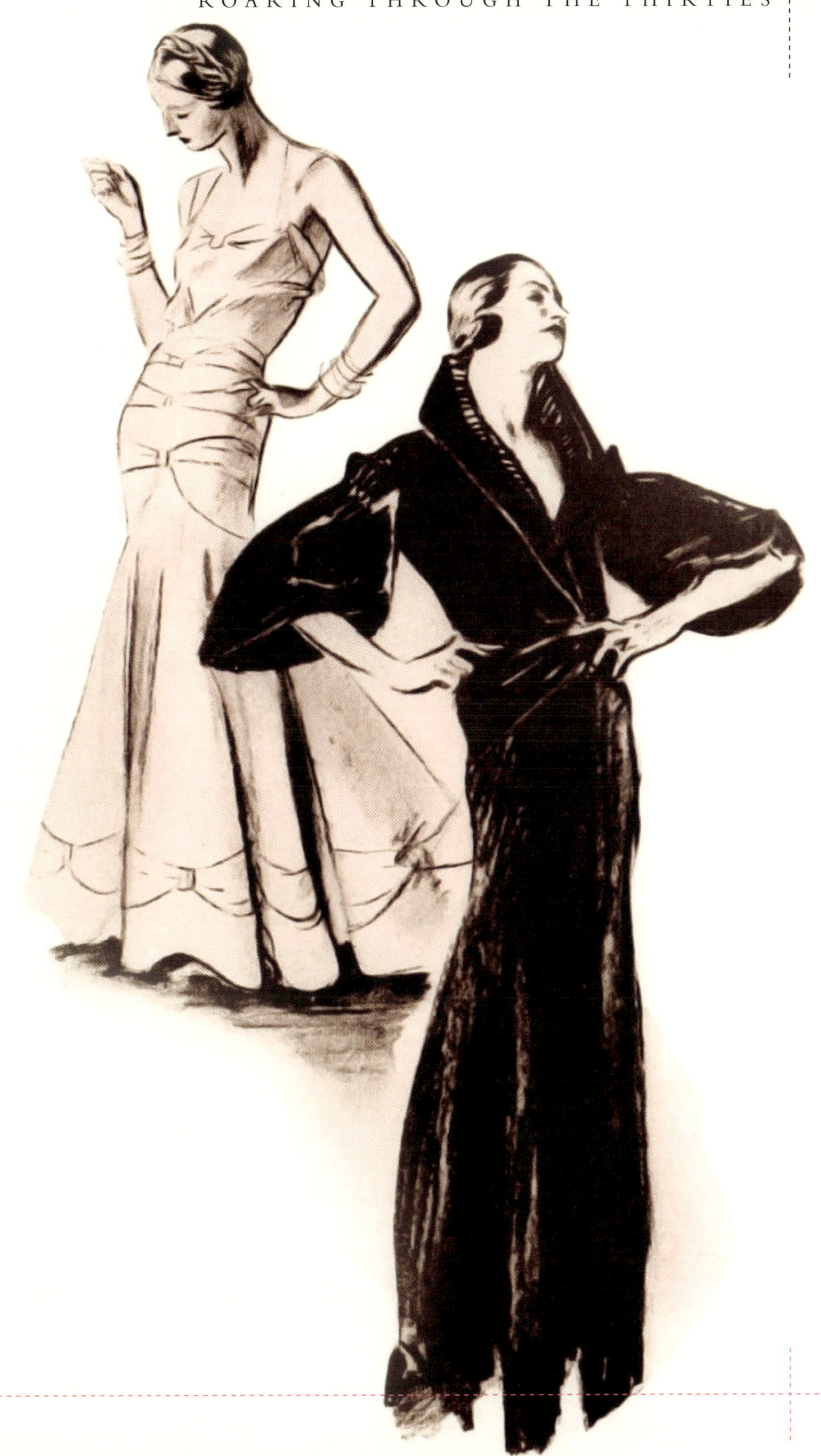

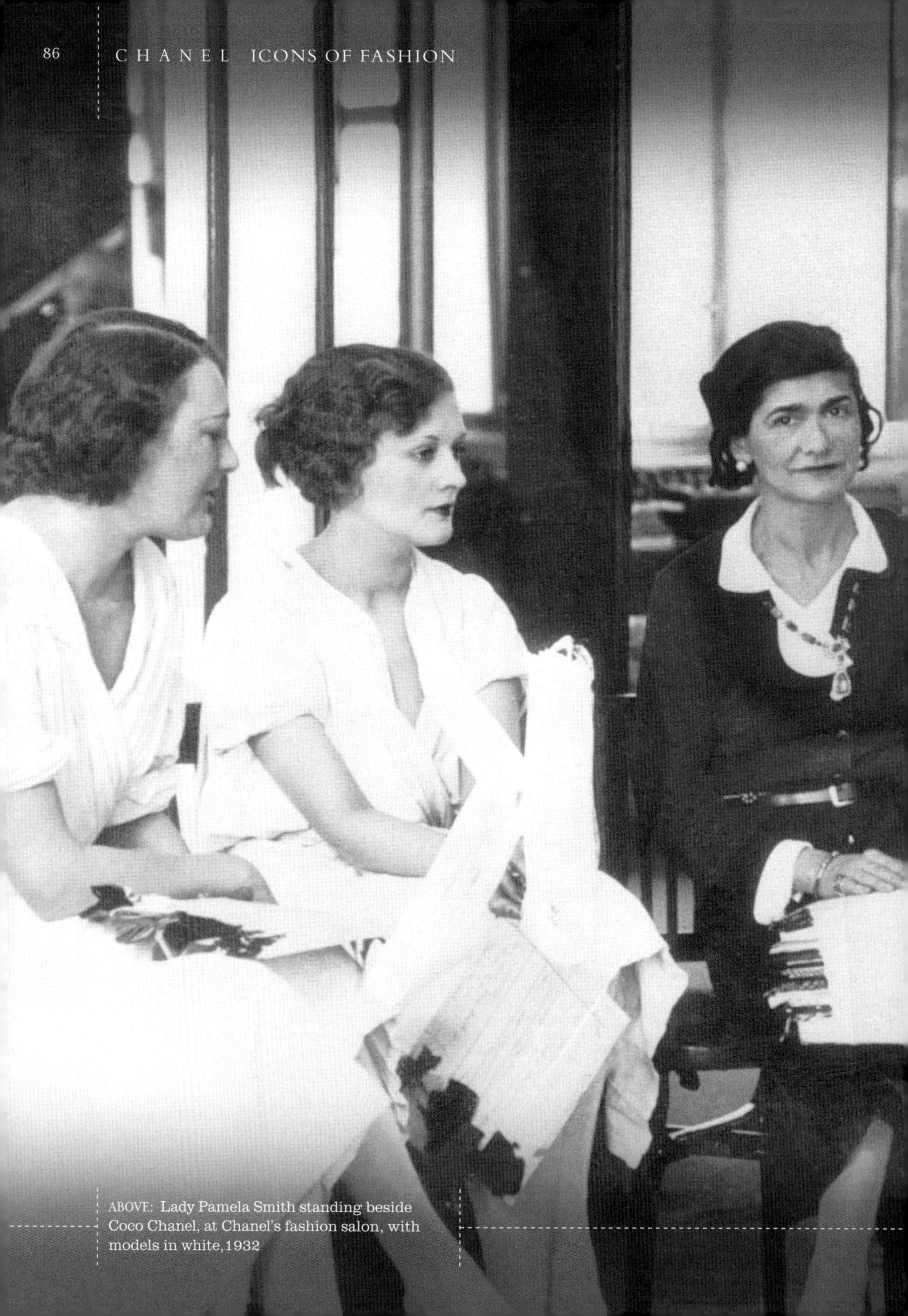

ABOVE: Lady Pamela Smith standing beside Coco Chanel, at Chanel's fashion salon, with models in white, 1932

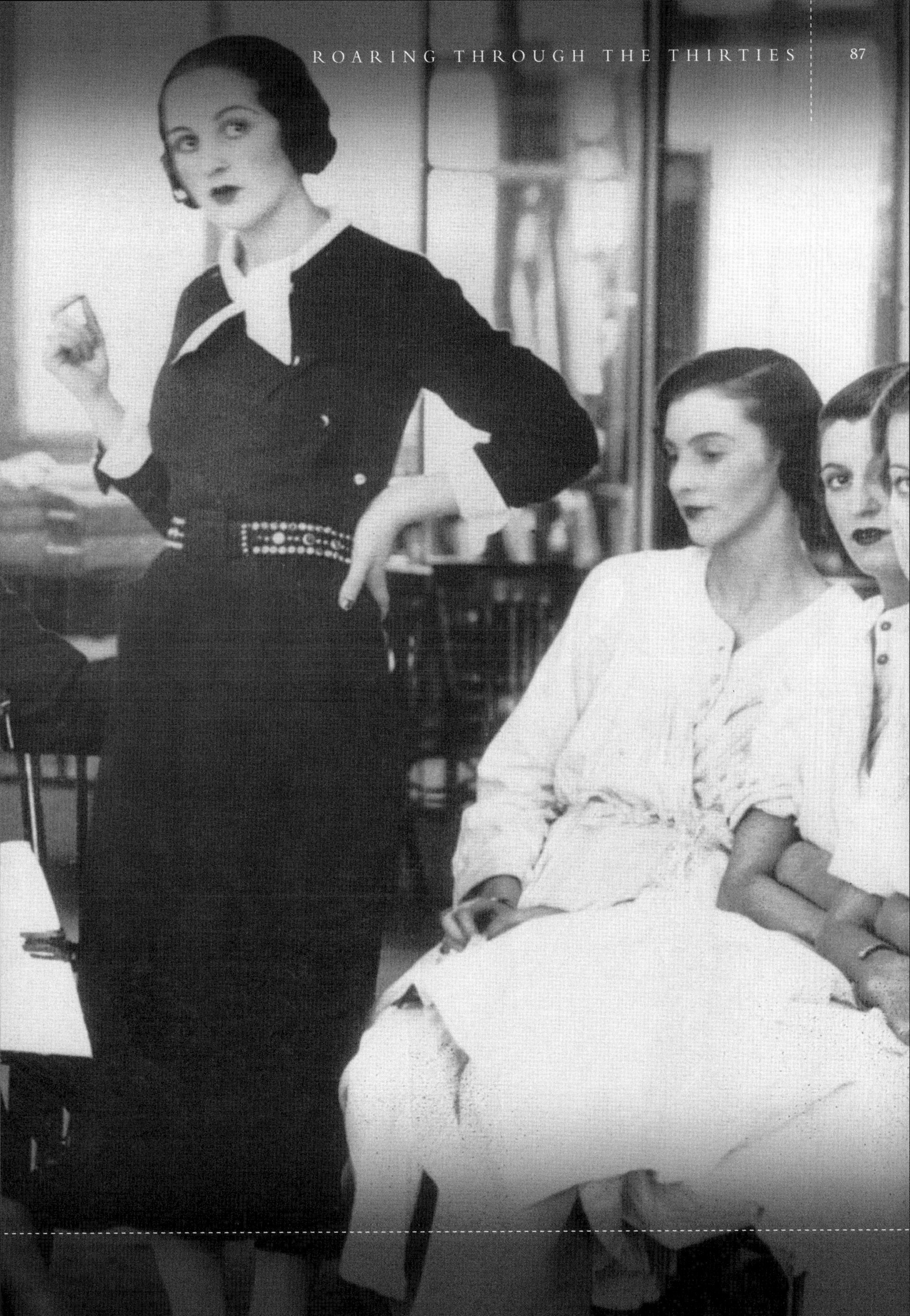

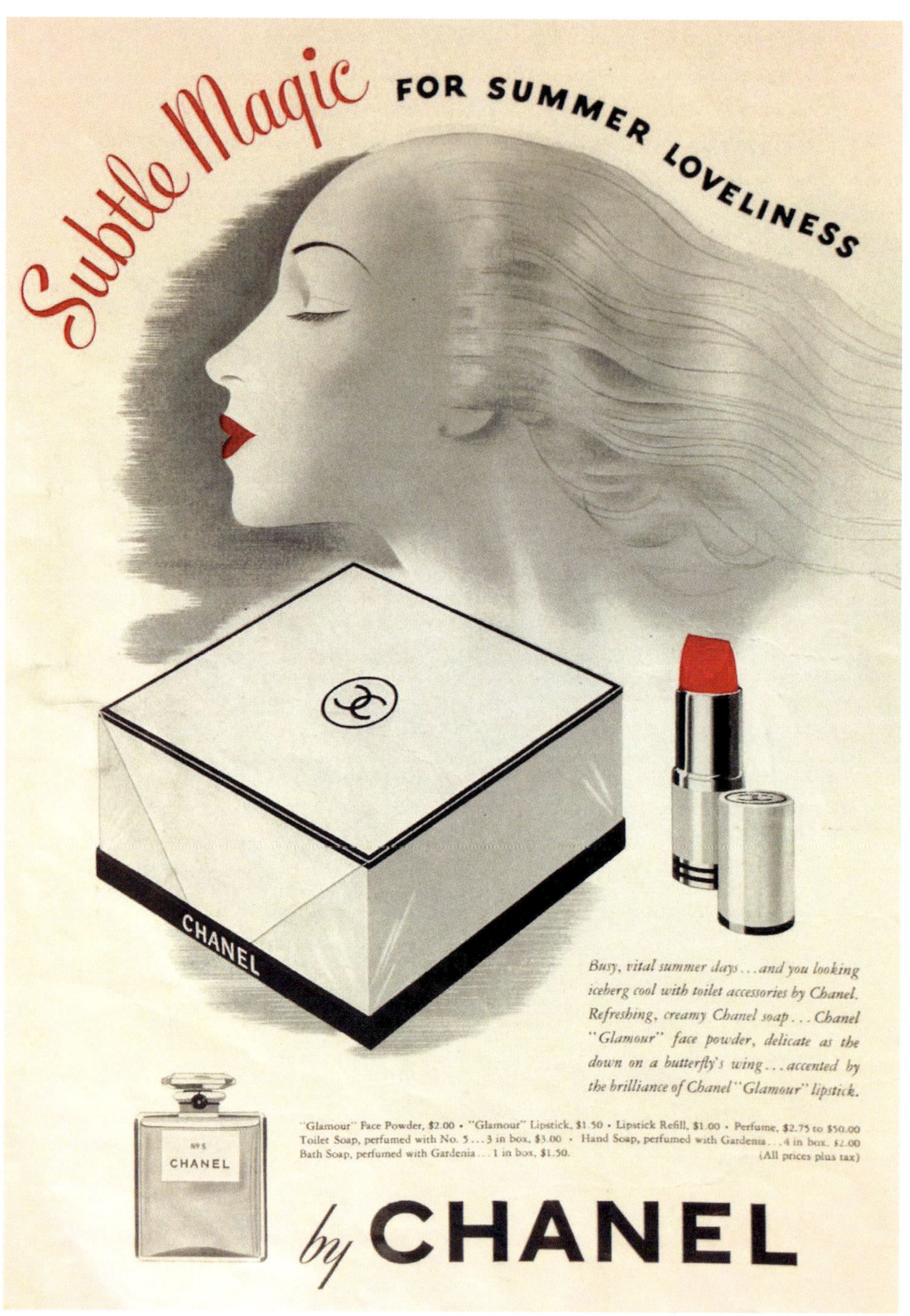

ABOVE: Chanel advert, circa 1936
RIGHT: Bouché sketch of Chanel's gypsy dresses,
Vogue 1938

imminent. In keeping with all of her previous lovers, Iribe, of Spanish descent, was a womaniser and charmer, softly-spoken and as ambitious as she. The deep connectivity between the couple was based on shared values and characteristics. She evidently valued his wit, which was peppered with provocation, professional self-propulsion and the right-wing inclinations, which – to what degree is uncertain – also informed her own life.

She had commissioned illustrations from Iribe way back in 1908 and had helped to support his nationalistic, antisemitic newsletter, Le Témoin, which had featured Coco as a model for the illustration of Marianne, the historic symbol of France. His professional fame had seen his life move along on an upward trajectory into financial and societal success, in parallel with Coco's.

In one of her 'thoughts' intended for public consumption, she said she considered him to be '… the most complicated man I ever knew', which seems an anodyne, if not penurious description of such an important relationship.

'There is time for work and time for love. That leaves no other time', is another of Coco's sayings. For her and Paul there was, indeed, no other time – in 1935, whilst playing tennis at La Pausa, Paul Iribe simply collapsed and died.

The court was never touched again.

Once more, Coco reached for the veil of silence to draw across her life with him. But considering that theirs was a relationship that so upset her, Coco was so distraught that even her beloved La Pausa was now an emotional burden.

Repression was no longer sufficient to cope with the pain. Watching her lover die was too enormous a psychological weight to bear without assistance, so she sought solace in an 'aperitif', as she once called it, a sedative injection which she would eventually take each night before sleep for the rest of her life.

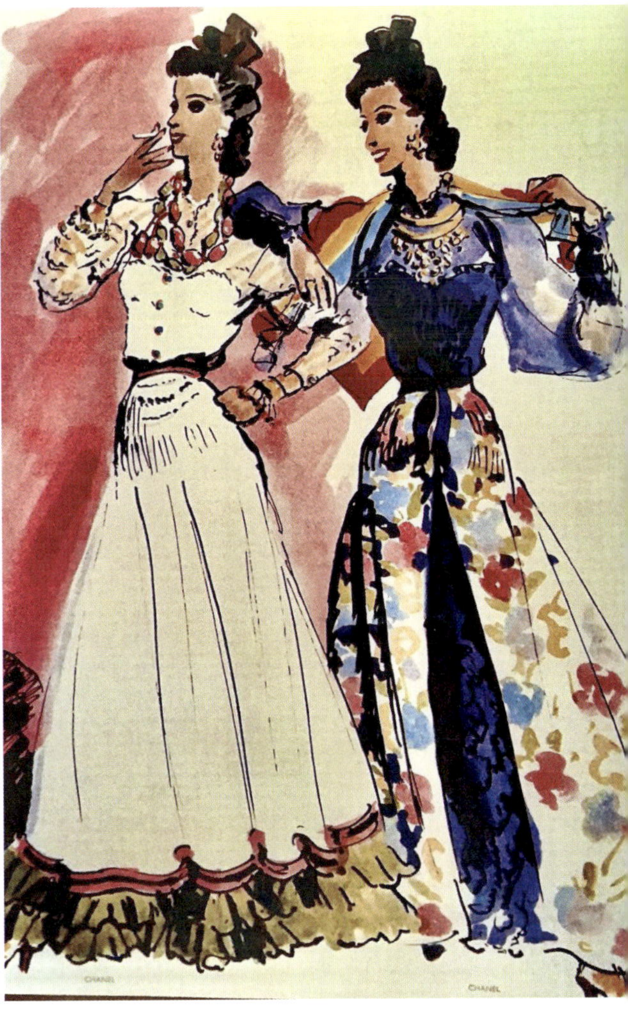

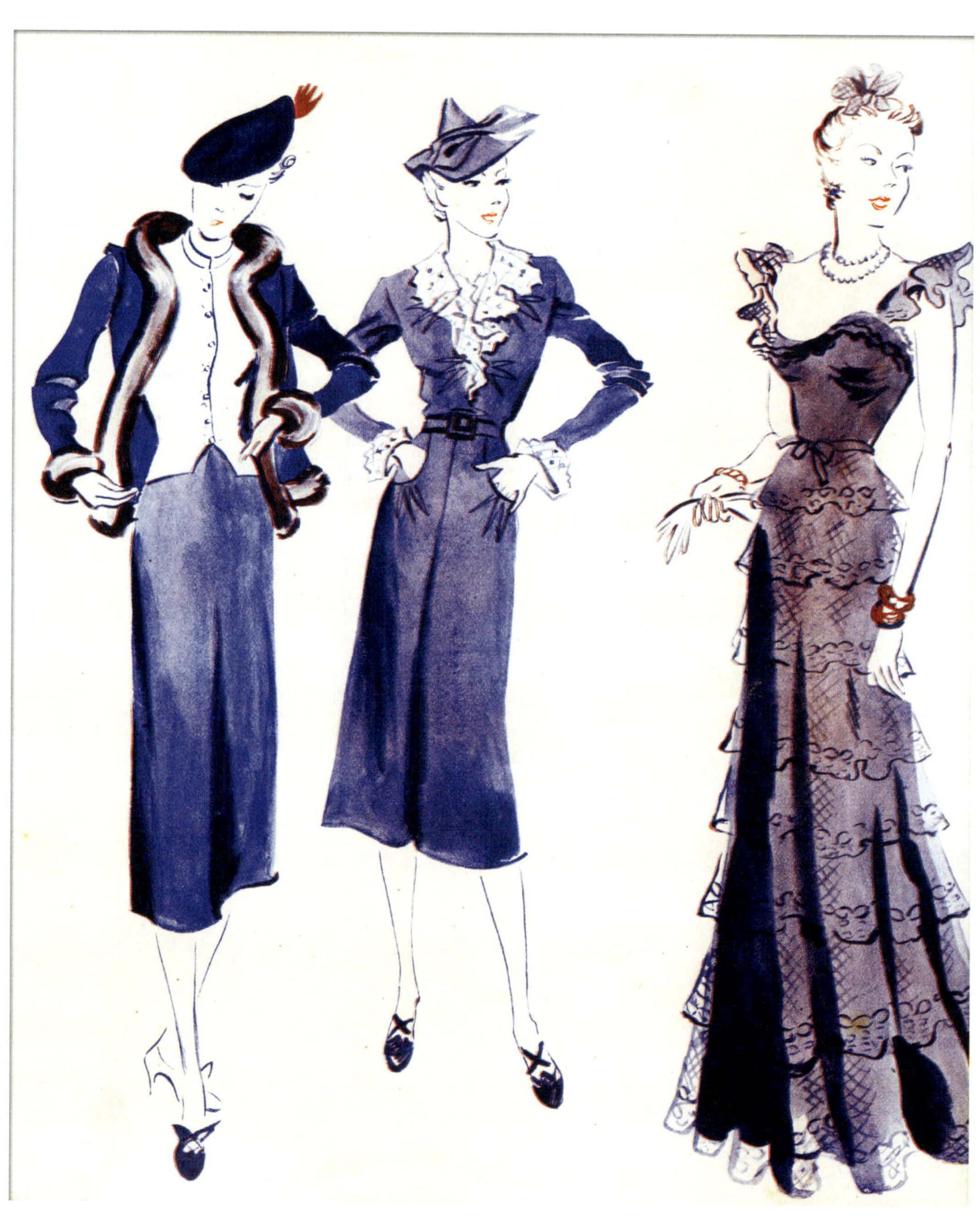

ABOVE & RIGHT: The 1938 autumn collection,
featured in Marie Claire, "The Great Designers
and Their Collections," No. 82, 23 September 1938

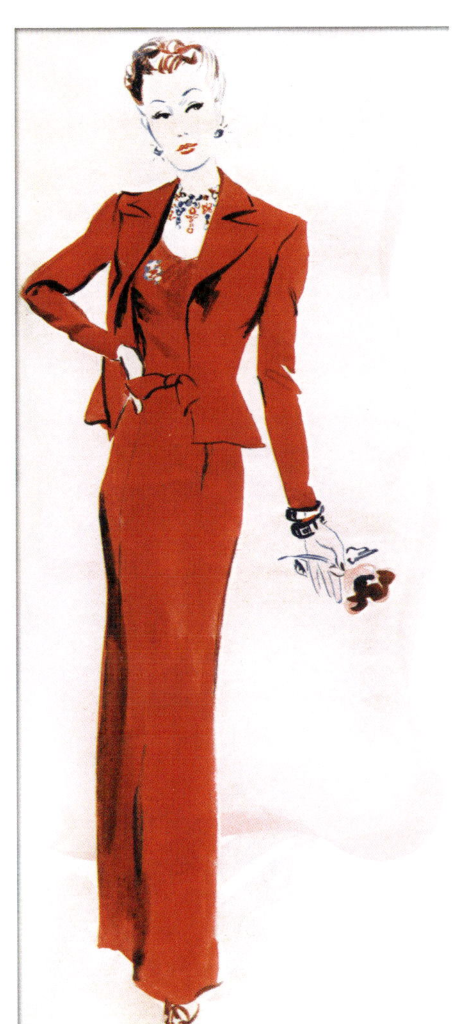

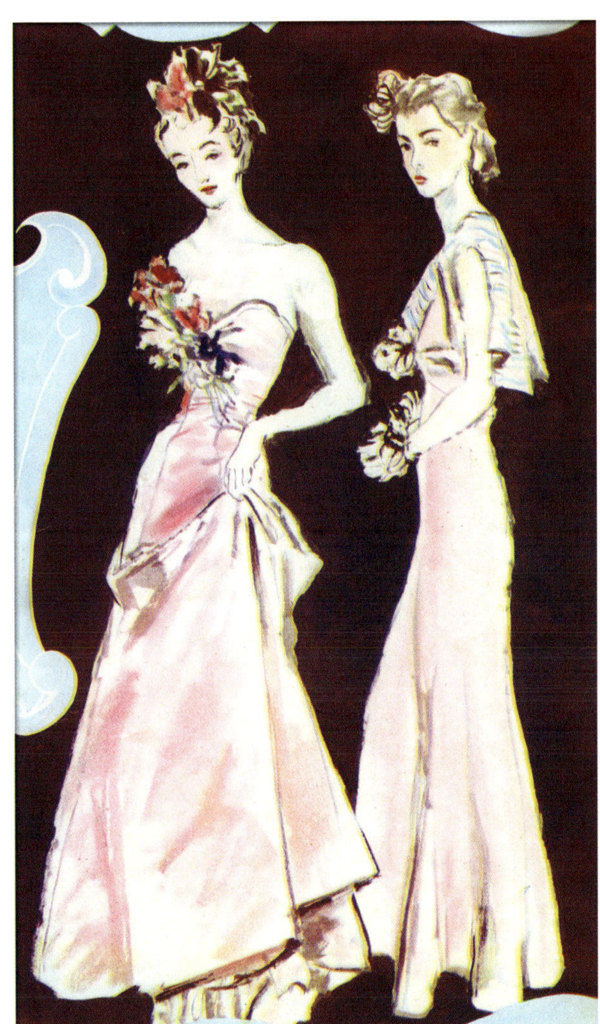

INTO THE SHADOWS 1939

"I stopped working because of the war. Everyone in my place had someone who was in uniform—a husband, a brother, a father. The House of Chanel was empty two hours after war was declared."

Although Chanel was still a successful enterprise in the 1930s, with 4,000 employees, there was now a new contender for the fashion crown that had, until then, indisputably belonged to Coco.

She was Elsa Schiaparelli, Coco's Italian counterpart, whose surrealist designs were attracting the likes of the Duchess of Windsor. The Duchess allowed herself to be dressed by Schiaparelli in a skirt with a life-size print of a lobster on it.

Coco found that her minimalist aesthetic and 'garçonne' look suddenly seemed tired in comparison.

Even worse, Schiaparelli, who had studied philosophy at the University of Rome, was of aristocratic stock, possessed the invaluable connections which Coco had discovered early on were such an asset. In New York, Schiaparelli had met the artists Marcel Duchamp and Man Ray through her work with the French art critic and writer Gaby Picabia who had been married to artist Francis Picabia, a French Dadaist.

The House of Schiaparelli had begun in Paris in 1927, and 10 years later, was beginning to encroach on Coco's terrain. 'Schiap', as Elsa had been affectionately nicknamed, was rubbing shoulders with Marlene Dietrich, Greta Garbo and Jean Cocteau. Like Coco, Schiaparelli understood the power of advertising and was no stranger to the pages of *French Vogue* magazine. She even had her own successful standout creation, a black sweater topped with a white trompe l'oeil scarf, and she appropriated a colour known as 'Schiaparelli pink'.

Also someone who excelled in overturning expectations and established fashion norms, Schiaparelli had added evening wear to her collection in 1931, and relocated her shop premises to 21 Place Vendôme, snappily known as the 'Schiap Shop'.

She collaborated with Salvador Dalí to produce the striking 'shoe hat', an evening gown painted with trompe l'oeil rips and tears, the 'tears dress', and a black gown incorporating padded areas intended to resemble bones. It was hard for Coco to compete with those achievements, which all combined to make the little black dress seemed dated if not dull.

RIGHT: Portrait of Elsa Schiaparelli in 1935 Paris

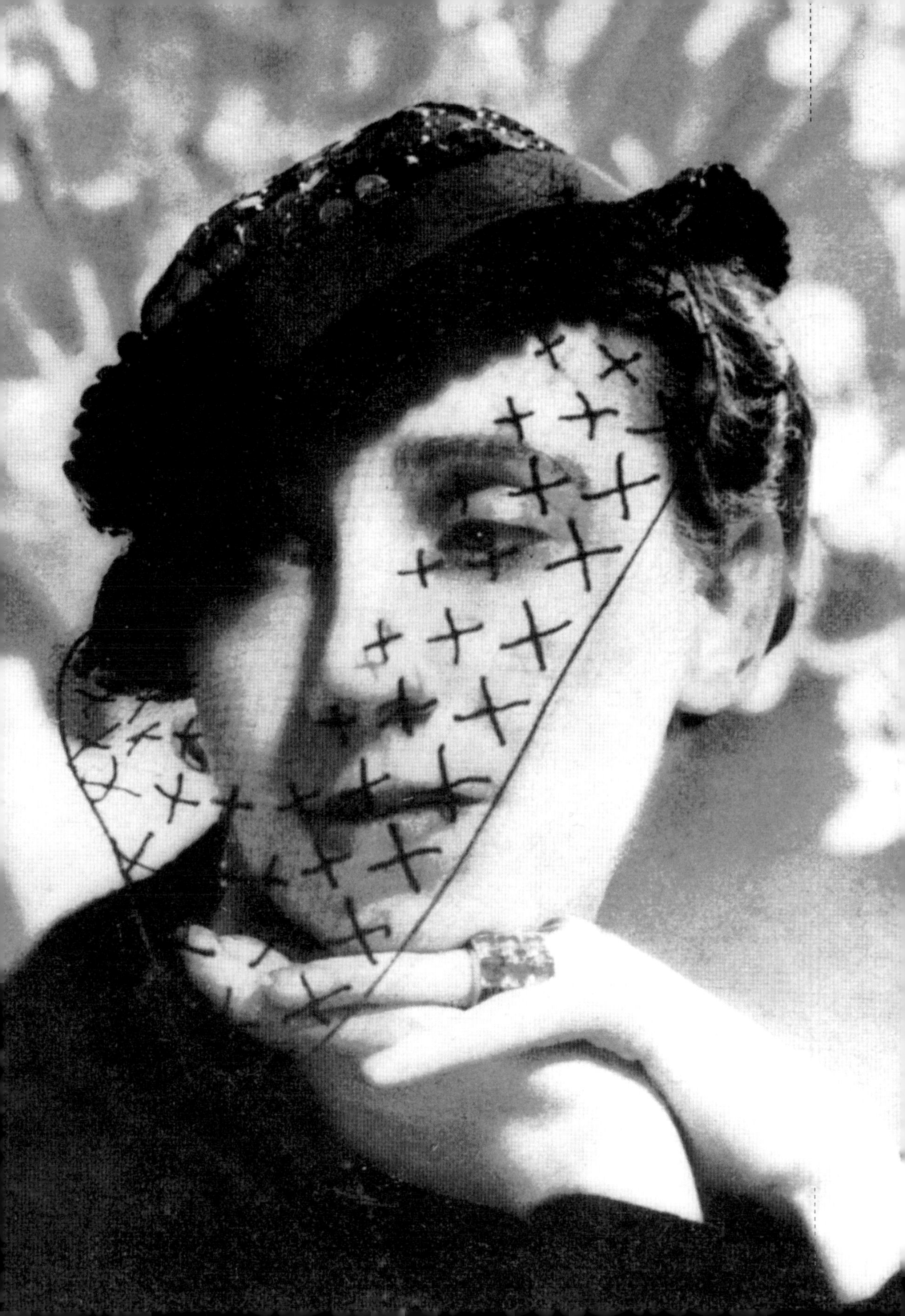

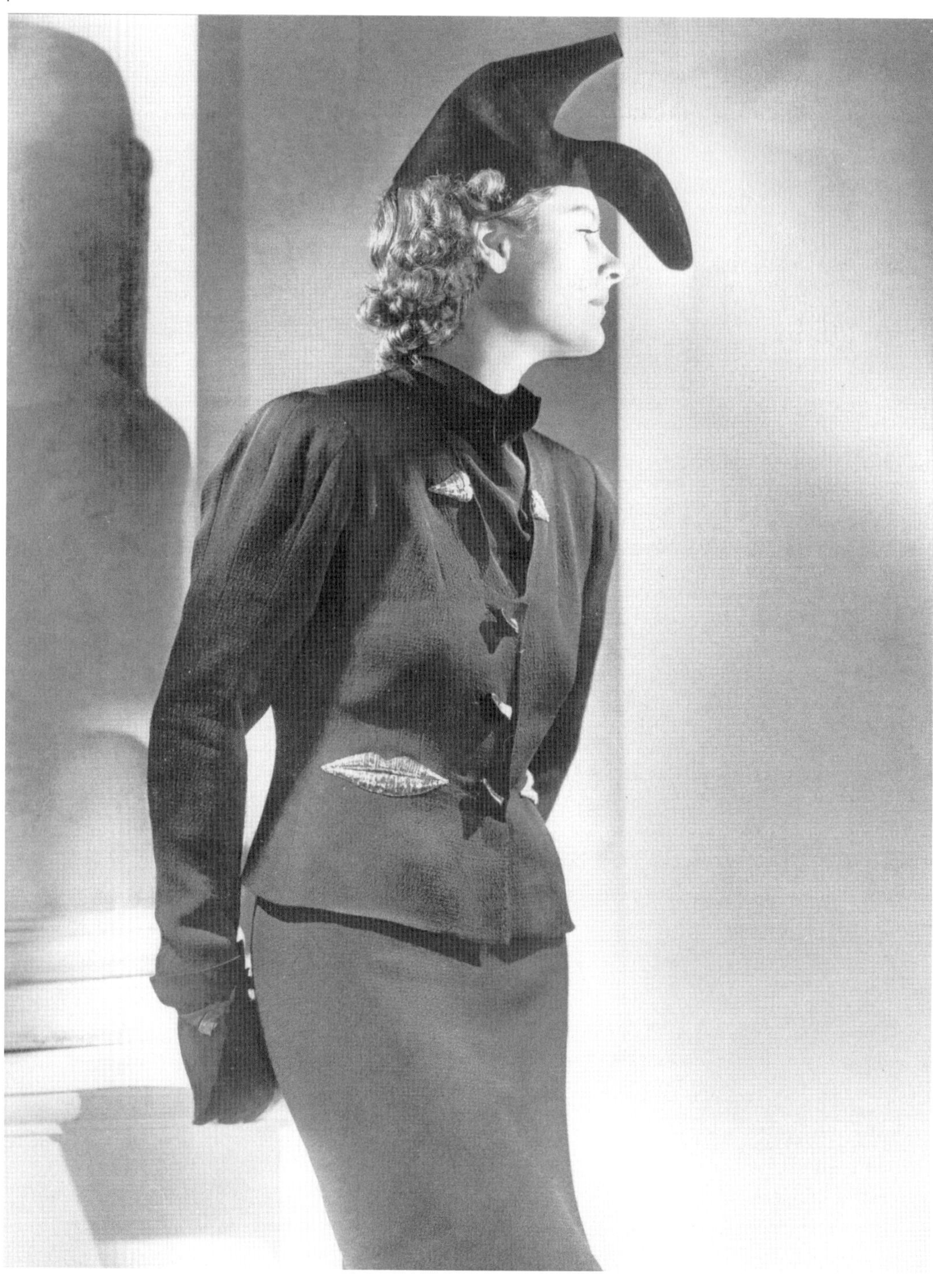

ABOVE: Schiaparelli's 'Shoe Hat'
TOP RIGHT: Schiaparelli's 'Tears Dress' &
Salvador Dalí

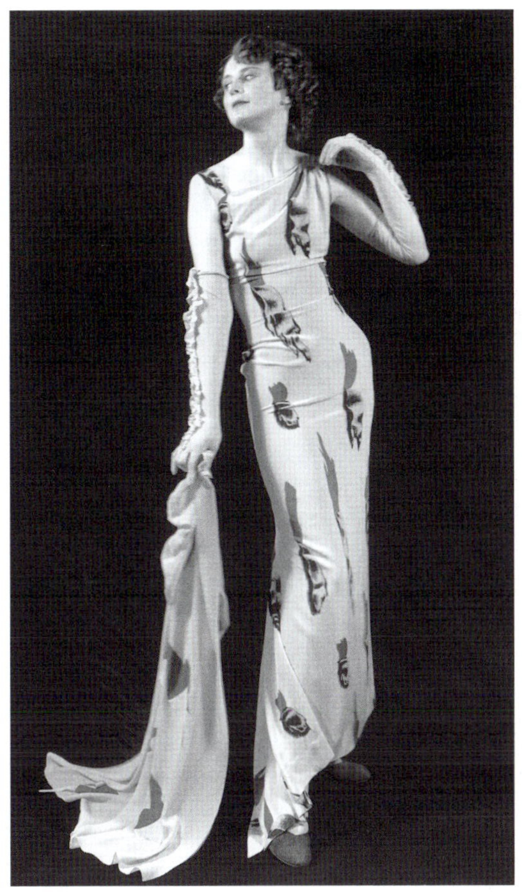

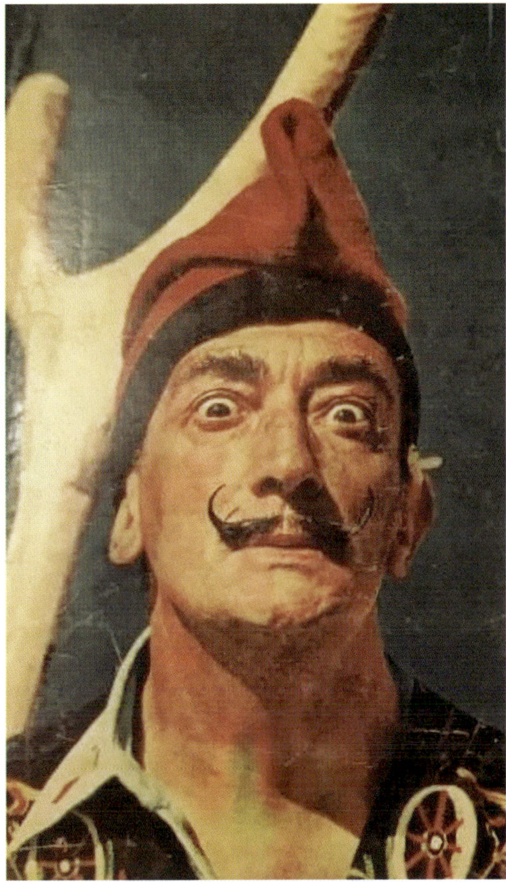

It had after all been designed for the flapper era, which had already been consigned to history by the fast-moving world of fashion.

Coco could hardly complain; as she herself maintained: 'Fashion should die and die quickly, in order that commerce may survive … The more transient fashion is the more perfect it is. You can't protect what is already dead.'

Meanwhile, Chanel's own personal life adventures continued when, in 1936, the 30-year old Italian aristocrat Luchino Visconti di Modrone, Count of Lonate Pozzolo, arrived in Paris. He was hoping to break into filmmaking and chose Paris because it was a pre-eminent artistic and intellectual centre before WW2 and where he hoped to gain access to the influential figures of the day.

Coco's 'feminine beauty, masculine intelligence, and outstanding energy' impressed Visconti greatly when they met and they began an affair, despite his being openly gay. Through her relationship with Visconti, Coco met the renowned film director Jean Renoir, who had hired Visconti as his assistant on his next film, 'Partie de campagne',

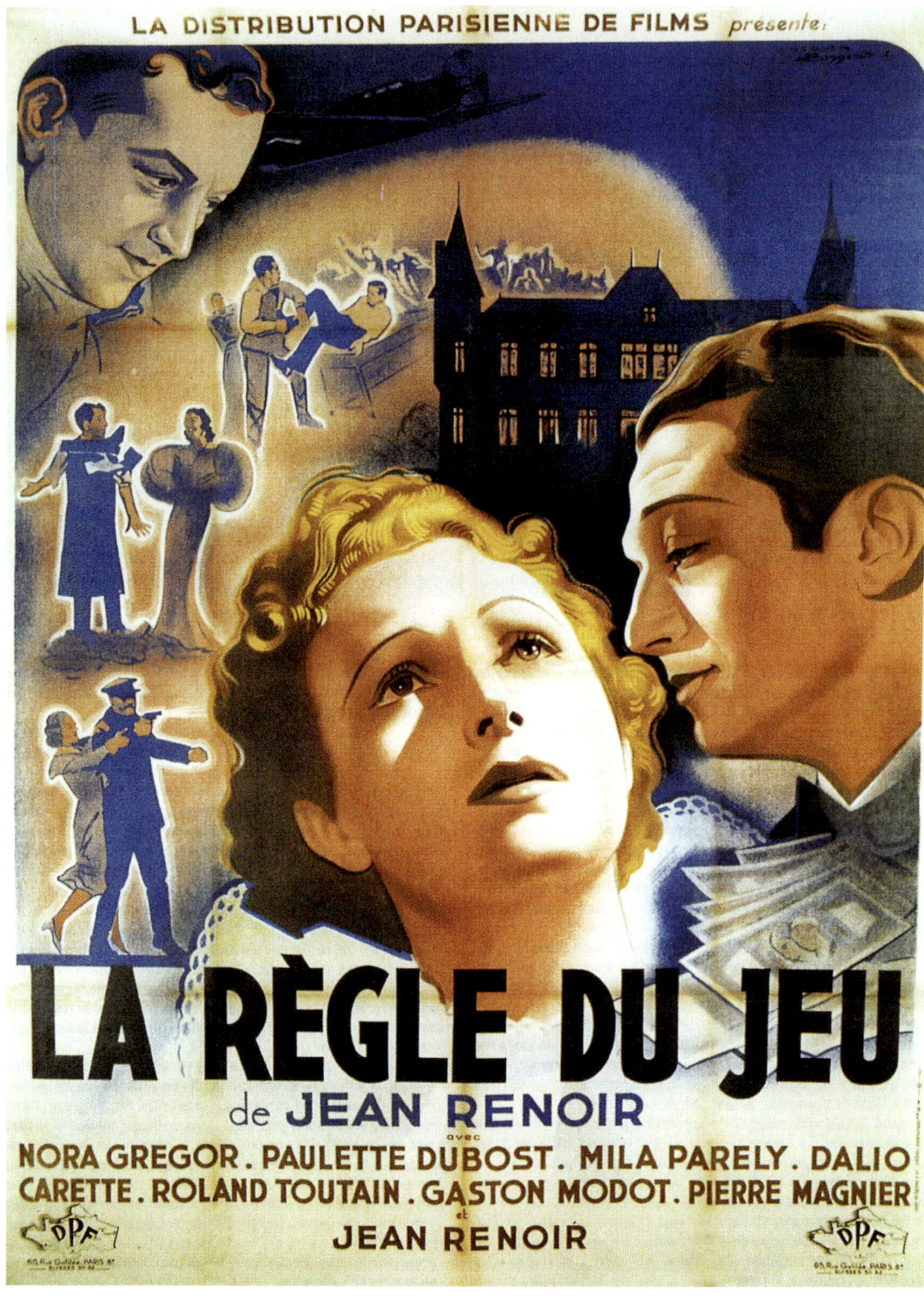

ABOVE: Poster for Jean Renoir's 'La Règle du Jeu'

'A day in the country'. It was the start of a brilliant career as a director for Visconti.

Coco then moved on to Salvador Dalí – perhaps 'sleeping with the enemy' was her counter-attack on Schiaparelli. But sleeping with the enemy was soon to become a dangerous side-line.

In an attempt to claw back her professional reputation, Coco turned her attention to another innovator; her long-time friend Jean Cocteau, and created the costumes for his 1937 play, 'Oedipe roi'. However the job backfired badly, when her costume designs were mocked as resembling mummies or accident victims.

Undaunted, she went on to create many costumes for him including those for the film that he premiered in France in July that year, 'La Règle du Jeu', (The Rules of the Game), a film that has, retrospectively, been accorded the accolade, 'one of the greatest films of all time', for its portrayal of the moral callousness of wealthy Parisians as Europe's tensions increase.

Defiantly, Coco also turned her attention to the Ballet Russes production of 'Baccanale', in tandem with Dalí, one of nine the surrealist would design. At the same time Coco began designing a gypsy collection, featuring 'divine brocades', 'dégagé' skirts, 'roses in the hair' and 'little boleros'.

But all such artistic endeavour was soon overshadowed by the dark insatiability of Nazism, which was gradually, but with growing confidence, crawling out of Germany.

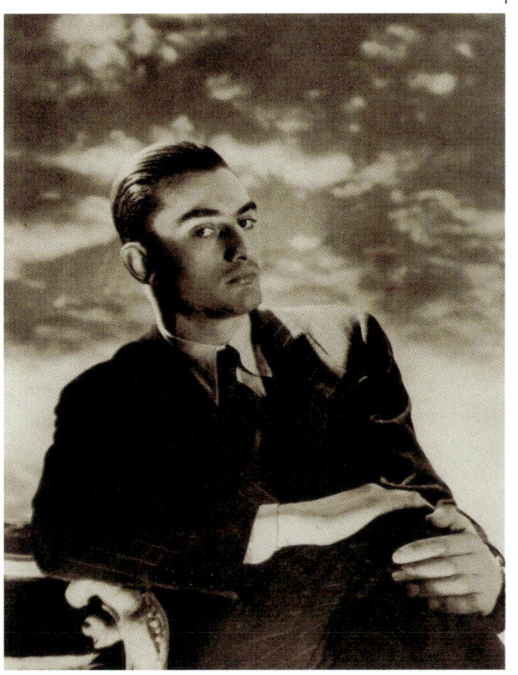

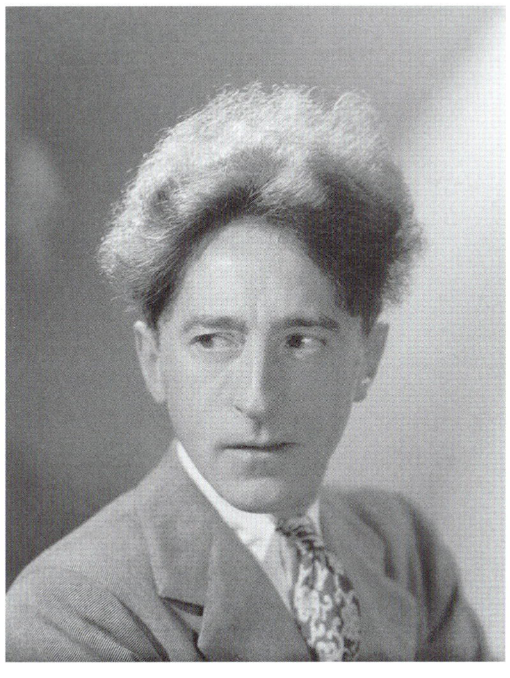

ABOVE: Jean Renoir
TOP: Luchino Visconti

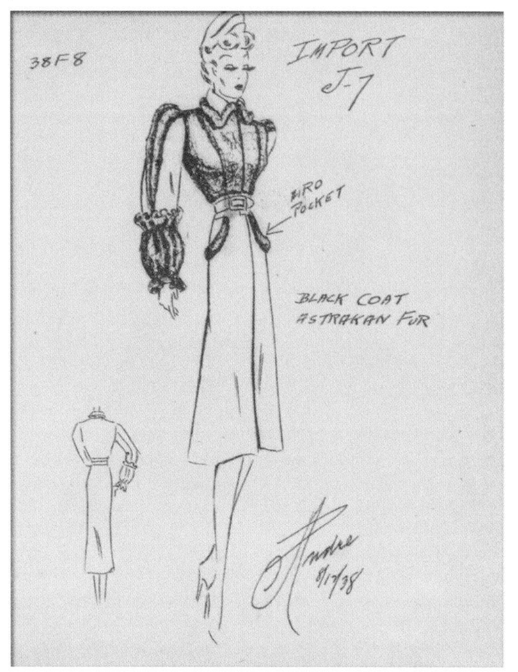

38F8
IMPORT J-7
ZIRO POCKET
BLACK COAT ASTRAKAN FUR
André
9/17/38

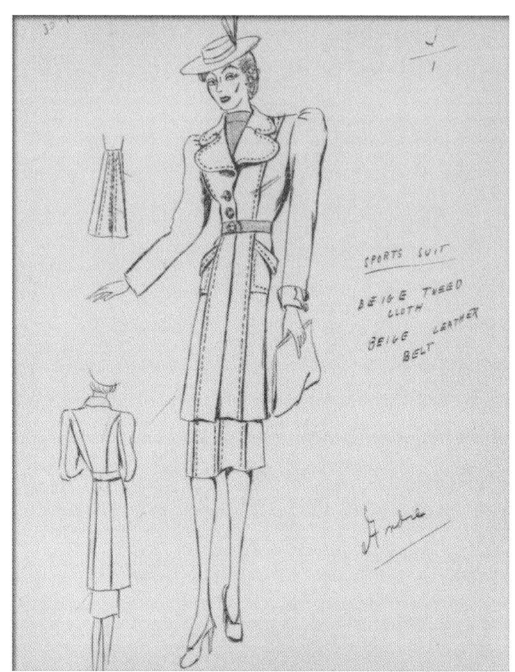

J / 1
SPORTS SUIT
BEIGE TWEED CLOTH
BEIGE LEATHER BELT
André

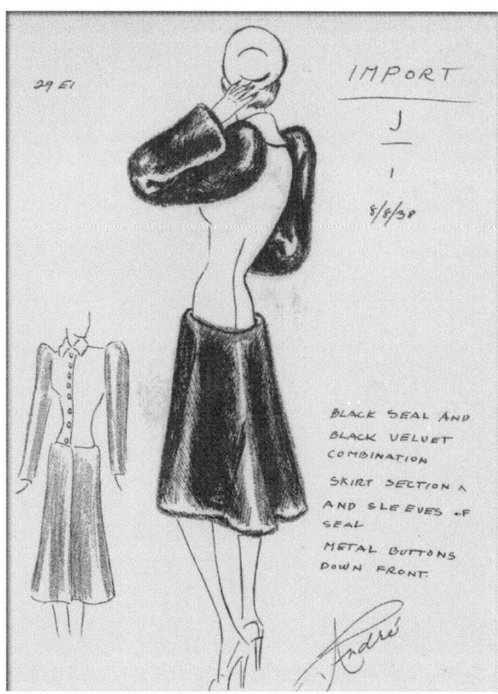

29 E1
IMPORT
J / 1
8/8/38
BLACK SEAL AND
BLACK VELVET
COMBINATION
SKIRT SECTION
AND SLEEVES OF
SEAL
METAL BUTTONS
DOWN FRONT
André

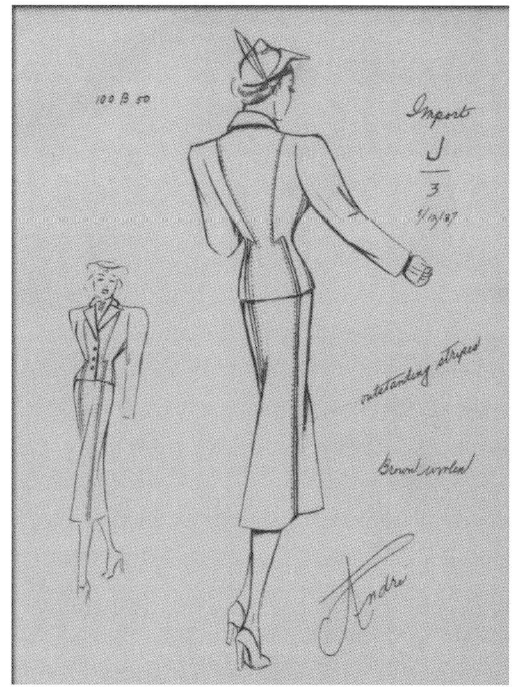

100 B 50
Import
J / 3
outstanding striped
Brown woolen
André

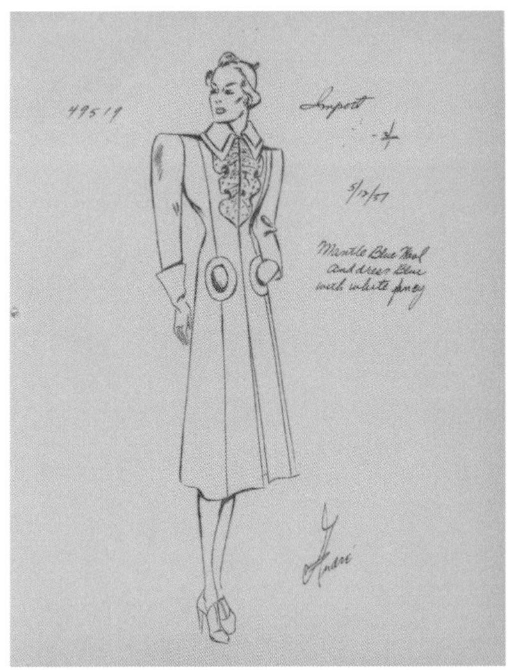

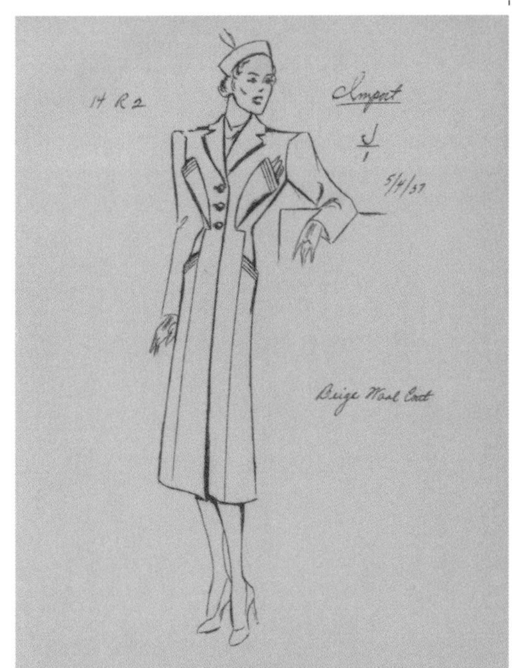

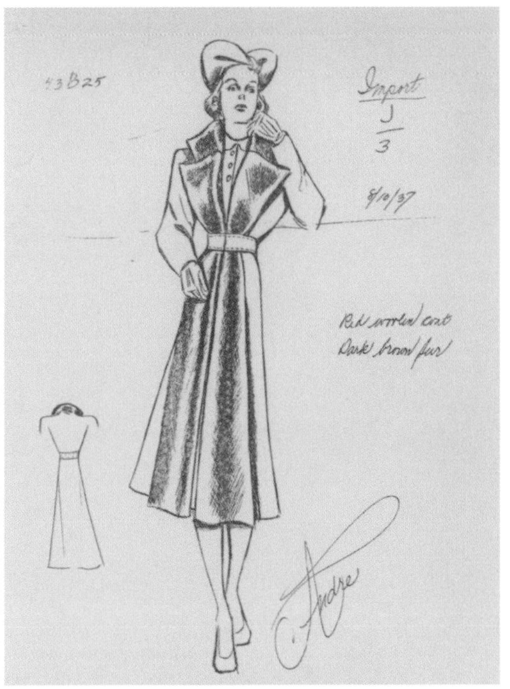

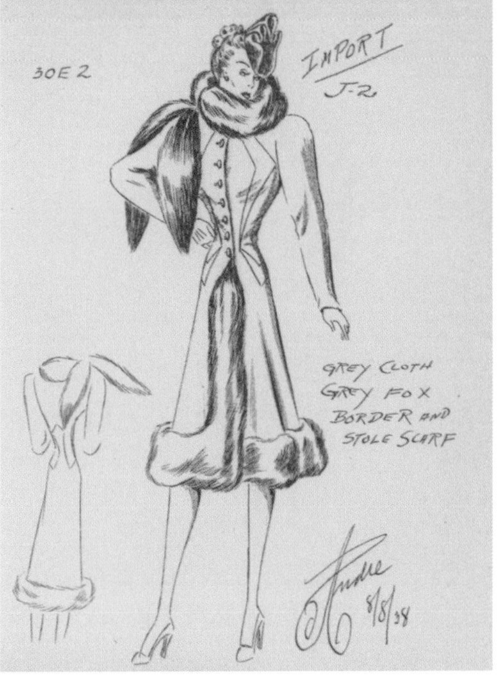

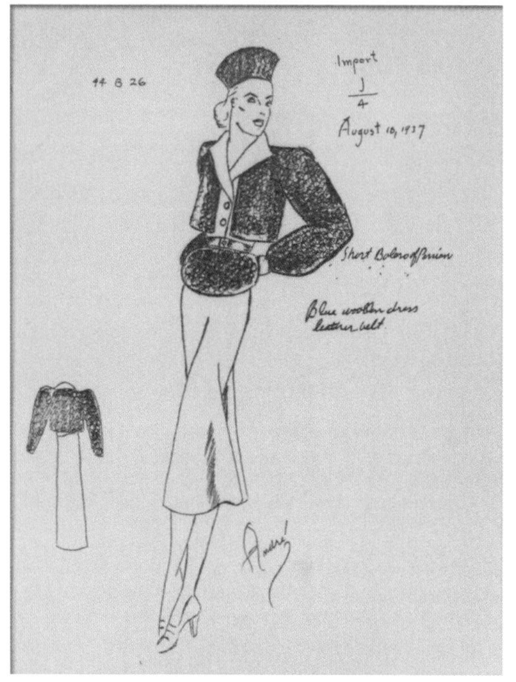

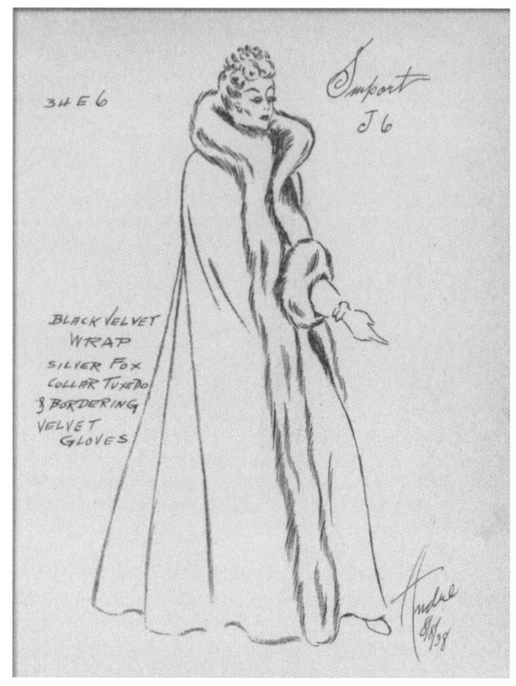

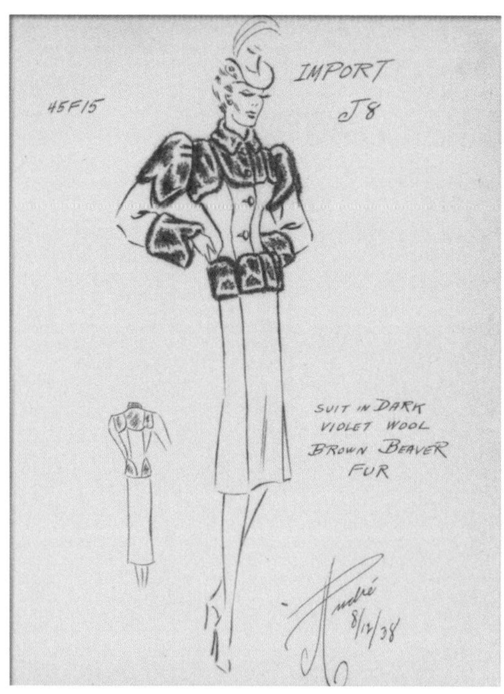

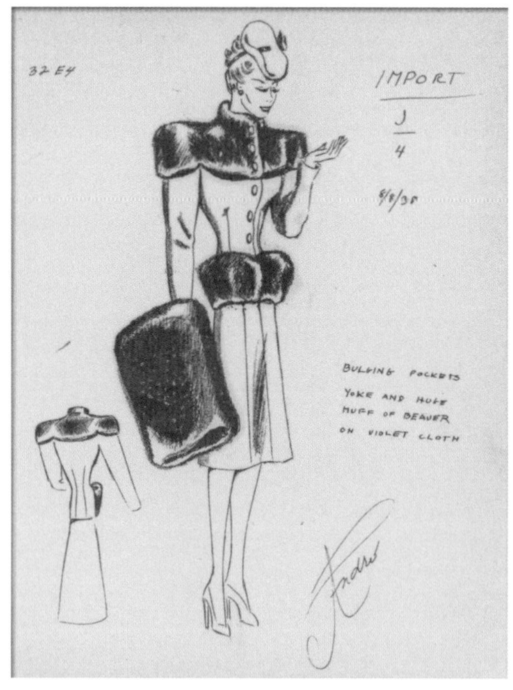

Various Chanel designs. André Studios 1937 – 39

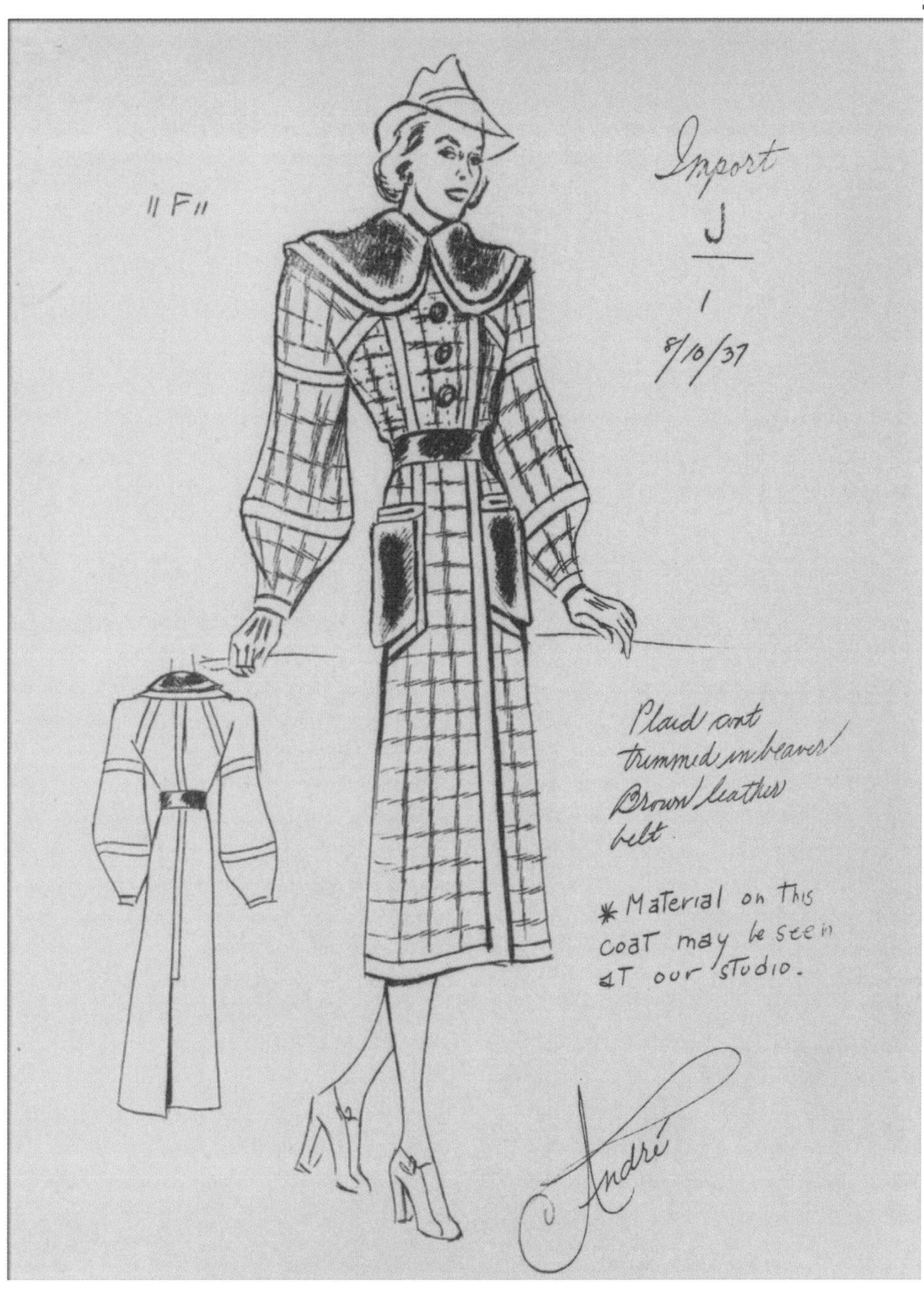
"F"
Import
J
1
8/10/37
Plaid coat
trimmed in beaver!
Brown leather
belt.
* Material on this
coat may be seen
at our studio.
André

THE DARK AGE OF COCO CHANEL 1939-1945

"The most courageous act is still to think for yourself. Aloud."

Following the outbreak of war between Britain and Germany on 3 September 1939, Paris fell to the Nazis on 14 June 1940. Schiaparelli, who employed 600 people in her business, left Paris for New York shortly afterwards, abandoning the field to Coco and her House of Chanel.

Apart from returning for a few months early in 1941, Schiaparelli stayed in New York until the war was over (she was bankrupt by 1959).

But the field she had vacated was burdened with an extreme threat. Coco dealt with it in the only way that she knew how – as an extreme opportunist. Coco had already decided to close the House of Chanel within two hours of the declaration of war; announcing that 'This is no time for fashion'.

Just a few staff were retained at Rue Cambon, those who were needed to sell perfumes and accessoires. Her action was considered reprehensible at the time, plunging her thousands of employees into instant unemployment. Was this a spiteful act on her part, revenge against those workers who, in 1936, had gone on strike for higher wages and shorter work hours during a general workers' strike in France? Some thought so, obviously.

Despite protestations of poverty herself, Coco initially continued living at the Ritz Hotel in Paris with her servant, although the atmosphere in Paris became more and more eerie as the people vanished from the streets and air raid sirens wailed.

But Coco fled Paris when the German forces thrust towards the capital. She had been advised wisely not to use her Rolls-Royce to do so and abandoned Paris in a car belonging to her driver, accompanied by several of her employees.

Her first port of call was the house she had acquired for André Palasse, her nephew, in the Pyrenees.

By 22 June it was all over for France, which from that date on was occupied by the Germans. The Franco-German armistice which divided the country into an occupied Northern zone and a nominally unoccupied southern zone was signed in the forest of Compiègne, a place of great significance for Coco, for it was amongst those trees that she and Etienne Balsan had enjoyed horse riding 30 years previously. For Coco, such

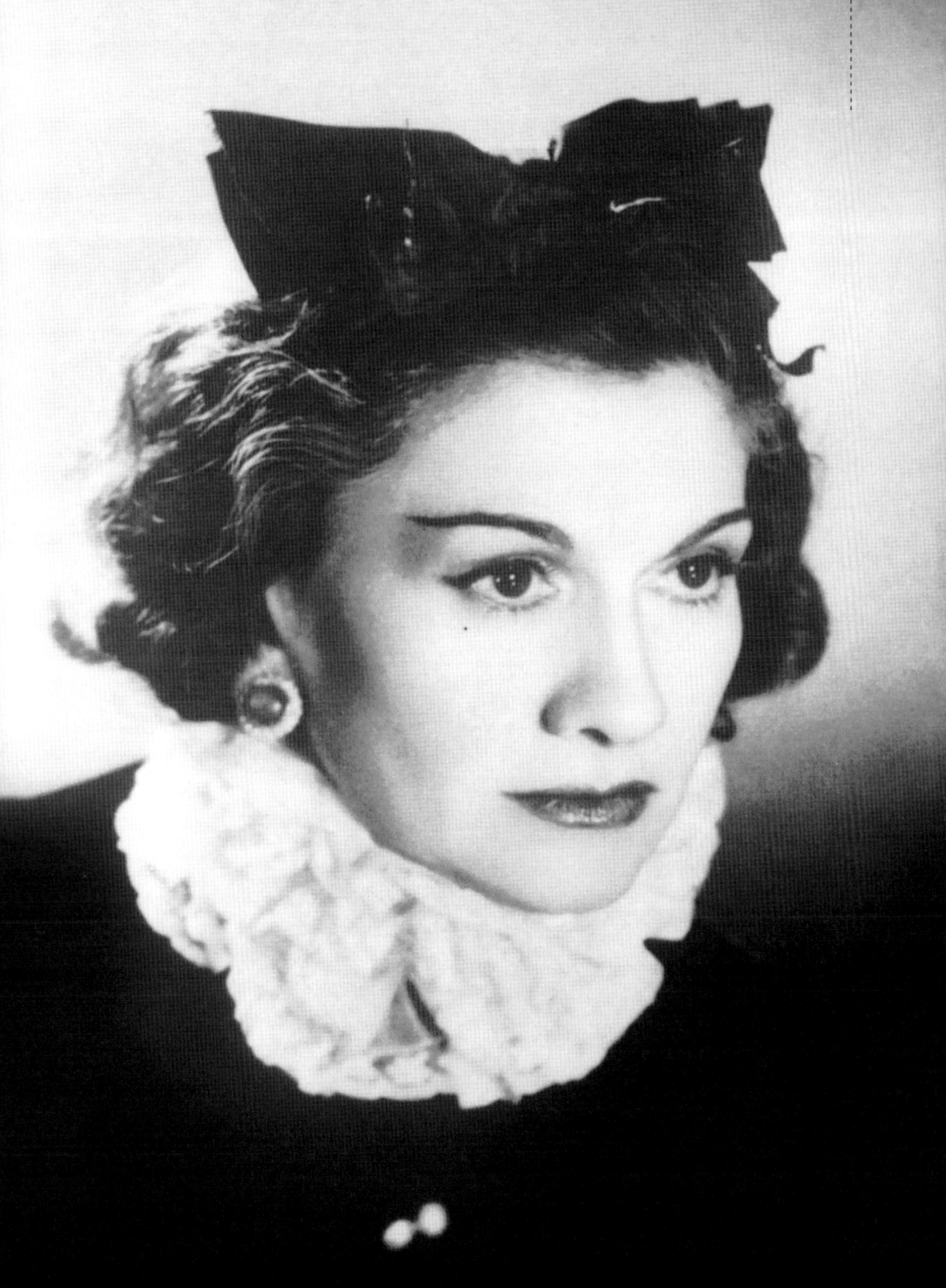

French capitulation was a deep wound, and she could not hold back her tears.

Once war had congealed into an uneasy peace, with Marshal Philipe Pétain assuming the role of leader of the puppet Vichy government for the south of the country, Coco was anxious to return to Paris.

Balenciaga, Lelong and her other rival couturiers had decided to keep their businesses alive during the Nazi occupation, thus entering, as would Coco, a strange twilight world that was a defeated France.

The 'système débrouillard' – a French term for being resourceful and making do – reigned, with the result that the lines defining moral actions became indistinct, resentments would fester and righteous indignation turn, later, into savagery.

People struggled to make sense of the altered reality and tried simply to survive. Consequently the fashion houses all sold what they could to the wives and mistresses of the German military men.

Coco undertook the journey back to Paris with her friend, Marie-Louise Bouquet, finally arriving in August 1940 only to find that her suite at the Ritz was no longer available, most of the hotel having been commandeered by the Nazi military.

Coco went into battle herself for her right to stay in the Ritz, and managed to squeeze a concession from the relevant German commander who granted her a small bedroom on the top floor. As a civilian, she was not permitted to use the entrance reserved for the Nazi hierarchy on Rue Vendôme. In the meantime, the Resistance built a network amongst the hotel staff.

At some point during her time in occupied Paris, Coco became re-acquainted, and later romantically involved with Baron Hans Günter von Dincklage. By the time the war started, 'Spatz' (sparrow), as he was known, had been an attaché at the German Embassy in Paris for four years.

Tall, blonde and with a reputation as a playboy, Spatz had engaged in many affairs with wealthy, educated women in Paris – and had divorced his half-Jewish wife the same year that he took up his post in Paris in 1935. Although he was another charming womaniser, he was also described as ruthless and indifferent to others' feelings or pain. The French believed him to be a German agent under the auspices of the German military intelligence service, the Abwehr.

Nevertheless Coco sought his help to get André, her nephew, who had joined the French Army when the war started, released from captivity in a German detainment camp. At some point after 1941 onwards their renewed contact developed into an affair. Coco was 58, Spatz 45.

It is nigh on impossible to gauge Coco's true state of mind at this time. Her former lover Bendor had been a pro-German advocate of right wing political positions prior to the war, as his membership of the right wing movement 'Link' proved. Coco's current disdain for the Germans 'en masse' did not preclude her own alignment with some of the Nazi ideology. She was certainly moving among high circles of the German occupying force.

Initially, Coco's life slipped easily into its usual trajectory, more or less, but now with Spatz at her

AU REVOIR

Coco suffered several losses in the early years of the 1940s.

- 1940 – The Wertheimers, Coco's partners in the Parfums Chanel business – and under no illusions about their fate under the Nazis – departed for Brazil and then New York in 1940. Nonetheless, they succeeded in keeping their French business running, despite the Nazi's attempts to seize it.

- 1941 – Coco's brother Lucien died of a heart attack.

- 1942 – Coco's former lover Dmitri Pavlovich, Grand Duke of Russia died at the age of 50. Dmitri had contracted tuberculosis around 1929 and undergone several operations. He had entered hospital in Davos in Switzerland, where, on 4 March 1942, he had organised a Russian festival for himself and the staff. He died the following day after succumbing to an attack of uraemia, related to kidney failure.

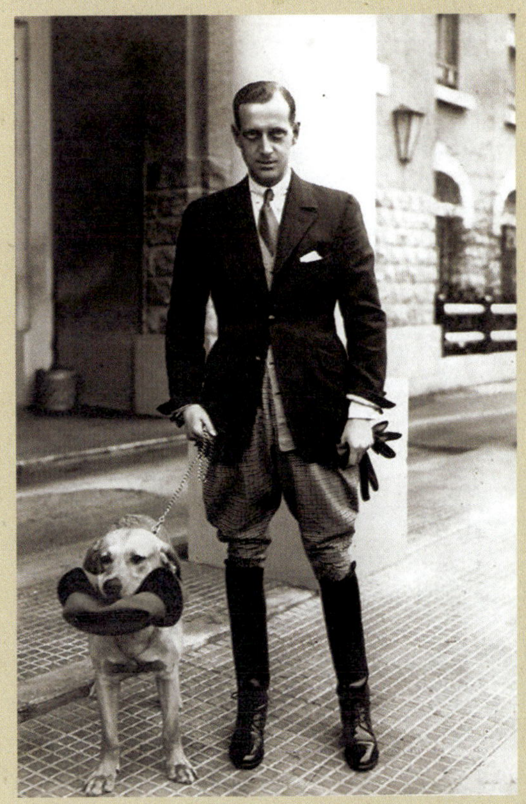

ABOVE: Grand Duke Dimitri Pavlovich

side. There were visits from close friends Misia, Jean Cocteau and Ukrainian Serge Lifar, whose dance outfits she designed, as well as trips to La Pausa. She seemed preferred to ignore the fact that her country was occupied, and treated the occupiers with the hauteur she could activate so lethally.

In a further example of her 'business as usual' approach she even tried to gain control of the Parfums Chanel company in 1941, hoping to be aided by the anti-Jewish Nazi laws.

Coco was awash with contradictions in her dealings with Jews, often quoted as holding them responsible for any problems encountered with the French currency, the franc, yet counting many wealthy Jews amongst her friends and clients. It seemed that she could compartmentalise business and friendship as necessary to safeguard her interests.

'Parfums, Chanel has been legally "abandoned" by its owners', she wrote to Nazi officials. 'I have an indisputable right of priority. The profits that I have received from my creations since the foundation of

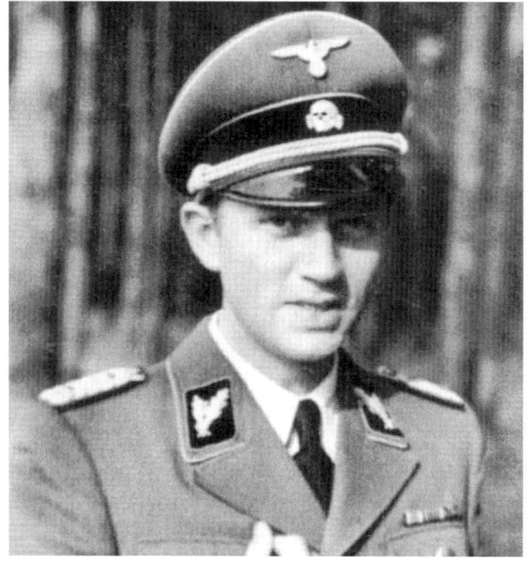

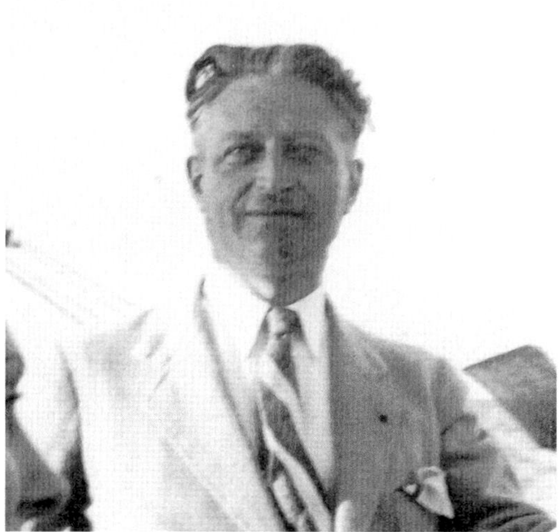

this business… are disproportionate'.

But she ultimately failed in her bid to exploit the anti-Jewish laws prohibiting non-Aryans from owning businesses, because the two Wertheimer brothers were a step ahead of her and the Nazis. They had handed over their assets and stake holdings in Bourjois and Chanel to French aeroplane constructor and industrialist Félix Amiot, in trust. It was extraordinary that the Nazis allowed themselves to be held at bay by this move. But to the benefit of all, throughout the war years, Chanel Nº5 continued to be sold to Nazis and their wives and mistresses in occupied Paris and all over Europe. After the war, Amiot returned ownership to the Wertheimers.

Meanwhile Coco was still trying to get her nephew out of the POW camp, and in 1943 Spatz suggested she consult Theodor Momm, a senior Nazi officer in Paris who had taken charge of the administration of the local textile industry for the German Reich. By now the war in the east had turned against

the Germans and many in the Nazi hierarchy, including the Chief of German foreign intelligence General Walter Schellenberg, had seen the writing on the wall. Schellenberg commissioned Momm to sue for a separate peace accord with Britain, or at least, convey the message that German commanders had detached themselves from Hitler's increasingly paranoid conduct of the war.

The timing was perfect – Coco appeared at Momm's door just as he was searching for someone with connections to the British prime minister Winston Churchill, to deliver such a missive.

Her excellent connections to Churchill, established via Bendor, the Duke of Westminster, made Coco the perfect go between and she was duly selected for a secret mission, with the code name Operation Modelhut. Her willingness to undertake the liaison role was, over time and together with other of her actions, to put a question mark over exactly where

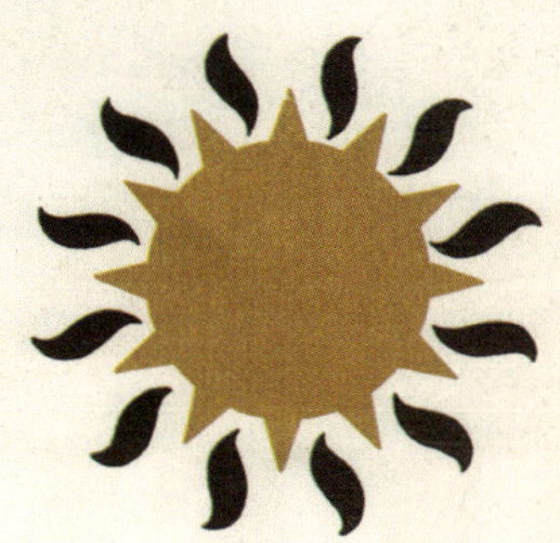
LES
PARFUMS
CHANEL
PARIS

her allegiance lay – with the Allies or the Nazis?

For now, she was assigned the codename 'Westminster'; and became agent F-7124. Files later released by British MI6 and German authorities confirm these details.

Initially, the plan involved her travelling to Madrid to meet Sir Samuel Hoare, the British Ambassador to Spain, someone else that Coco counted amongst her acquaintances. From here she was put in contact with Baron Louis de Vaufreland, a former Gestapo agent in Morocco.

Agent F-7124 then proceeded to introduce an unwanted element of uncertainty when she insisted that her friend, and former Chanel brand ambassador, Vera Bate accompany her to Madrid. The problem was that Vera, now living in Rome and married to Italian Fascist, Alberto Lombardi, was suspected of being a British spy.

From then on recollections vary, which has blurred the facts of the matter.

Vera claimed that she had received a letter from Coco asking her to return to Paris, to support the reopening of the House of Chanel, an offer which she declined. Several weeks later she was arrested, under suspicion of being a British spy. She blamed Coco, an accusation that Coco refuted saying that she had in fact worked to get Vera released.

Whatever happened, Vera was then released from a brief time in custody and did travel to Madrid with Coco. But once there, Vera informed the Spanish that Coco was a Nazi spy while she, Vera Bate Lombardi, was loyal to the British Crown.

However the accusation fell on deaf ears and Vera was detained in Spain for several years. Coco returned to Paris and that, it appeared, is as far as stage one of Operation Modelhut ever got.

But a year later, came stage two.

Still hoping to get her nephew released, Coco was said to have gone to Berlin, where she was then asked to contact Churchill, again with the intention of persuading him to enter into a separate peace accord. This attempt faltered, too, when Churchill caught pneumonia.

And even though the French Préfecture de Police also had their suspicions about Coco, nothing was ever revealed about her second mission which would clarify her involvement with Operation Modelhut.

From Coco herself, of course, not a word would seep out about what really happened. Whatever the motivations for her actions, opportunism or concern for her nephew – who was eventually released in 1944 – her involvement with the Nazi high command meant that the word 'collaborator' would never quite leave her thereafter.

Many who had done far less were submitted to vicious reprisals once Paris was liberated. Some 20,000 French women who were accused of 'collaboration horizontale' – sleeping with the enemy – would suffer retribution which ranged in ranging from being paraded through the streets with shaven heads and swastikas painted on their faces, to being tortured and beaten.

Yet Coco Chanel, who openly associated with the

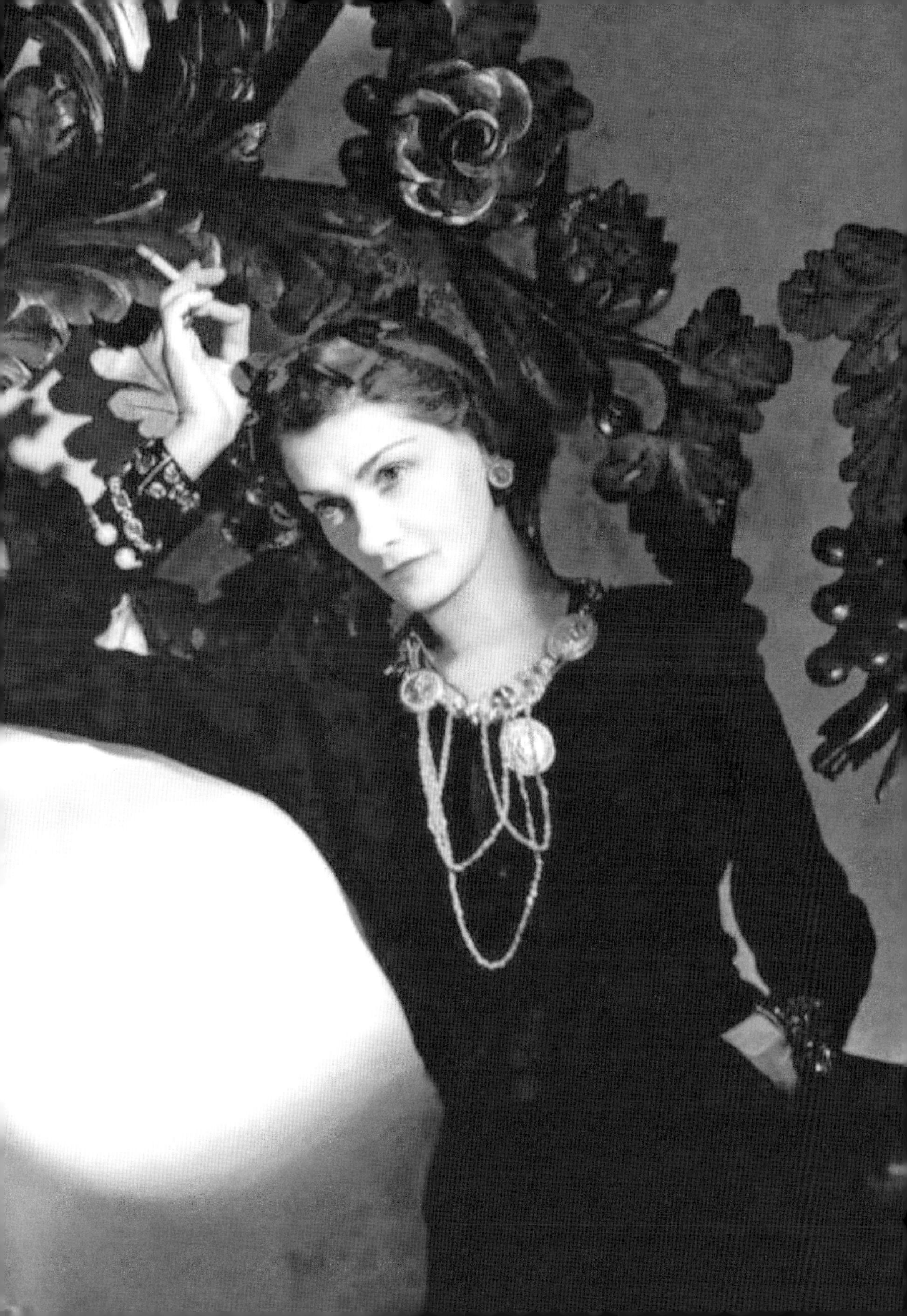

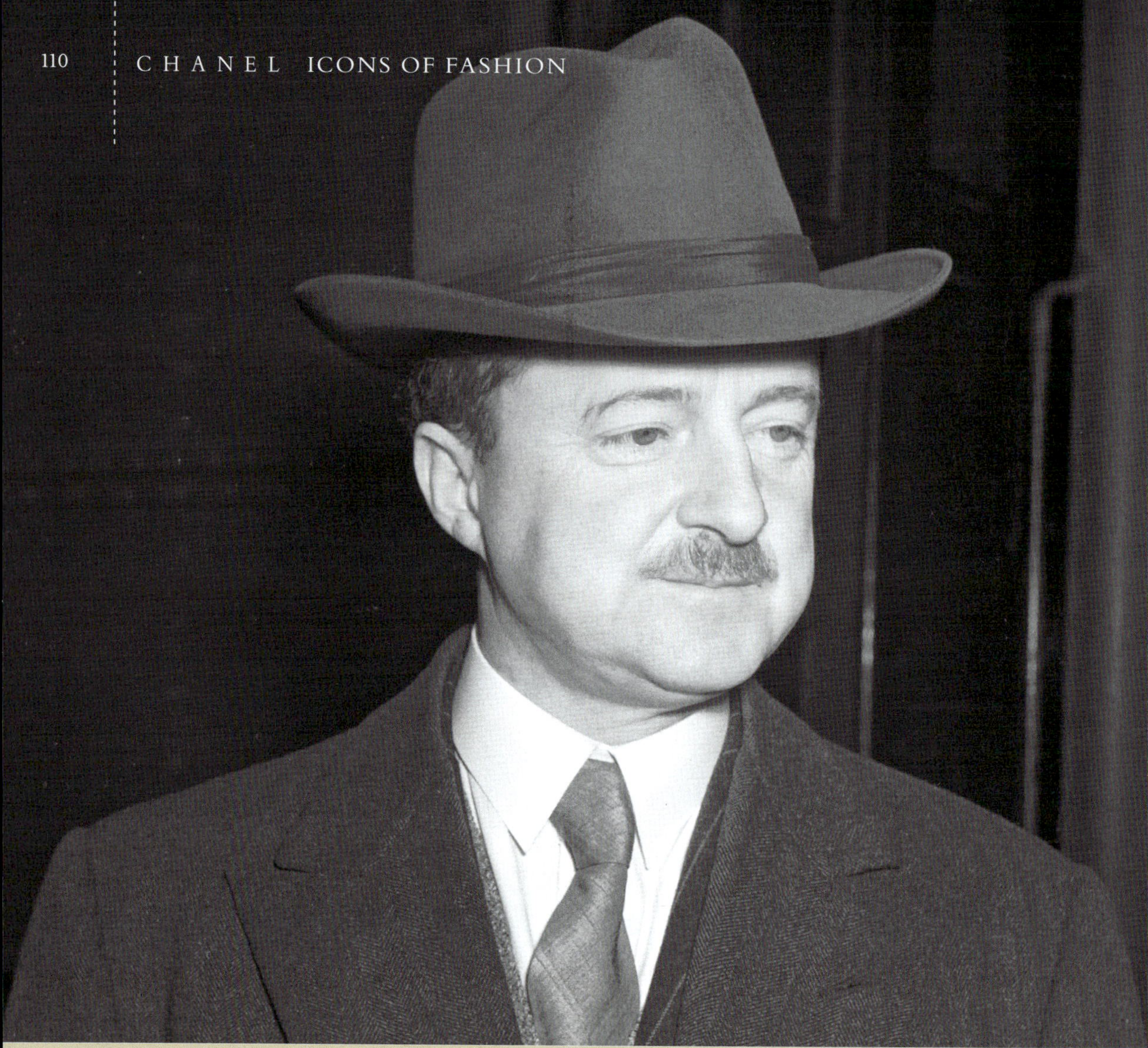

PAYING THE PRICE

In another act likely to raise questions about exactly where her wartime loyalties lay, Coco paid the medical bills and funeral costs of the SS German functionary Walter Schellenberg, the man behind the scenes of Operation Modelhut. To protect himself from a longer prison sentence he had testified against the SS in the post-war Nuremberg trials but still received six years for his role in the murder of Russian prisoners of war. Having been released from prison in 1951 on the grounds of ill health, two years into a six-year sentence, he died in March 1952. His memoir, published posthumously, did not mention Coco's activities, nor her friendships with the Nazis.

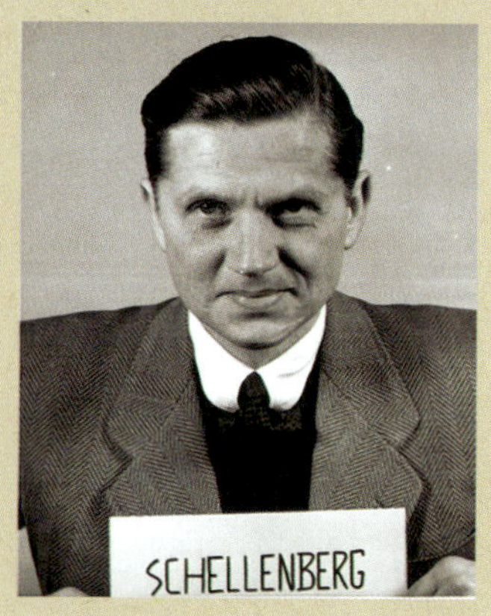

Nazis day in day out, did not suffer any such fate.

However, once Paris had been liberated in August 1944, two men from the Forces Françaises de l'Intérieur came to the Ritz and arrested Coco as a collaborator.

Although she was brought in for questioning, there, was no documentary evidence to convict her of spying for the Germans. Unlike thousands of others, she was released just a few hours later. Such a short detention was bound to raise more suspicions about her activities and friends. Was Churchill responsible for her quick liberation? The whole truth has never emerged.

Tantalisingly, Gabrielle Palasse-Labrunie, Coco's great niece, remembered Coco saying that 'Churchill had me freed'. Did Gabrielle know, or was it simply an informed guess? Had the British been afraid that she might reveal pro-Nazi sympathies amongst British royalty, the wealthy and politicians?

Once the war was over, Coco did appear in a French courtroom to account for testimonies from Baron de Vaufreland claiming that she was connected to the German Abwehr. She maintained that she only made contact with Vaufreland because he had intimated that her nephew would be freed if she did so, and that there was no further interaction.

'I could arrange for a declaration to come from Mr. Duff Cooper', she had confidently informed the presiding judge as she offered him a character reference. Rumours abounded that Cooper, ambassador to France in 1944, had been instructed by Churchill to protect Coco.

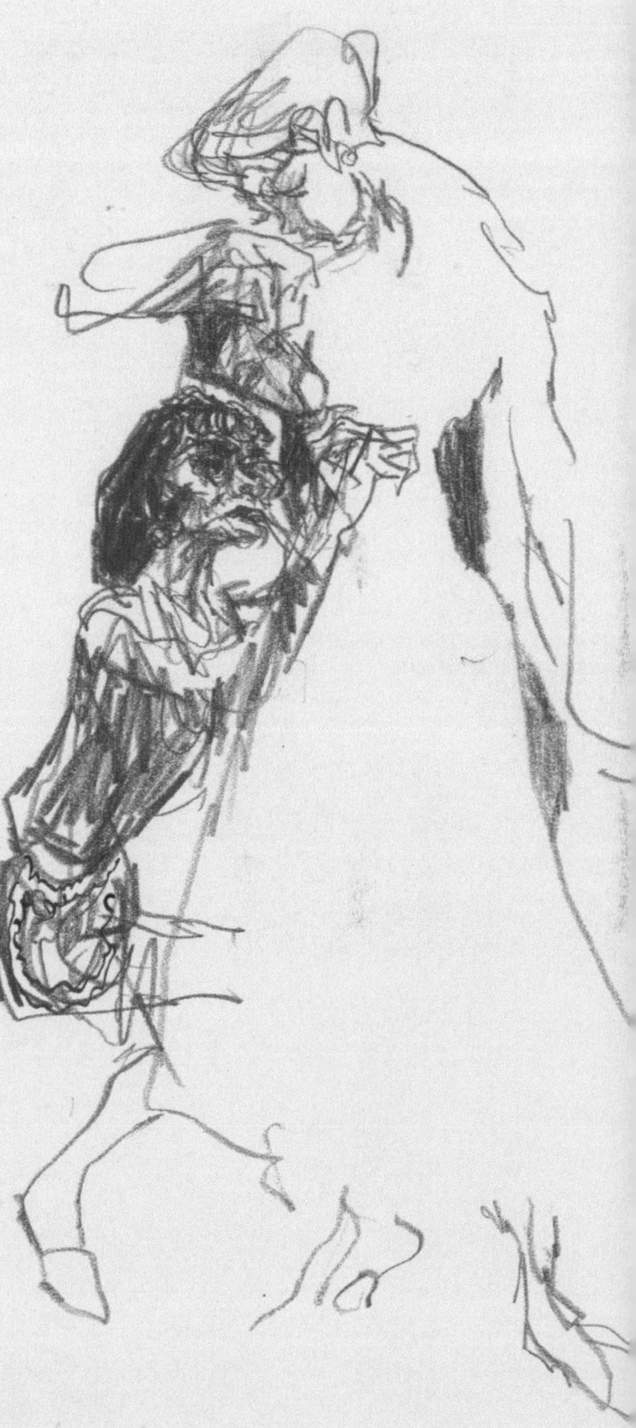

ABOVE: A sketch of Coco Chanel adjusting the outfit on a tall model, by Polish-born British expressionist painter Feliks Topolski, circa 1950

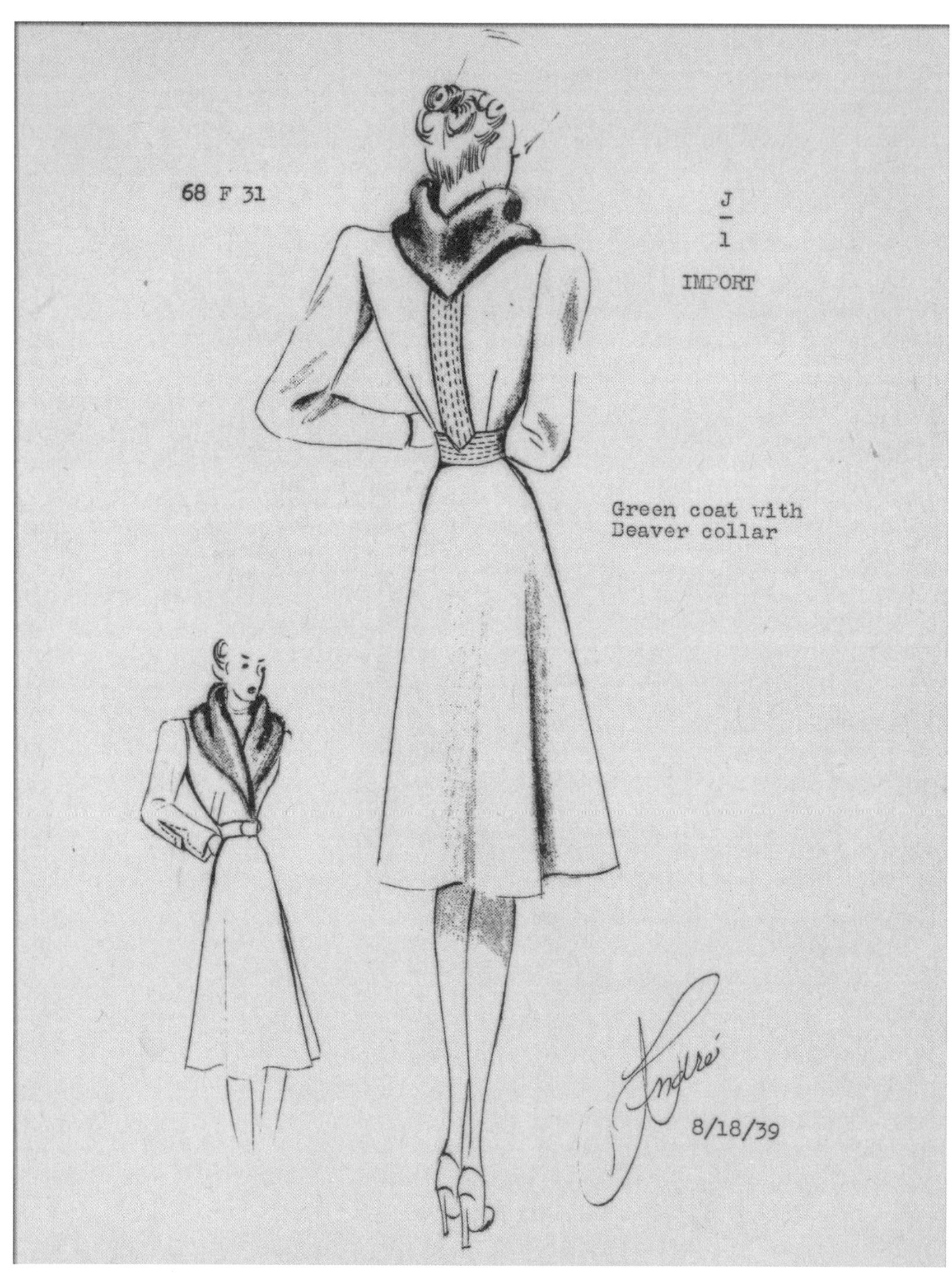

68 F 31

J
1
IMPORT

Green coat with
Beaver collar

8/18/39

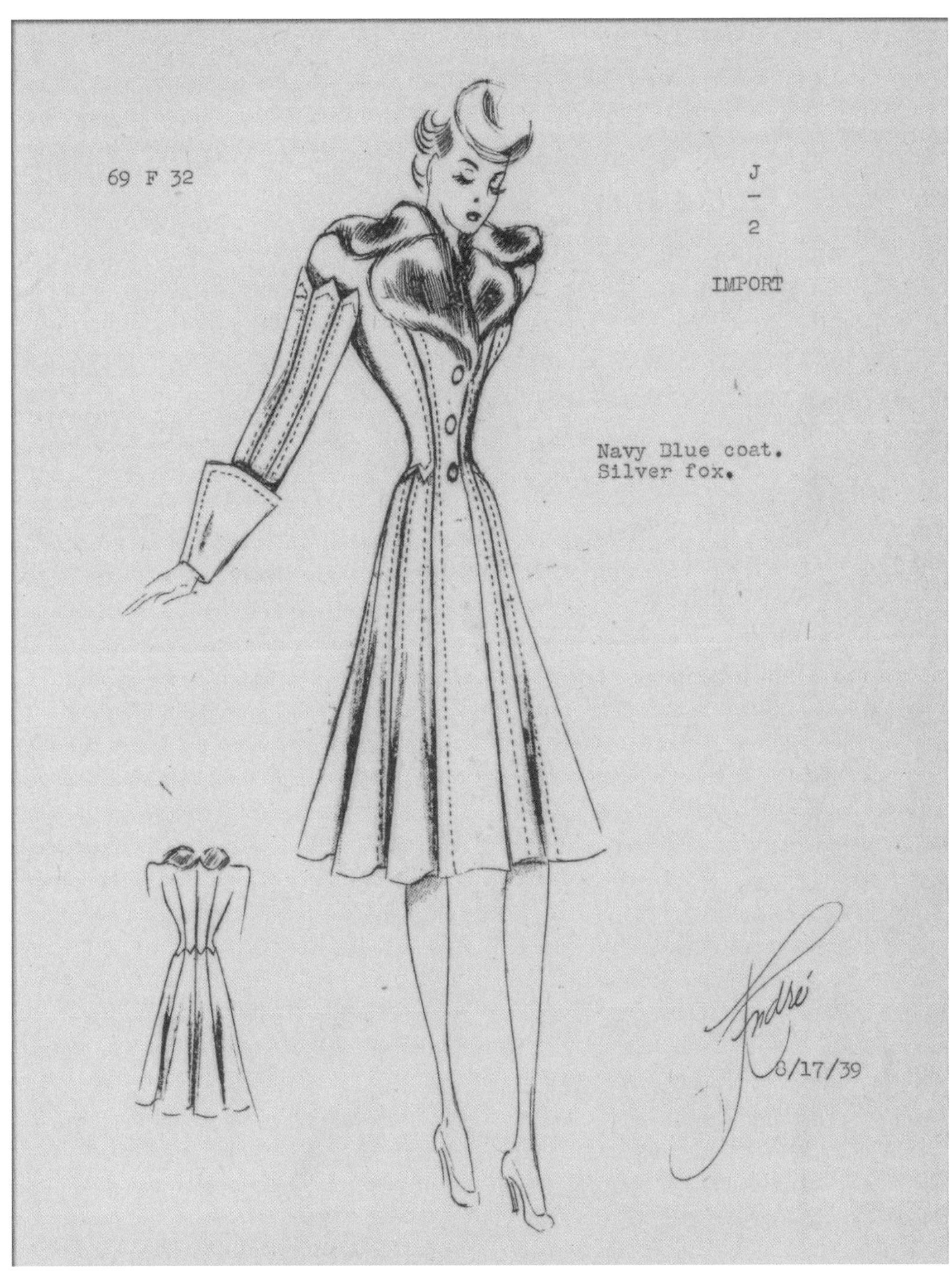
69 F 32
J
—
2
IMPORT
Navy Blue coat.
Silver fox.
André
8/17/39

COCO KEEPS HER HEAD DOWN 1945–1954

"I am not saying goodbye for long. I am not thinking of anything, but when the moment comes, I feel I will pounce on something that will be within my reach."

Despite her release without charge for collaboration with the Germans, Coco Chanel found she was now persona non grata in France, and elsewhere.

Her German Baron lover, Spatz, had fled France for the safety of Lausanne in Switzerland in 1944 and so it seemed prudent to follow him into exile until the wind had changed. So it was that Coco decamped to a hidden spot in the woods above Lake Geneva and resumed her affair with Spatz. She was also reunited with her nephew André, released but still suffering from the years of detention in a Nazi camp.

Without Coco's financial support, Spatz would have been penniless, but he now revelled in luxury again. Their affair continued until the early 1950s, when Spatz moved to Spain and the Balearic Islands, where he could be sure of being looked upon favourably under General Franco.

Even after his separation from Coco, the pair remained friends and she granted him a monthly financial allowance. As she had been with several other favoured lovers, Coco was generous, even after the romantic sparks had died away.

She could afford to be bountiful as she was now wealthy beyond her wildest dreams. Coco had continued her challenge against the Wertheimer's holdings in 'Les Parfums Chanel' after the war by creating a further range of perfumes with Mademoiselle Chanel emblazoned in red letters across the front. They were a defiant challenge to The Wertheimer brothers, who were astute enough to know the potential of the three rival scents, No. 1, No. 2 and No. 31, and to realise that they could best maintain their own success and domination of the perfume market by cooperating over a new deal with the feisty Coco.

So it was that Coco began to earn around one million dollars every year from perfume sales alone.

Her life of luxury continued in Switzerland, much as it had in France, as she socialised with the great and good as ever. She would drink champagne in the Boulevard Palace Hotel, where she had booked a suite. The Lausanne Palace Hotel was another of

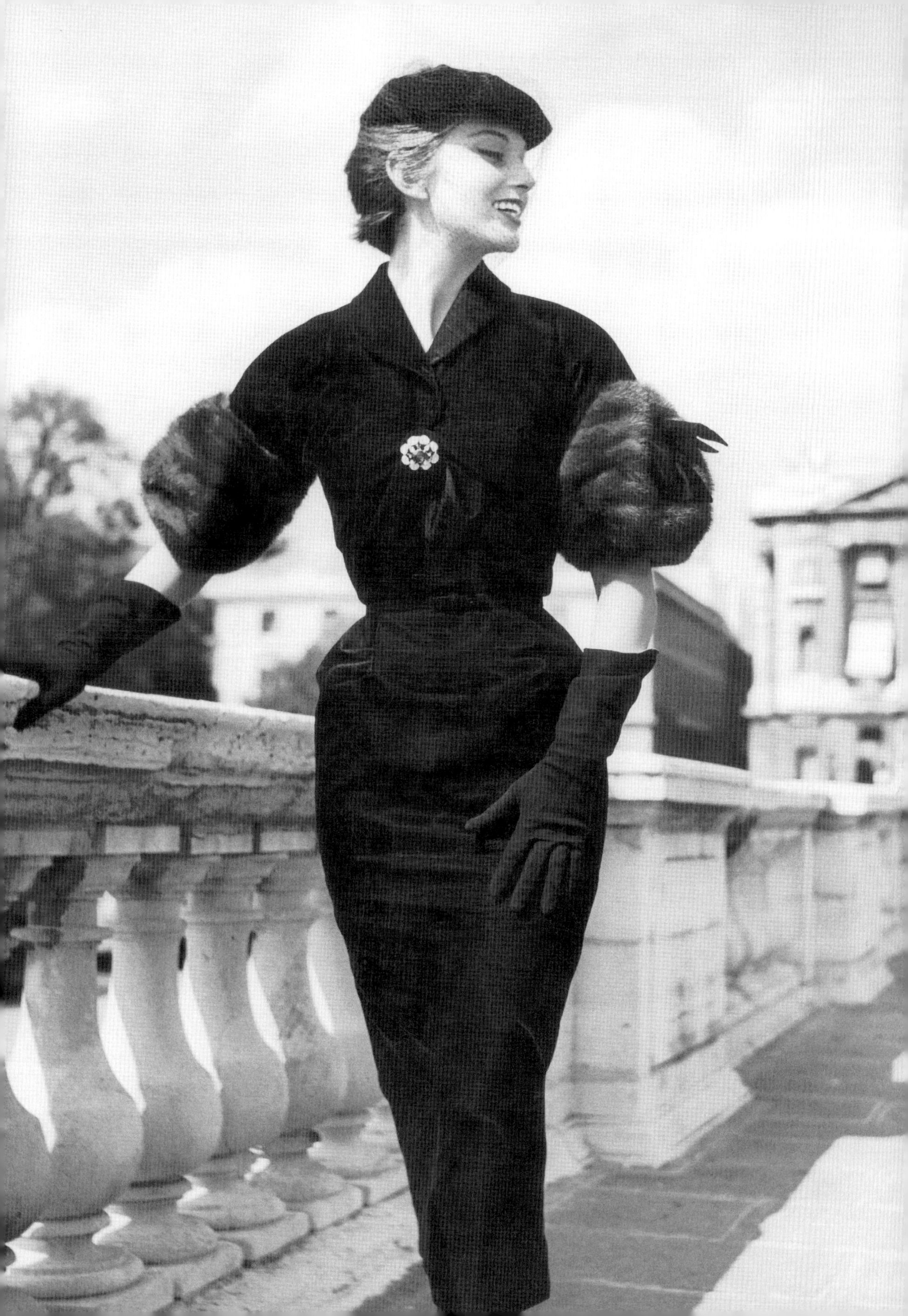

her haunts. She also visited the Valmont Clinic for beauty treatments and, according to one writer, to undergo facial surgery as well.

Coco appreciated not just the peace of the place, but also the security that she said could only be found in Switzerland. She enjoyed the country so much that she would eventually buy a house there, (in 1966 in Le Signal) high in the wooded hills above Lausanne.

By 1954 Coco was 70 and she had outlived most of her closest friends and lovers. Both Étienne Balsan and the Duke of Westminster had died in 1953; Vera Bate Lombardi had passed away in Rome in 1948 and Misia Sert had died in 1950.

With Spatz moving to Spain, Coco, as she told Marlene Dietrich, was now 'dying of boredom', alone in Switzerland. She became ever more disgruntled with her state of relative inertia, was prickly and

FRIENDS TO THE END

Although their friendship undoubtedly had its up and downs, there was evidently some strong connection between Coco and Misia Sert, who had known each other since 1917. There were even rumours that they had once been lovers. Whether because of that, or because Misia was one of the few people left with a real link to her glorious past, Coco was by Misia's side when she died in Paris on 15 October 1950.

During the years before her death Misia had gradually succumbed to the use of morphine, as had her ex-husband José-Maria. No longer capable of caring who knew, Misia would inject in public situations, straight through her clothes.

On the day of Misia's funeral, Coco made sure her old friend was 'properly dressed' as befitted a 'rare being who knew how to be pleasing to women and artists' – she had after all in her time been painted and adored by artists from Renoir to Toulouse Lautrec and a friend to Proust and Picasso.

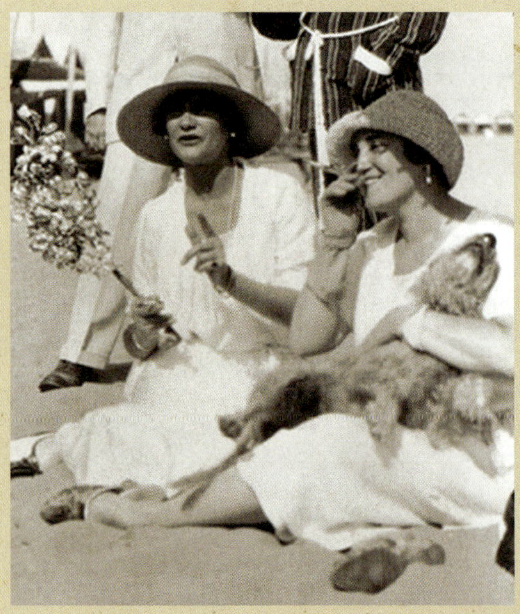

Coco clothed Misia's body in white, surrounding her with white flowers, her face properly made up, her neck hung with jewels. Coco said of Misia, a woman who shared her scorn for personal boundaries: 'We love people only for their faults. Misia gave me ample reason to love her'.

contradictory, liberally apportioning blame for imagined or real faults to others.

She had self-isolated herself from Paris and the fashion world where there were now new ideas and new designers had made their name including Hubert de Givenchy, Christian Dior, Mary Quant, Pierre Cardin, and Yves Saint Laurent.
Dior's success particularly embittered Coco. She was particularly unimpressed by his 1947 'New Look'

collection featuring padded bras, stiff jackets, full skirts and nipped-in waists, which she dismissed as 'illogical designs'.

And so, unhappy with the sense that she was on the side lines, Coco began to plan her re-entry into the fashion world to reclaim her abandoned 'top spot'.

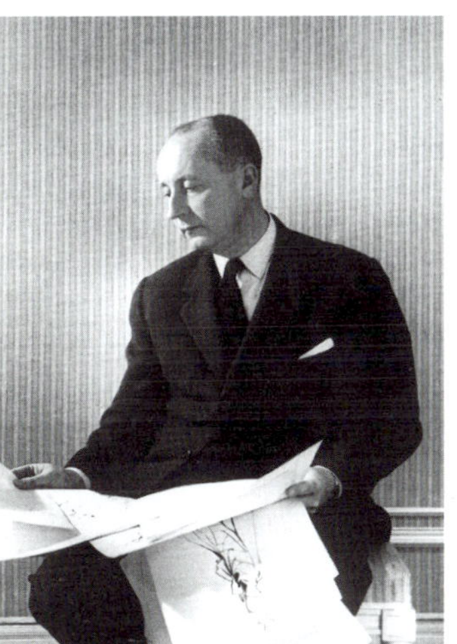
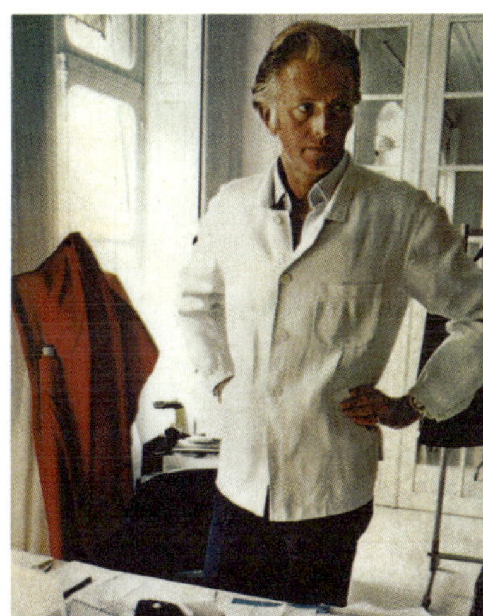
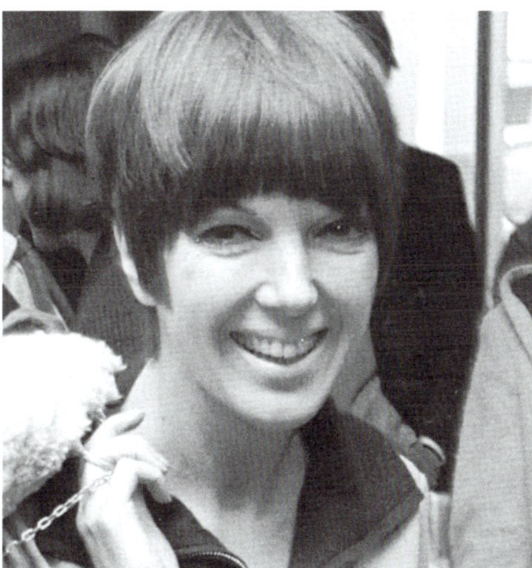
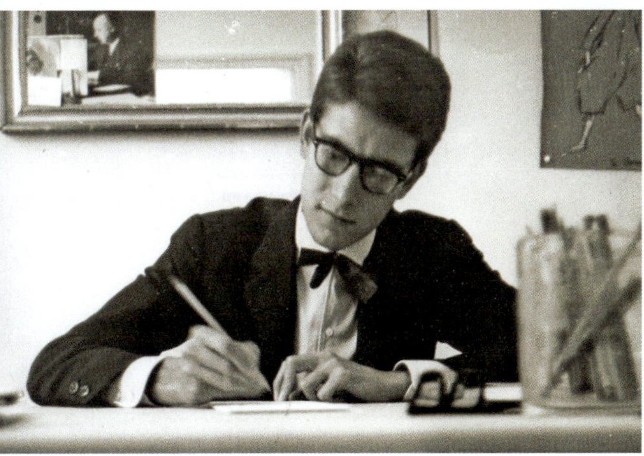
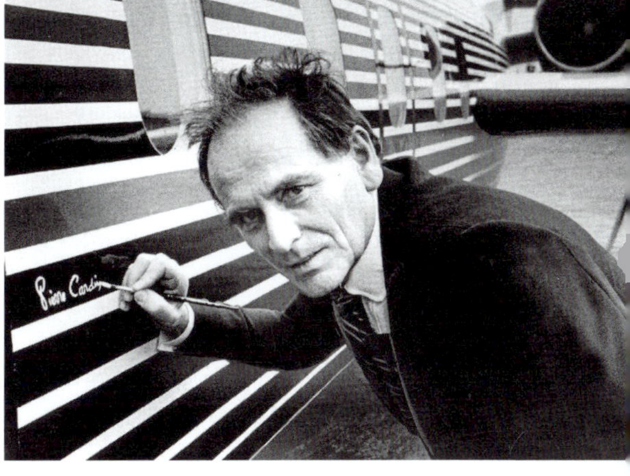

ABOVE - CLOCKWISE FROM TOP LEFT:
Christian Dior; Hubert de Givenchy; Mary Quant; Pierre Cardin & Yves Saint Laurent

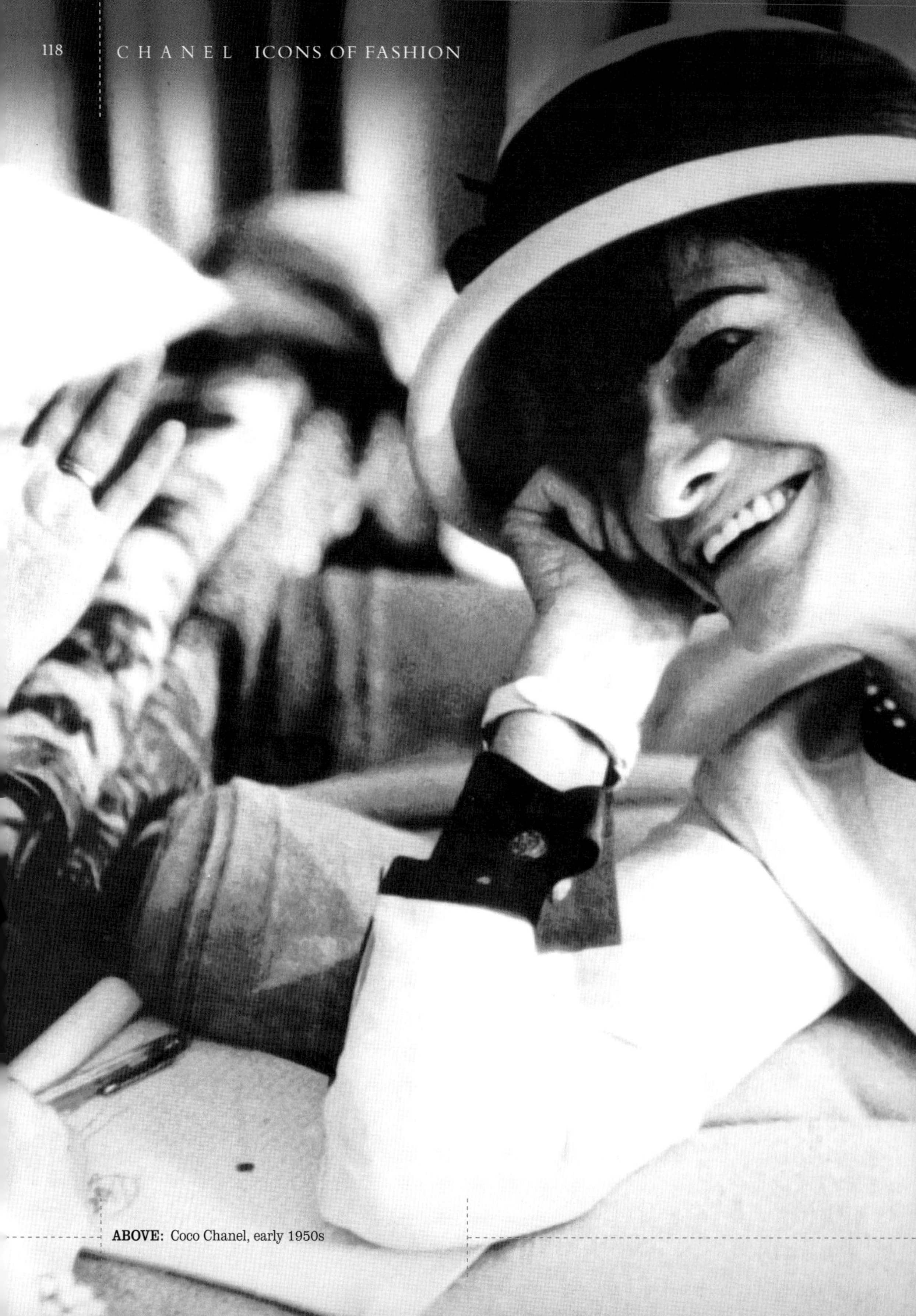

ABOVE: Coco Chanel, early 1950s

COCO ON LOVE IN OLD AGE

Speaking about love as she grew older, Coco would say: 'Love? For whom? An old man? How horrible. A young man? How shameful. If such a terrible thing happened to me, I'd flee, I'd hide'.

She contented herself instead with a multitude of short-term lovers, acquiring a reputation for being promiscuous in later life.

COCO IS BACK
1954–1964

"Elegance is not the prerogative of those who have just escaped from adolescence but of those who have already taken possession of their future."

Coco's return to business in Paris was funded by the Wertheimer brothers, Paul and Pierre. After months of lengthy discussions Coco had agreed to sell her business to the Wertheimers, who underwrote the business and acquired all rights to Coco's name. In return they would pay all her expenses, which included her bills at the Ritz Hotel and those incurred elsewhere. Coco would retain creative control, plus receive the royalties from Les Parfums Chanel. The financial running of the company was now entirely in the hands of Pierre Wertheimer, consequently dubbed the 'King of Perfume', by *Time* magazine.

Despite their fraught dealings in the past, Pierre was known to have supported Coco without reservation, even against the naysayers in his company, who were less convinced about the prudence of the association.

Despite the deal giving her such vast wealth, Coco always bore a grudge against Pierre, believing that Pierre had once 'stolen' her perfume company, as she saw it. Consequently she could never bring herself to thank him, nor to recognise that he had made her success possible on each occasion they had combined their talents. Her resentment even raised its head when his horse won at Ascot; Coco feigned ignorance of the event so that she could avoid offering him congratulations.

Entirely free of the burden of the business side of things, 71-year-old Coco could now concentrate on her first love, clothing design. She worked tirelessly, knowing that she would very likely face great and pent-up hostility.

She presented her comeback collection on 5 February 1954. It went down well in America where orders poured in after *Vogue*'s American fashion editor Bettina Ballard declared 'Chanel Designs Again' in a feature showing a more youthful Coco in black with a long pearl necklace. The piece also included photographs of the 1950s 'face of Chanel', model and actress Marie–Hélène Arnaud wearing a red dress with a V-neck, complemented with ropes of pearls, a navy jersey mid-calf suit, and a tiered seersucker evening gown. Other designs featured included a loose open jacket, a navy straw hat with ribbons, and a white blouse.

However the French press was not so keen.

Combat magazine said the collection was a ghost

OUT WITH THE OLD

As Coco returned to Paris in 1954, her old rival Elsa Schiaparelli closed The House of Schiaparelli. Having returned from New York, she too discovered that the new wave of designers was dominating the market and, unlike Coco, decided against re-entering the fray.

Instead, she wrote her autobiography, *Shocking Life*, and then for the years before her death in 1973, she divided her time between an apartment in Paris and a house in Tunisia. One of her lasting legacies to the fashion world was the wrap around dress, which American designer Diane von Fürstenberg brought back to life in the 1970s.

of the 1930s, depicting the past not the future, and described as, 'a pretentious little black figure' who was vanishing at speed.

Le Figaro similarly oozed contempt, whilst the British were only too glad to jump on the bandwagon with headlines such as 'Flop' and 'Fiasco'.

As the knives struck home in the Rue de Cambon, Coco's only defence against the press onslaught was to keep going, to work, despite the rheumatism in her once agile fingers which would often stop her from doing so.

Doubtless the sting of criticism was greatly eased when a month later she received a huge boost from America's largest circulation magazine, *Life*, which published an article celebrating '... the name behind the most famous perfume in the world'.

Instead of lambasting her for her retro look, they revelled in its 'elegant dash and easy fitting suits'.

This 'retro' look became more popular than Coco could ever have foreseen, and her second collection that year was, according to *Life* magazine, creating nothing less than clothes that were a revolution and 'shaping the future'.

In fact Coco had not revolutionised her designs and was indeed harking backwards; but in doing so, she had judged the mood of women correctly again.

Just as at the beginning of her career when she had made basic straw hats, simplicity was the name of the game. Coco was shaping the future by giving women what they wanted – not what others – often male fashion designers – wanted them to have.

STRIKE A POSE

While Coco may never have taken to the catwalk herself, she was always a great model for her clothes. Her way of standing was an art in itself, described as, '… an impertinent chic; one foot forward, hips forward, shoulders down, one hand in a pocket and the other gesticulating' by Bettina Ballard of *American Vogue*.

RIGHT: Bettina Ballard combines lunch and work, while viewing contact strips for *Vogue*

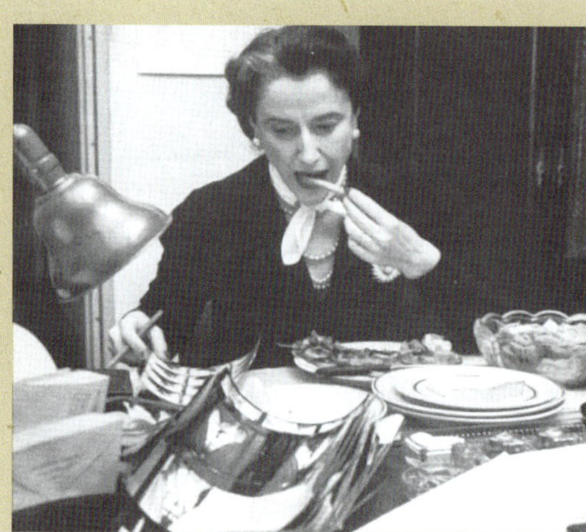

Coco's clothing range expanded adding bell-bottoms and pea jackets, and her emblematic trimmed tweed suit made its re-appearance, this time to even greater acclaim.

What was it about Coco's designs that so attracted her customers? Her clothes were so simple in style as to once have been described as hardly fashion at all.

Maybe it was because Coco never wavered in her belief that 'Fashion goes out of fashion, style never does'. How right she was. Whether it was Scottish tweeds, the jersey of the war years, the 'style anglais' or the summer bathing outfits for the Côte d'Azur, simplicity, elegance, and freedom of movement were indispensable features of her clothes.

Her signature jacket, for example, was silk lined and fitted with a thin chain in the lower seam to ensure it slid seamlessly into the Chanel 'vocabulary of style symmetry'. The cut was perfect, enabling a woman to swing her arms, the pockets placed just so to permit her relaxed, hand-in-pocket stance.

The time for the jacket's renaissance had now arrived, adorned with embossed gilt buttons and grosgrain ribbon.

Then in February 1955, Chanel premiered a handbag that was to achieve iconic status; the 2.55. Named after the month and year of its launch, the bag featured a 'double strap' which could be worn long from the shoulder. Coco explained that she had become fed up with having to hold her purses in her hands and then losing them. As an active woman, she wanted the ease of being able to use her hands freely. The signature quilting with its diamond stitching was a direct inspiration from the grooms' equestrian jackets that could be seen at the racetracks she adored, where belts, leather, buckles and chains were plentiful. The 2.55 would later be joined in its exclusive ranks by the 11.12.

With this 'shoulder strap' Coco was revolutionary and not 'harking back' at all. Amazingly, the 2.55 was the first handbag to feature a long strap. Now, even high society ladies not so ready to be active could

RIGHT: Model wearing a tweed suit designed by Coco Chanel, in Coco's suite at the Ritz Hotel, Paris, 1956

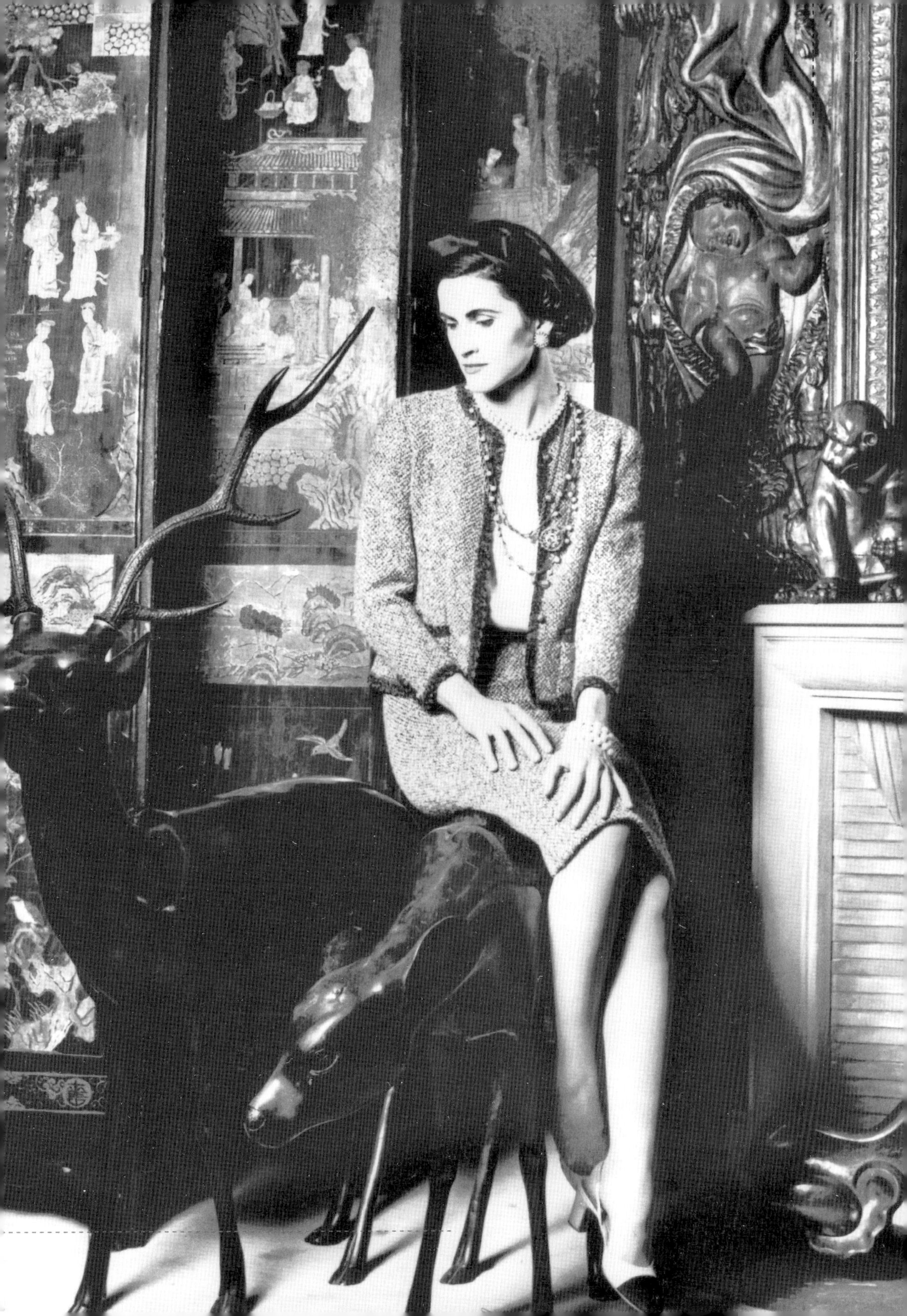

FIVE DROPS OF CHANEL NO 5

When Marilyn Monroe said in a 1952 interview that all she wore in bed was, 'Five drops of Chanel No 5' she reignited the popularity of the then 30-year-old fragrance.

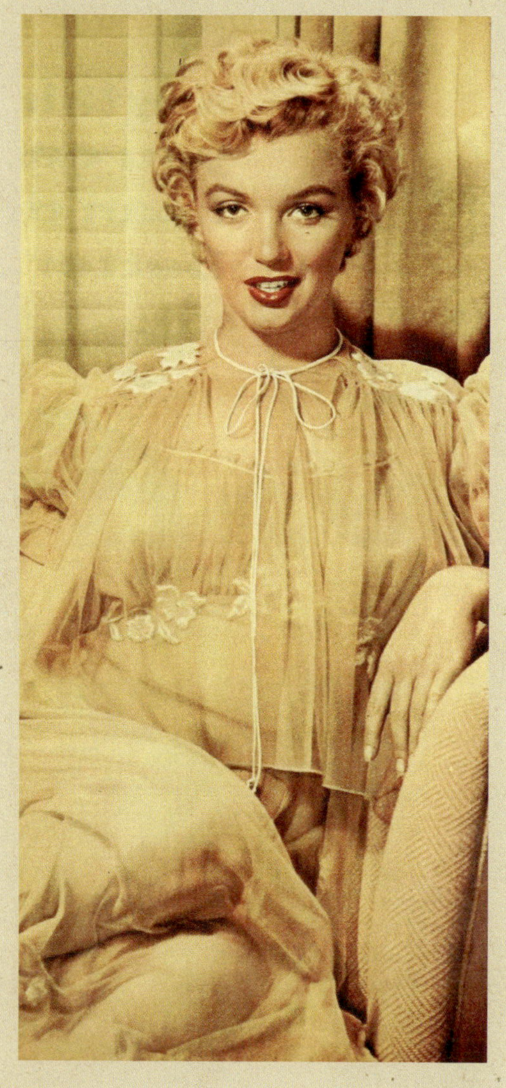

at least stay balanced, holding their champagne in one hand and a cigarette in the other, while not needing to worry about their handbag.

Going from strength to strength, Coco followed up this success with another design for Chanel which would become iconic – her two-toned slingback pumps, introduced in 1957. Firm reminders of the era in which Bendor and his friends would sport two-tone shoes on the golf course, Chanel's timeless version complemented a variety of wardrobes and situations. Its short heel was comfortable, the black, squared toes that made the foot look shorter while the beige main body of the shoe gave the impression of lengthening the leg.

It was understandably a hugely popular design.

A 74-year-old Coco had reconquered the heights and stars and starlets, the famous and would-be famous all beat a path to her door in the Rue Cambon once again.

Despite her declaration; 'How mean, how hard, how awful Paris was', Coco was on another roll. She was asked to design costumes for the play, 'Thé et Sympathie', being staged in Paris by Ingrid Bergman in 1956, while her clothes were worn by Brigitte Bardot, Jeanne Moreau and Catherine Deneuve.

Now a renowned film director himself, Luchino Visconti repaid Coco's friendship to him back in the 1930s by having her clothe Romy Schneider, in his film, 'Boccaccio '70' in 1962.

Coco's kudos spread beyond Europe's borders,

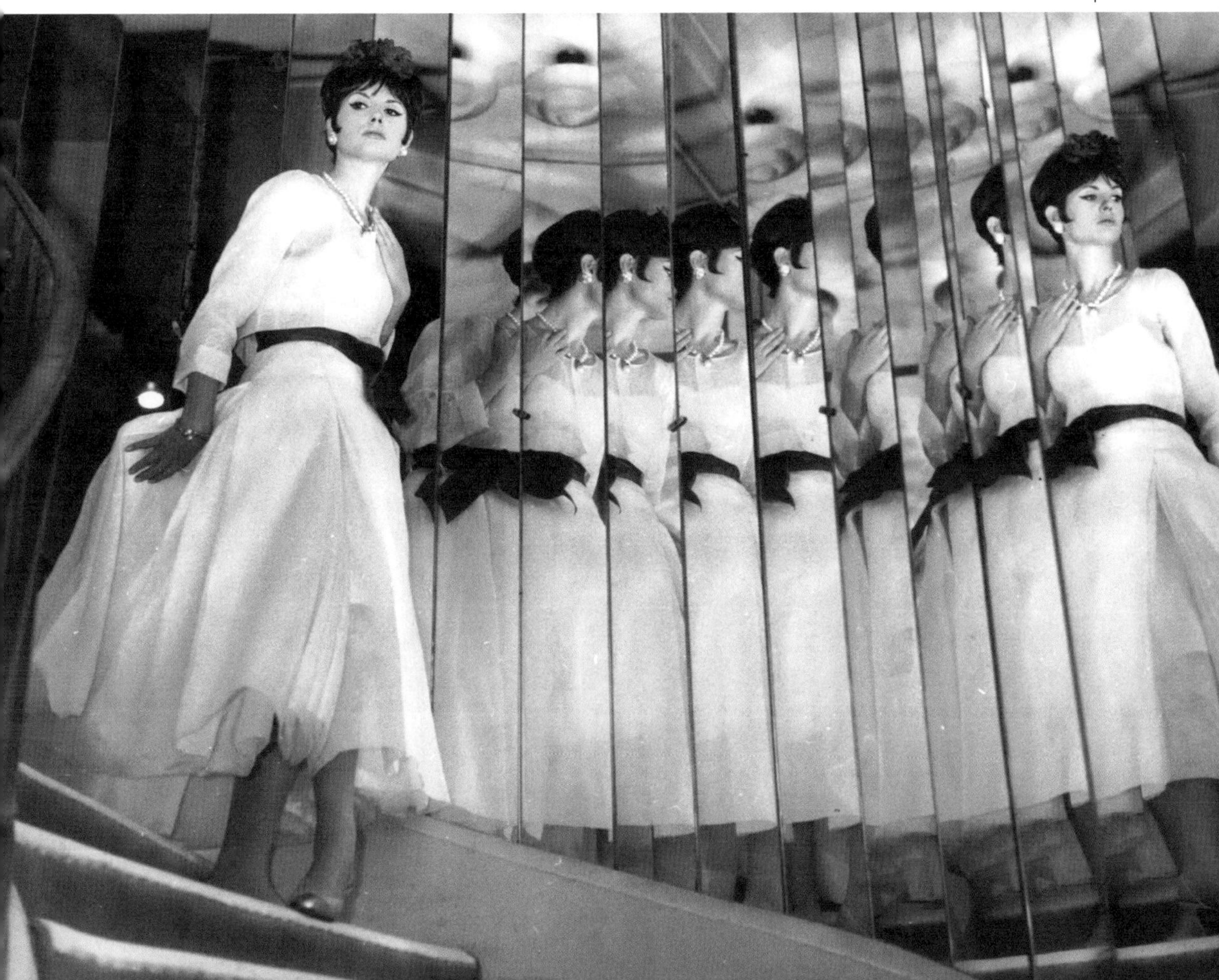

and America once again opened its doors wide for her work. Such illustrious star names as Jane Fonda, Marilyn Monroe, Elizabeth Taylor and Grace Kelly could be seen out and about in Chanel. In September 1957, the US department store Neiman-Marcus handed her a fashion award as the most influential designer of the 20th century.

Even the American First Lady Jackie Kennedy had been seduced by Chanel. In August of 1959,

when her husband was still an ambitious senator, *Life* magazine ran a photograph showing Jackie behind her husband wearing a pastel pink dress and pearls. Then, most famously, Jackie was wearing a pink bouclé Chanel suit when her husband President Kennedy was shot on 22 November 1963.

A Chanel suit sadly immortalised as Jackie wore it, complete with bloodstains, for the rest of the day.

ABOVE: A glimpse of Coco Chanel's new 1963 line

COCO THE MUSICAL

While the idea for a Broadway musical based on Coco's life had been floating around since 1954, it wasn't until 1964 that the show eventually began to come together.

With music by André Previn and lyrics by Alan J. Lerner, a man Coco trusted to do right by her reputation, the show 'Coco' would cover the period between early autumn 1953 and late spring of 1954, when she had made her 'comeback'.

However on learning that the celebrated actress Katharine Hepburn would play her, Coco was not best pleased, tersely dismissing her as 'too old'. This was even though Katharine was 24 years her junior and Coco herself had been 70 at the time the show was set. However Coco had initially been sold the idea of the show with the promise that it would cover her early career and that plan was changed to accommodate Katharine Hepburn, who was making her debut in a stage musical.

There were however many parallels between Katharine and Coco. Katharine was another modern woman, who was also happiest in simple and sleek clothing that allowed her freedom of movement and did not make her appear too 'feminine'. Both women were highly successful and famous, indomitable, independent, feisty, strong-willed and slim as reeds. They also both found fulfilment in their work, which saved them from being alone.

Once she had come to terms with the change to the content of the show, Coco met with British designer and photographer Cecil Beaton, who had been hired to make the costumes and design the sets.

Beaton visited Coco in Paris in 1965, at her Rue Cambon premises still bursting with opulence, gold lacquer and crystal. He found Coco to be buzzing with activity and ideas, wearing her favoured beige, wielding her scissors and chattering without cease in her clipped manner. The never-ending monologue caused Beaton to wonder if she was talking to him or to herself. Incidentally, Beaton also noted that Hepburn displayed an equally loquacious streak.

Eventually, in 1969, the musical opened in New York on 18 December.

Coco had been petrified at the thought of going to the première, watching her quasi-doppelgänger and seeing her life paraded on stage, even though she generally held the Americans in high esteem for their reverential treatment of her.

Her white evening dress adorned with sequins was ready, but just before Coco's departure for the US, fate decided to play a trick on her by paralysing the nerves in her right hand. So instead of the bright lights of Broadway, she faced the bright lights of a hospital bed.

The show ran for 329 performances, only closing two months after Katharine's eight-month contract ended. Although reviews had been lukewarm, audiences liked it and Katharine was nominated for a Tony award for her portrayal of Coco.

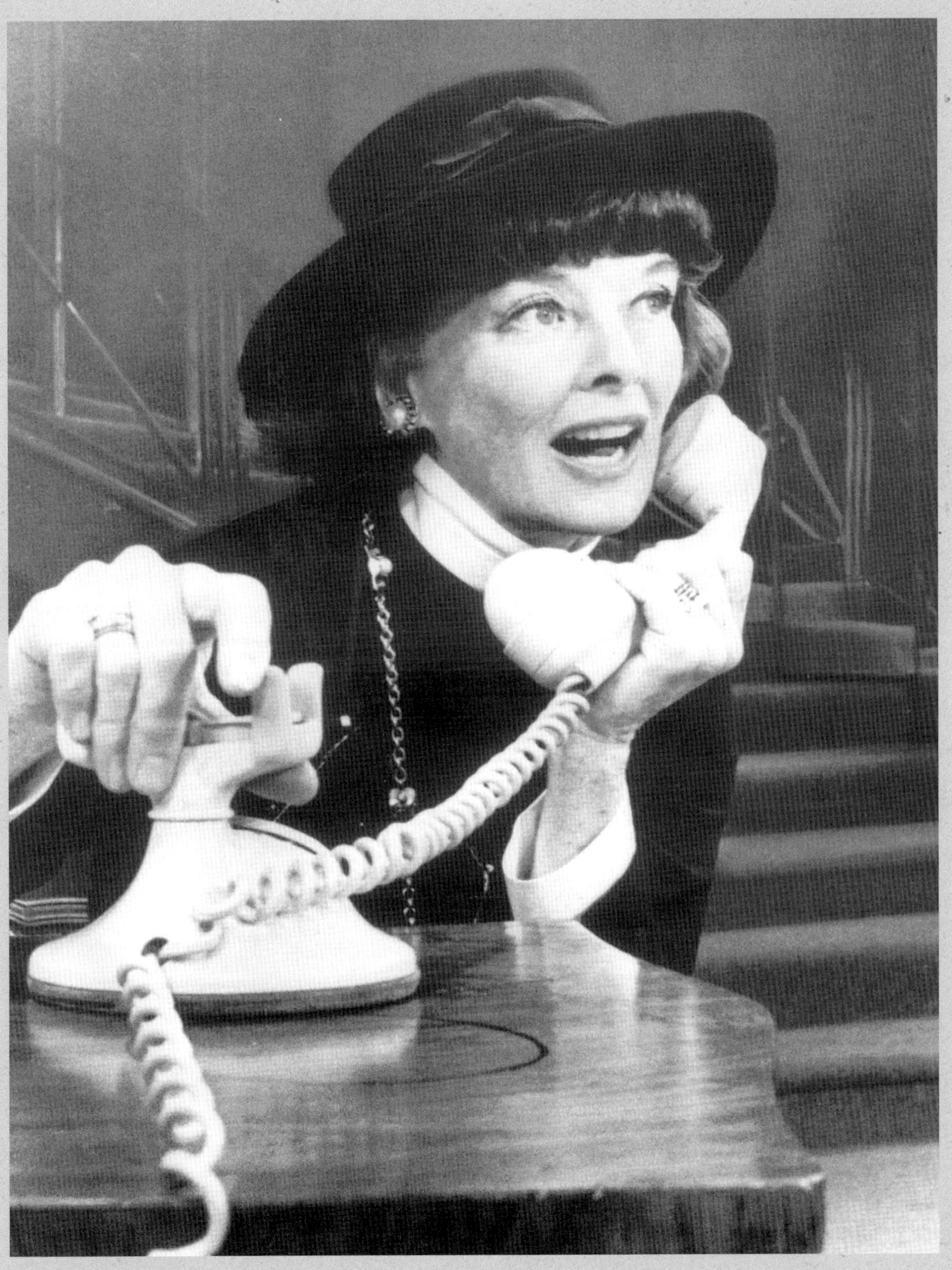

ABOVE RIGHT: Katharine Hepburn in 'Coco'

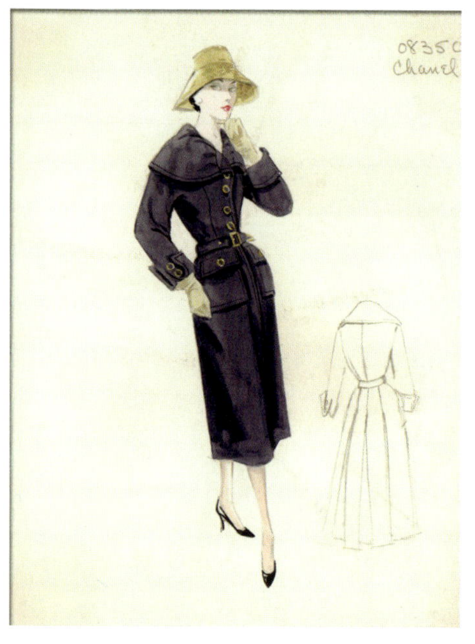

Chanel blue coat, spring 1955

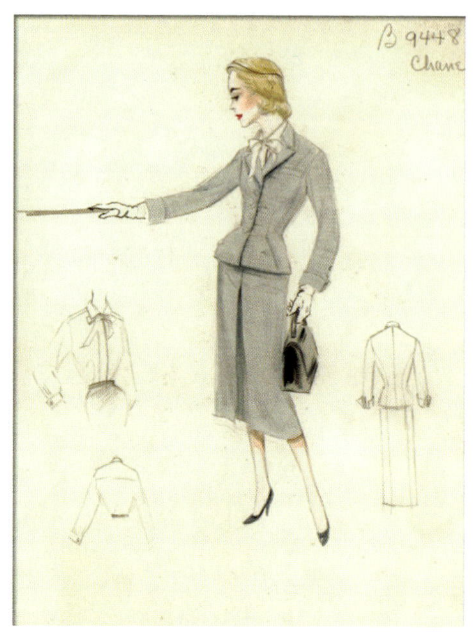

Chanel gray suit, 1955

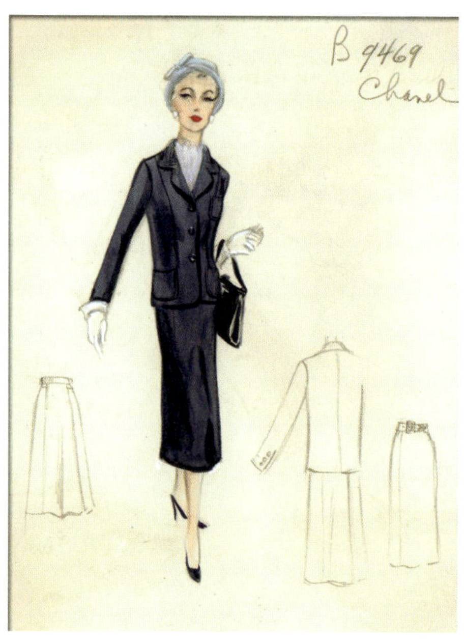

Chanel navy blue suit, fall 1955

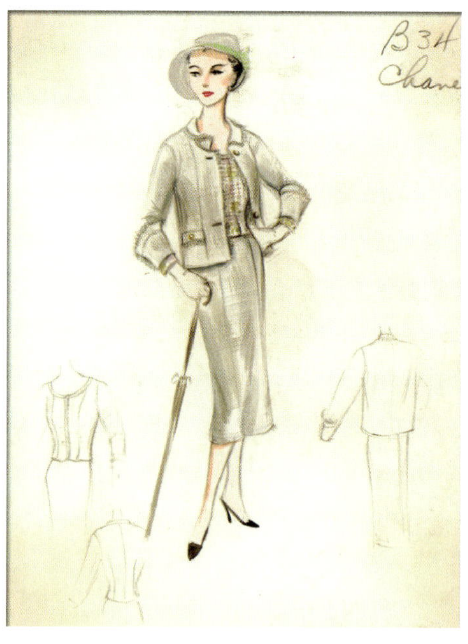

Chanel gray suit, spring 1957

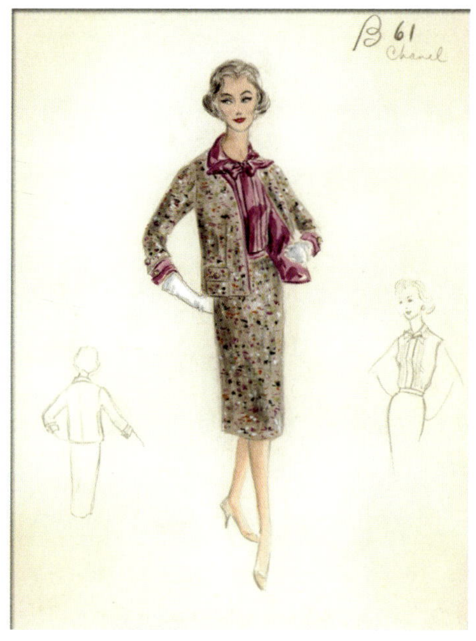

Chanel tweed suit, spring 1958

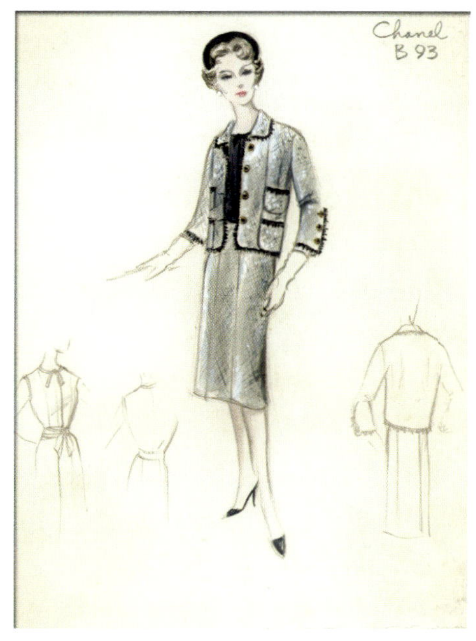

Chanel tweed suit with blouse, spring 1959

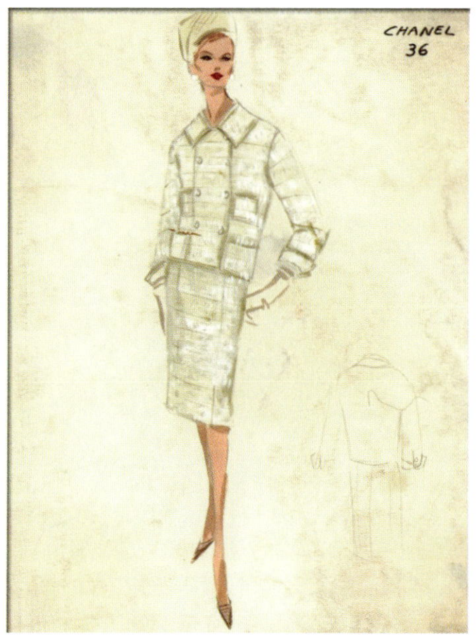

Chanel yellow and white tweed suit, fall 1961

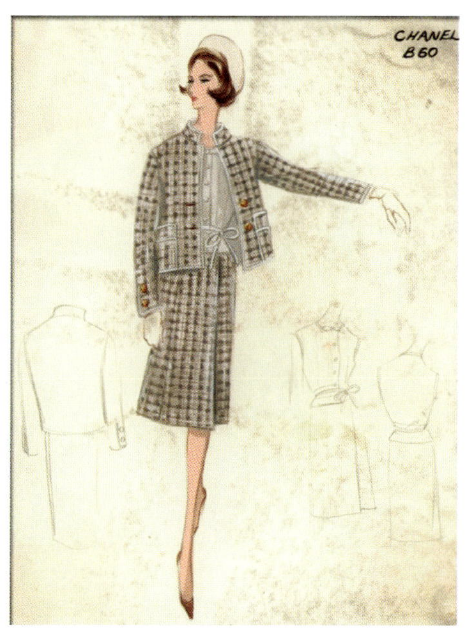

Chanel tweed suit with blouse, fall 1962

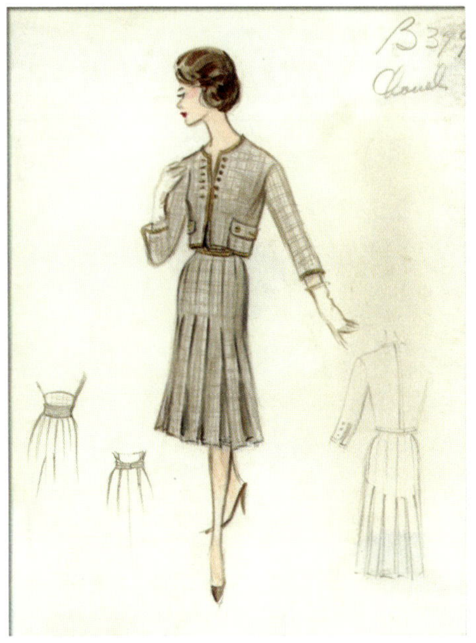

Chanel plaid suit, 1960

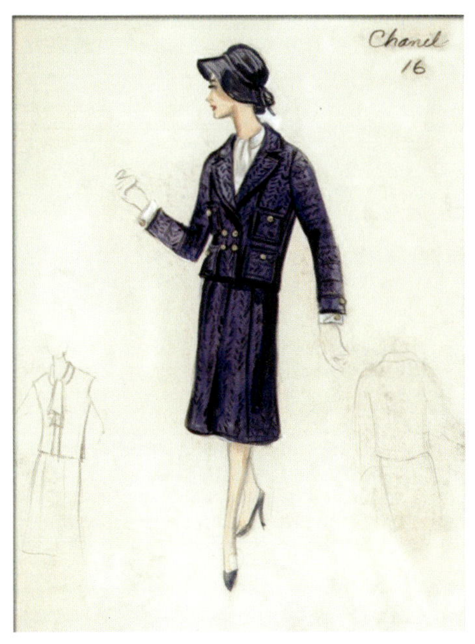

Chanel blue tweed suit, spring 1960

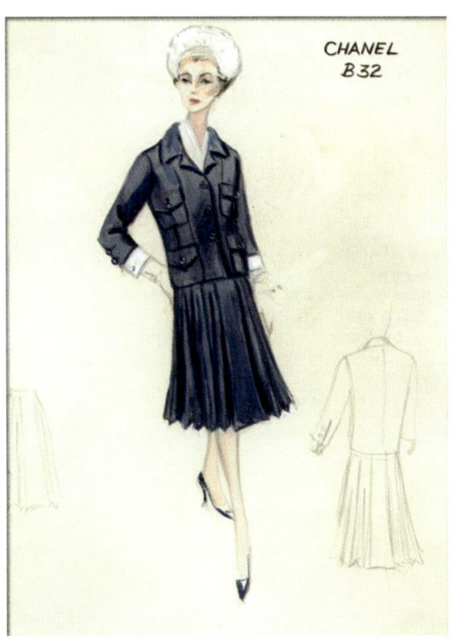

Chanel blue suit, spring 1961

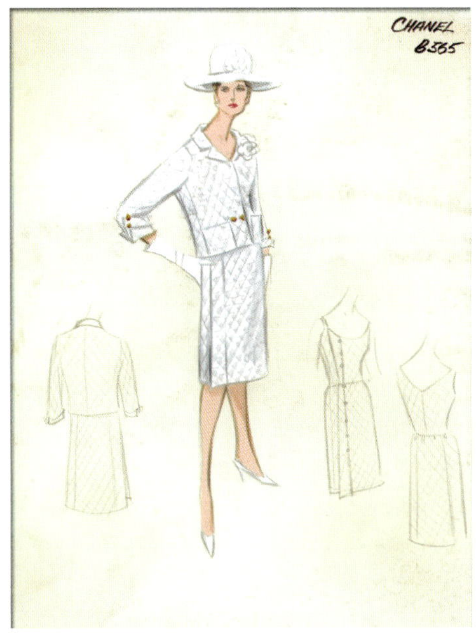

Chanel white day dress with jacket, 1964

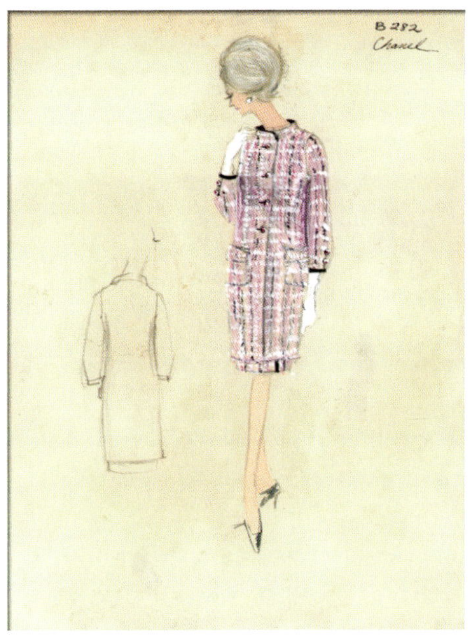

Chanel tweed coat, spring 1965

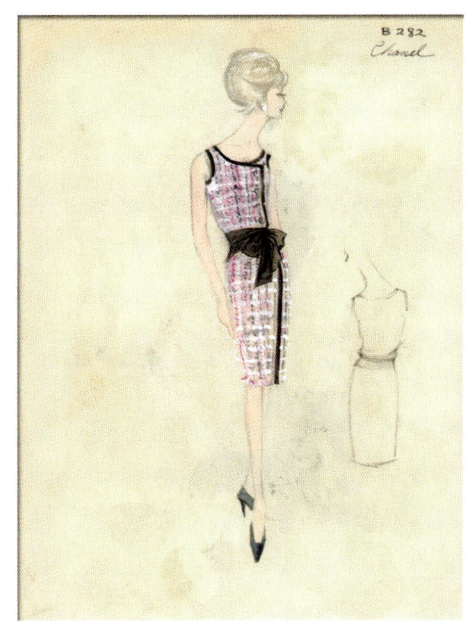

Chanel tweed dress, spring 1965

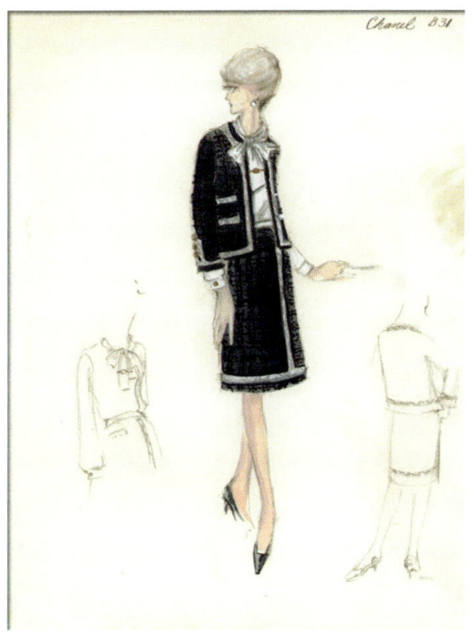

Chanel tweed suit with blouse, fall 1965

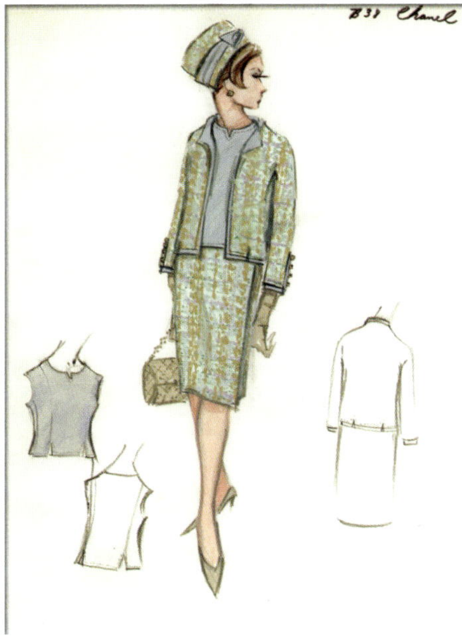

Chanel pastel tweed suit, spring 1966

THE LONELY YEARS 1964–1970

"There are many more attempts to define happiness than unhappiness. It is because people know all too well what unhappiness is."

Up until the issue with her hand, Coco had still wielded the scissors in the Rue Cambon, a tape measure hung around her neck even though she no longer needed to do the stitching herself. Pinning, cutting, re-pinning and re-cutting, she would exhaust her employees in the search for the perfect fit. Her dresses did not betray or desert her – they were constant and faithful companions who she could cut to size as she wished. She was an autocrat who reigned supreme in her kingdom.

But when the working day ended Coco found herself alone. Most of her former lovers and friends had died and she found life without men friends in particular, extremely hard. So she continued to work, in part, to distract herself and banish her loneliness.

'Work has always been a kind of drug for me', she once mused, 'Even if I sometimes wonder what Chanel would have been without the men in my life'.

'God knows I wanted love', she once mused. 'But the moment I had to choose between the man I loved and my dresses, I chose the dresses'. That was true, but perhaps, sometimes, she had wanted to choose the man. However the men in her life all made other choices.

Coco sometimes spoke about missing being noticed by a man who loved her, saying that without that, a woman would die. And she once said that an unloved woman was not a woman.

But what was Coco thinking as she aged? As her makeup became slightly heavier and her hair slightly thinner, she confessed to her great niece Gabrielle Palasse-Labrunie, that 'having your loved ones around you, leading a simple life, a husband, children, would be a 'real life'. She remained close to Gabrielle until she died. Another friend was the writer and psychoanalyst Claude Delay, a woman who wrote several Chanel biographies.

Claude said that Coco had spoken openly to her about her isolation. 'I often found her alone, sitting at the dressing table, gazing down into the garden, looking at the chestnut trees' she said.

'She was still so slender, thin as a girl in her white pyjamas, her eyebrows washed clean of their black makeup, her jewels put away beneath a chamois cloth, a silk scarf tied around her hair'.

For once, Coco admitted to having misjudged what was important in life, 'One shouldn't live alone', she told Delay. 'It's a mistake. I used to think I had to make my life on my own, but I was wrong.

RIGHT: Coco Chanel, rests on the stairs of her office in Paris on March 28, 1966

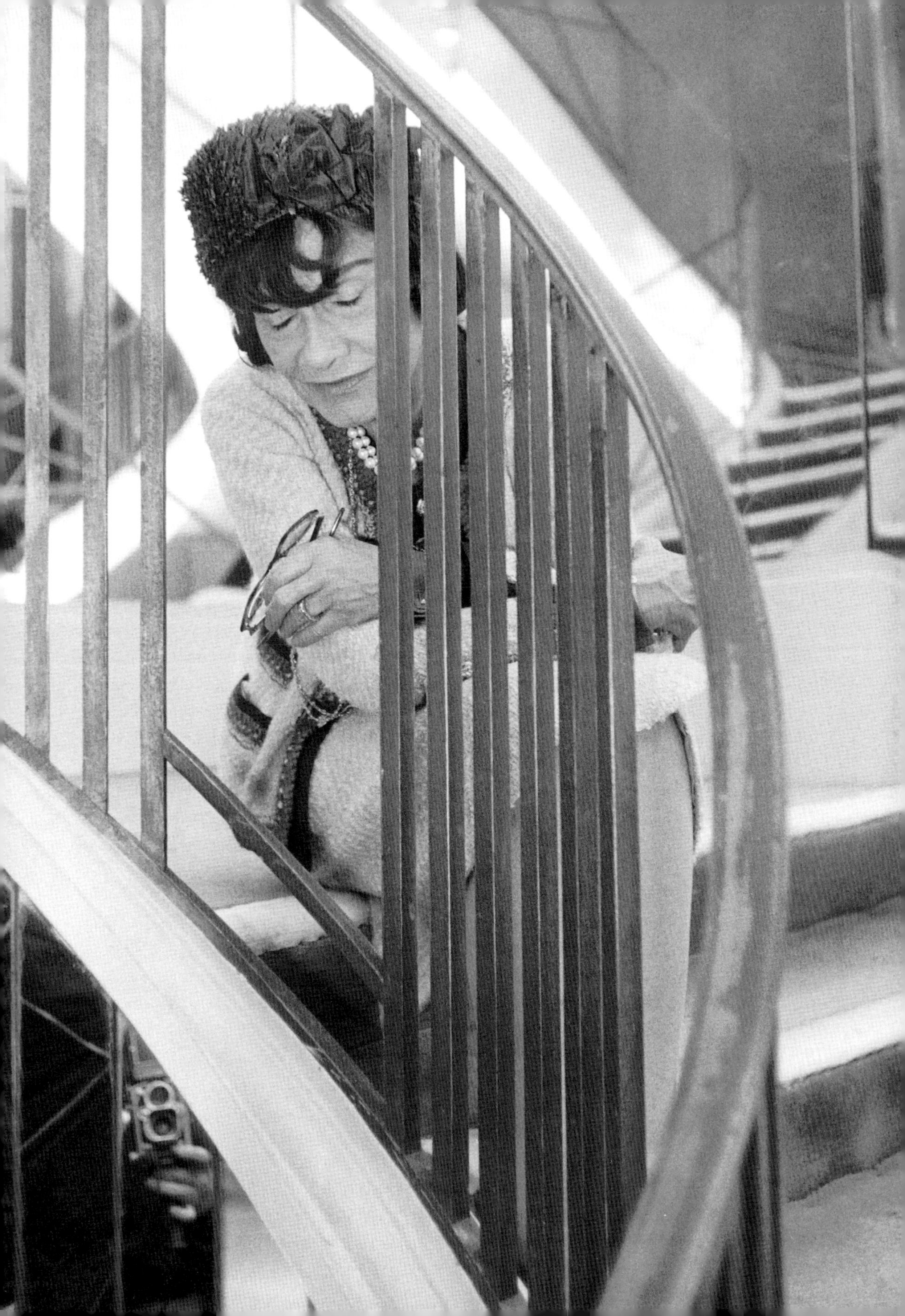

Coco also found little respite in sleep as she was plagued by nightmares, despite the opiates coursing in her veins. Bruises and cuts on her body towards the end of her life would tell of nocturnal terrors After darkness had fallen, she might sleepwalk or awaken suddenly, seated in front of her dressing table, shocked and scared to find her scissors in her hand having hacked and sliced her pyjamas. The door to her room at The Ritz, which had been her home for 30 years was locked, to prevent any sojourns into the hotel corridors, but she might still fall out of the bed or collapse in the bathroom. Unwilling to be seen by others when she was bleeding, she would carry out repairs to the wounds herself.

One nightmare was worse than the others, filled with recurring images. Claude said that Coco had told her: 'Out of the darkness of sleep, there would appear a white train with a scented coach full of flowers and COCO CHANEL written on the side. It was carrying a corpse inside – her own body'.

Aside from Gabrielle and Claude, Coco had her trusted servants; her maid Jeanne, her white-gloved butler François Mironnet, and her secretary Lilou Grumbach. On occasion, François would be invited to eat with Coco, something like a veal roast, with tiny peas, onions, carrots and potatoes, and at other times he and Lilou would play cards in a room adjacent to Coco's bedroom, to give a semblance of companionship while Coco fell asleep.

Others who lightened her dark hours included Jacques Chazot, dancer and socialite, and Aimée de Heeren, a Brazilian socialite and secret service agent, the society 'lioness', who all Parisian hostesses had once tried to entice to their gatherings. Although Aimée only resided in Paris for short periods each year, she and Coco could be seen wandering through Paris together, perhaps reminiscing happily about those halcyon days with Bendor, the Duke of Westminster, whom they had both known. Coco also liked to walk in the Cimetière du Père-Lachaise, the last resting place of so many famous names – although it was not where Coco had chosen to be buried.

RIGHT: Coco Chanel's suite at the Ritz Hotel, Paris, 1965

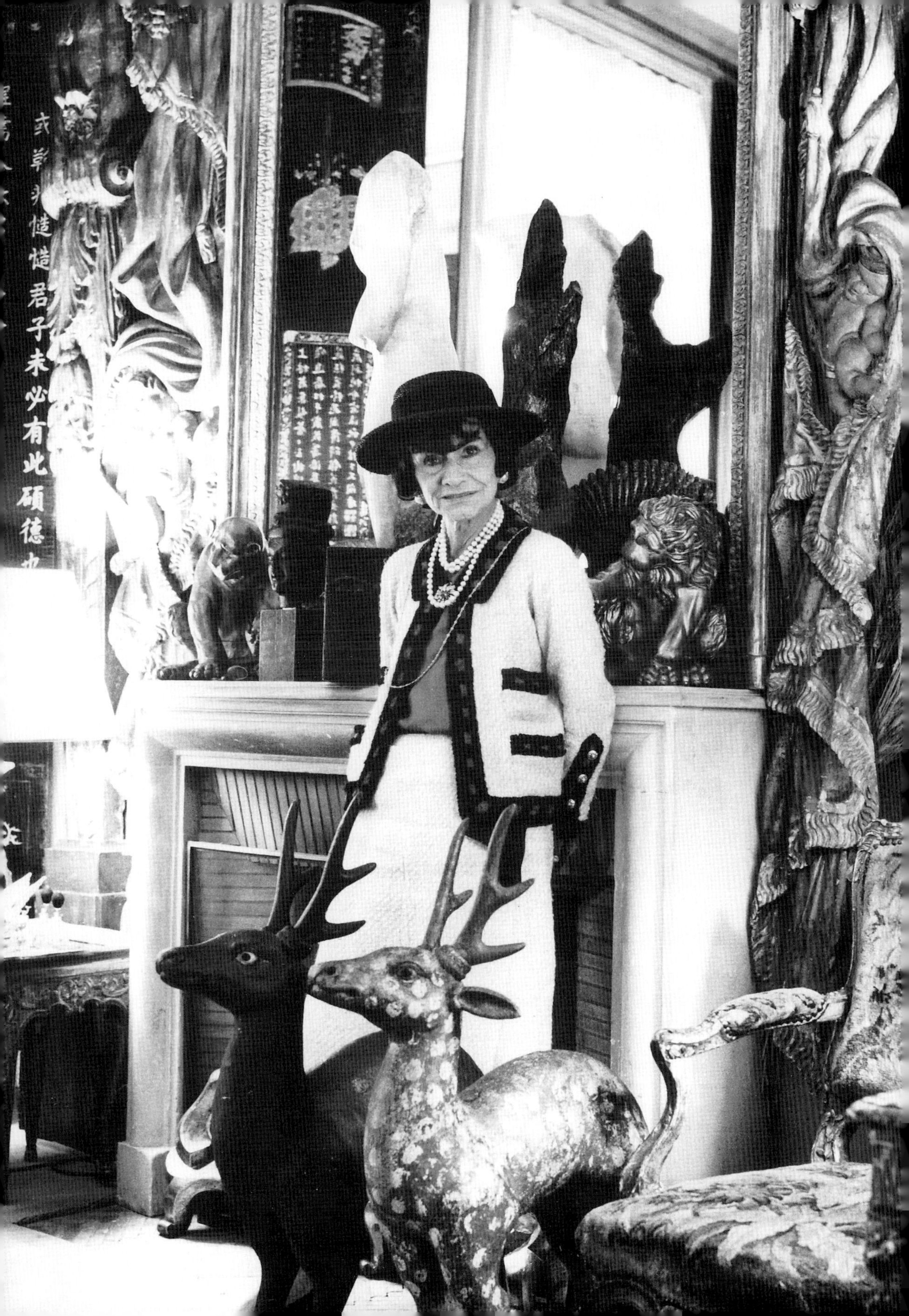

YOU SEE, THIS IS HOW YOU DIE
1971

"I am not young but I feel young. The day I feel old, I will go to bed and stay there. J'aime la vie! I feel that to live is a wonderful thing."

One Saturday morning early in January 1971, Coco, now an 87-year-old woman, was hurrying to finish her spring collection, due later in the month. She would have worked through the weekend had it been possible. Her staff recalled that she had worked in haste, and in retrospect her haste had seemed like a premonition they realised. 'She had wanted to get everything ready before dying', said one.

The next day, 9 January, Coco was visited in the Ritz by Claude Delay, and the two friends had lunch in the hotel, Coco made up immaculately as usual, wearing her favoured red lipstick. Even in old age she would wear the little straw hats that were similar to those she had worn as a young girl and which had set her off on her illustrious path. 'I still dress as I always did, like a schoolgirl,' she said. After their leisurely lunch, she and Claude went for a drive through Paris in the winter sunshine along the Champs-Elysées, not returning until the sun had already set. Claude went home, and Coco walked into the Ritz lobby alone, going straight up to her suite.

Feeling unwell, she lay down on the bed without undressing and at around 8.30pm she called to her maid Jeanne, complaining that she couldn't breathe and asking for her opiate injection.

As Jeanne helped her to inject herself, the needle pushing into her hip, Coco had just one last thing to say before 'the struggle', as she described old age, was over. 'You see, this is how you die', she said as she closed her eyes for the final time.

By the next morning, Jeanne had dressed Coco all in white as she had wanted; in a white blouse under a white suit, perhaps fulfilling her friend Diaghilev's wish, 'Promise me you will always wear white'. That is how Claude Delay saw her before the funeral as Coco lay in her suite on the second floor of the Ritz with a view over Paris and the Place Vendôme.

The funeral service took place at the grand L'Eglise de la Madeleine close to the Rue Cambon. Coco's coffin lay bathed in wreaths and spreads of white gardenias and orchids, azaleas, and camellias, with a single red rose glowing amongst the waves of white blossoms.

Among the mourners were the most celebrated names from the contemporary fashion world who came to pay their last respects: Yves Saint-Laurent, Balmain, Balenciaga, and Courrèges. Only Pierre Cardin stayed away. Perhaps Coco's oft-repeated criticism of him had soured any sense of allegiance he may once have nurtured.

The high society she had revelled in was represented by one of its prominent members, Marie-Hélène de Rothschild. Also paying their respects to 'La Grande Mademoiselle', as the press referred to Coco, was the actress and singer Jeanne Moreau and the artist Salvador Dalí.

Then there were her models in couture outfits. A fortnight later they would wear her final designs, the evening dresses in white and the ivory tweed suits, at the show Coco had worked on to the very last.

Although most of her 'golden era' friends had left the world before her, one was still alive, the choreographer and ballet dancer, Serge Lifar and he travelled from his home in Switzerland to pay his respects. Not once had Coco, his 'Queen of Fashion', missed any of his Parisian premières and Serge had become a regular visitor to La Pausa, and to Coco's retreat at Le Signal de Sauvebelin in the hills behind Lausanne.

And it was Switzerland that Coco had chosen as her final resting place, in the Cimetière du Bois Vaux in Lausanne. Back in the country that had offered her

exile and the security she craved during some difficult times in her life, her grave is every bit as stylish as befits her.

She lays under a mound of white flowers, because she said she did not wish to lie beneath a stone because, 'I want to be able to move... once I was put under, I would grow restless and would think only of returning to earth and starting all over again'.

She also expressed her belief, ' ... if you want to be close to a person who has died, you'll never find them in a graveyard'.

But many people do come to visit her grave, which bears a simple headstone, placed behind it, decorated plainly with a cross, her name and the dates of her birth and death. Across the top are five emblematic lion heads, the lion being a favourite motif she often featured in her designs for jewellery, buttons and bag clasps. Of course there are five lions – five being the number so synonymous with her business.

The greatest part of her estate was inherited by her nephew, André Palasse, and his two daughters.

PARIS WILL REMEMBER 1971

"I invented my life by taking for granted that everything I did not like would have an opposite, which I would like."

Coco Chanel was one of the last representatives of a gilded and cursed era – a mysterious figure whose story was filled with intriguing subterfuge, glamour, wealth, and pioneering creativity.

Attempting to unravel the entanglements that weaved in and around her life is a Herculean task. That is exactly how she had wanted it, having ensured that dead ends and 'fausses routes' were scattered everywhere to deceive and distract. Even her copious quote-worthy statements set up contradictions.

The little orphan girl had completely incredibly transformed herself, which took determination, ambition, and a streak of ruthlessness. She understood that power was money, money was strength, and strength delivered the independence she craved.

She morphed into a rebel, a fearless fashion pioneer propelled by the humble start in life, which she obliquely acknowledged had made her different. She retained a love of simplicity throughout her life – initially ignoring the laughter which had greeted her appearance, later biting back with humour and sharp sarcasm – understanding that the simplicity of her style was the secret of her success; 'I didn't look like anyone', she said.

As she got to grips with the rules of the game she needed to play to advance herself, she became the ultimate competitor, using whatever she had to find her way to the money she knew would benefit her. At first all that she possessed was herself, so that is what she used. As a very young woman, Coco could be found in the bedrooms of the upper classes and has been described as 'mistress to the wealthy' for the purpose of gaining entry into high society. But once she had arrived, she stamped her innovative and brave styles indelibly onto the fashion world, changing it dramatically as the world moved on and into the 1920s.

Once she had her business she promoted it just as fiercely as she had fought for her independence,

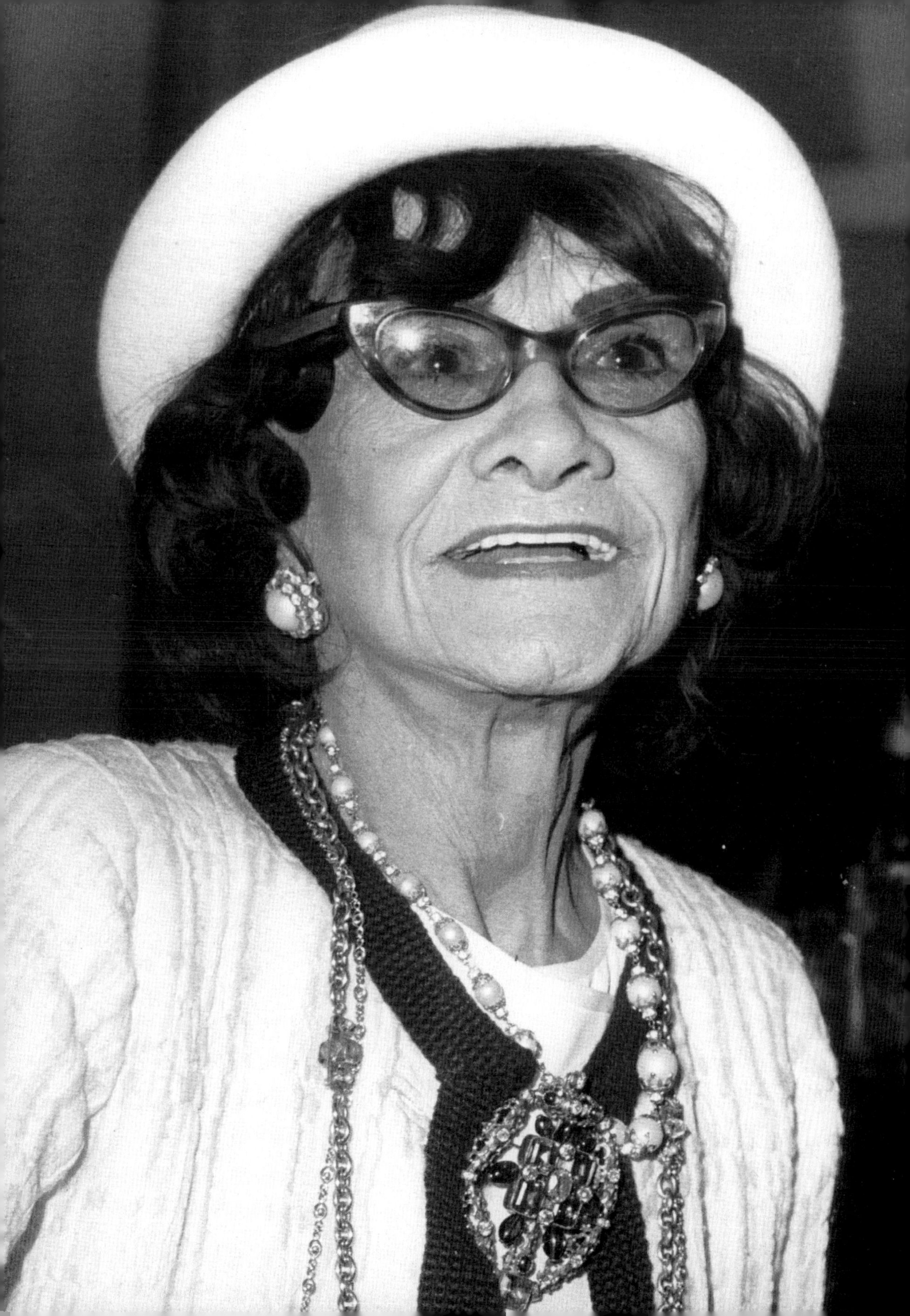

subsuming everything to see it flourish. For Coco, business was far more than a welcome means to earn money, it was inextricably linked to the essence of who she was.

The spare designs of her jewellery, little black dresses, jerseys and suits, enabled women to discard their corsetry and move more freely, whilst remaining stylish and chic. No wonder Chanel designs were seized on by women who had hitherto been forced into a breath-constricting, corseted silhouette. Chanel 'always dared, always strips, never adds, there is no other beauty than the freedom of the body', was French designer Pierre Balmain's comment about his rival. Her own assessment of herself in the latter years of her life was more mundane and succinct; 'I know women'.

Many people have tried to encapsulate what it meant to be the enigmatic Coco Chanel. The French writer Maurice Sachs, who briefly worked for her in the 1930s when she was designing for Sam Goldwyn, said: 'She was not regularly beautiful, but she was irresistible. Her speech was not dazzling, but her mind and heart were unforgettable'.

What was the special ingredient that made Coco Chanel so attractive to men such as Etienne Balsan, Boy Capel and the Duke of Westminster? Perhaps her avowed disdain for their ranks of the wealthy, whom she merely considered useful contacts? Her lack of the airs and graces that the women who were the equals of those men in social standing

were required to maintain by rigid etiquette? The freedom of spirit with which she also infused her designs? Whatever it was, her unique personality traits engendered friendships that lasted long after the passionate flames had cooled.

Her great niece Gabrielle Palasse-Labrunie, believed her success came about because, 'Nobody can possess her spirit — she was the embodiment of independence and freedom'.

But maybe, as so often, it was Coco who said it best. She was, after all, the only one with intimate knowledge of the truths, falsehoods, omissions and sentiments that informed her life. She professed that she was no heroine but had chosen the kind of person she wished to become, saying; 'My life didn't please me, so I created my life'.

She was indeed revolutionary, a woman who refused to be weighed down by her impoverished start, nor to allow those around her to subdue her spirit. That spirit found expression in the clothes she wore and then transformed into a fashion empire that brought the same freedom of clothing to women everywhere.

She would no doubt be pleased to know that her legacy would prove enduring, having once said: 'Reality is sad, and the handsome parasite that is the imagination will always be preferred to it. May my legend gain ground, I wish it a long and happy life'.

RIGHT: The grave of Gabreille "Coco" Chanel in the Cimetière du Bois-de-Vaux cemetary in Lausanne, Vaud, Switzerland with five stone lions on the headstone

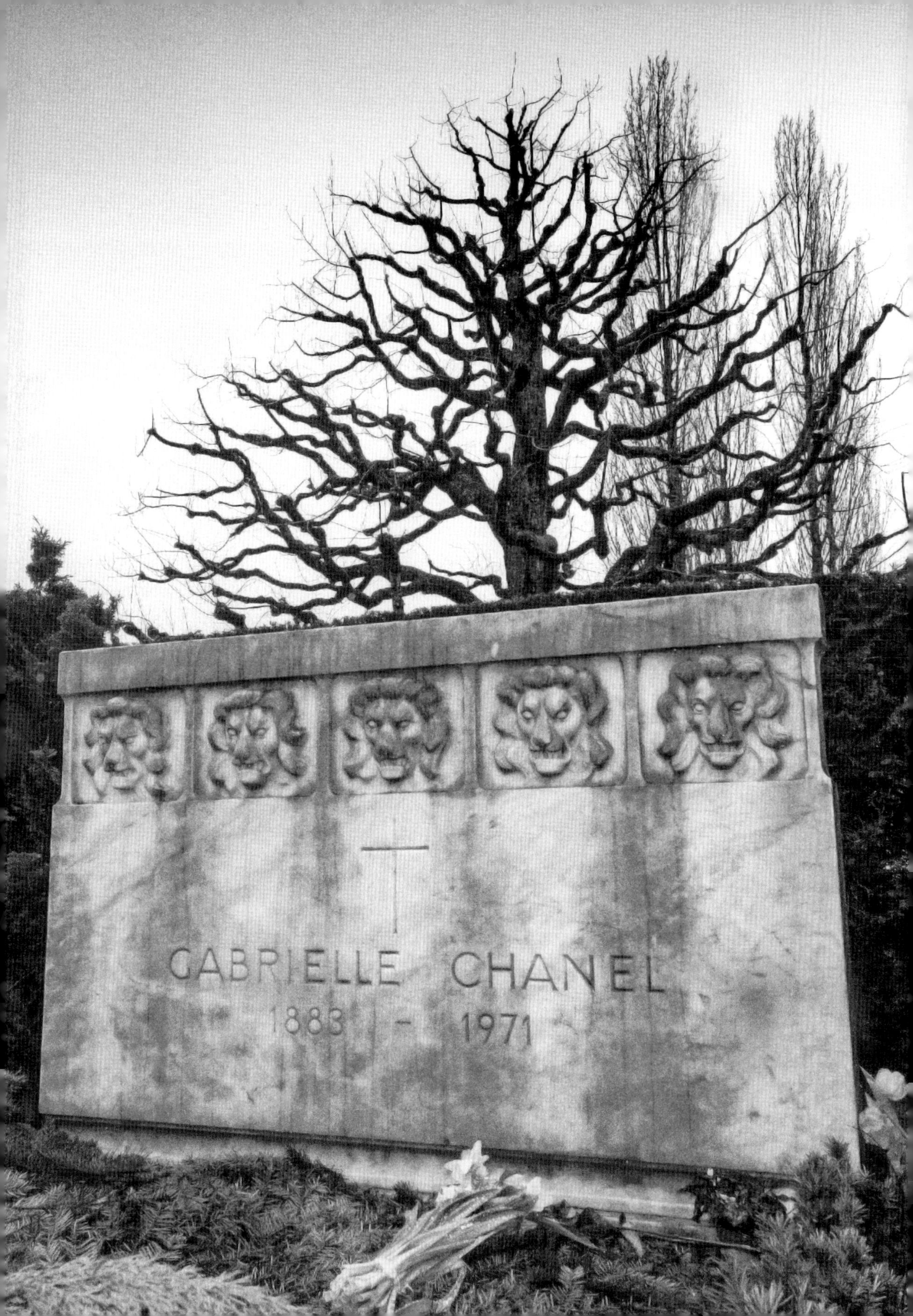

GABRIELLE CHANEL
1883 - 1971

CHANEL WITHOUT COCO

While Chanel without Coco at first seemed unthinkable, life – and business – goes on. Immediately following Coco's death, her assistants Jean Cazaubon and Yvonne Dudel took over the house, and were later joined by Philippe Guibourge who had been Marc Bohan's assistant at Dior. Coco's old sparring partner and Chanel's co-founder Pierre Wertheimer had died in 1965, and his son Jacques was now at the helm of Chanel, with the Wertheimer family now in full financial control of the company, having bought out the Bader family's 20 per cent share.

But Jacques didn't share Pierre's interest in fashion and perfumery, preferring to follow his passion for racehorses. So it wasn't hard for his son Alain to persuade him and Chanel's board of trustees to let him take over the company in 1974.

At this point, the company was in the fashion doldrums, relying on its perfume line for profits. There was plenty to do if Chanel were to return to its former glory days. And despite Alain's youth and inexperience – he was just 25 at the time – he knew what was needed to make Chanel relevant again. He began by making changes to the company's distribution network, so that its perfumes and cosmetics were no longer available on the 'high street' but became more exclusive. He also oversaw Chanel's first mass-produced,

ready to wear line of clothes, designed by Philippe Guibourge in 1978.

However the masterstroke came in 1983 when he hired fashion designer Karl Lagerfeld as Chanel's artistic director, luring him away from rival French fashion house Chloé. His brief was to revitalise Chanel couture. Just a year later, Lagerfeld took over the ready-to-wear lines as well.

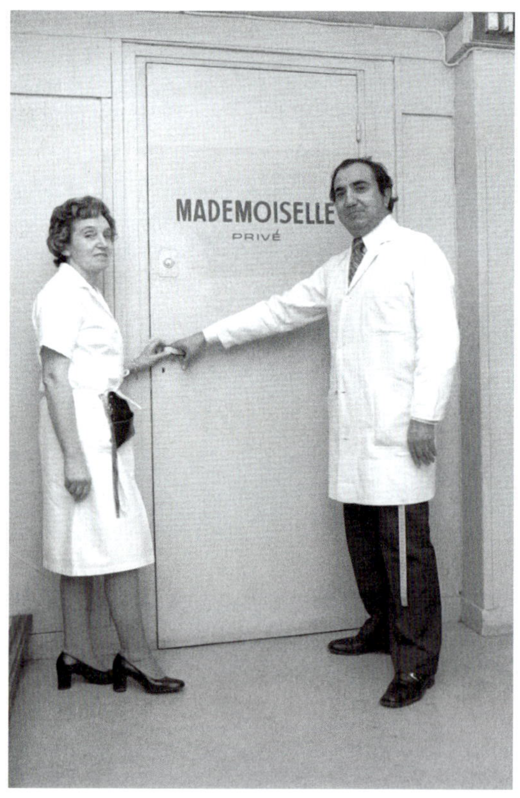

ABOVE RIGHT: Jean Cazaubon and Yvonne Dudel in front of the door of Coco Chanel's apartment in Paris on January 16, 1974, France

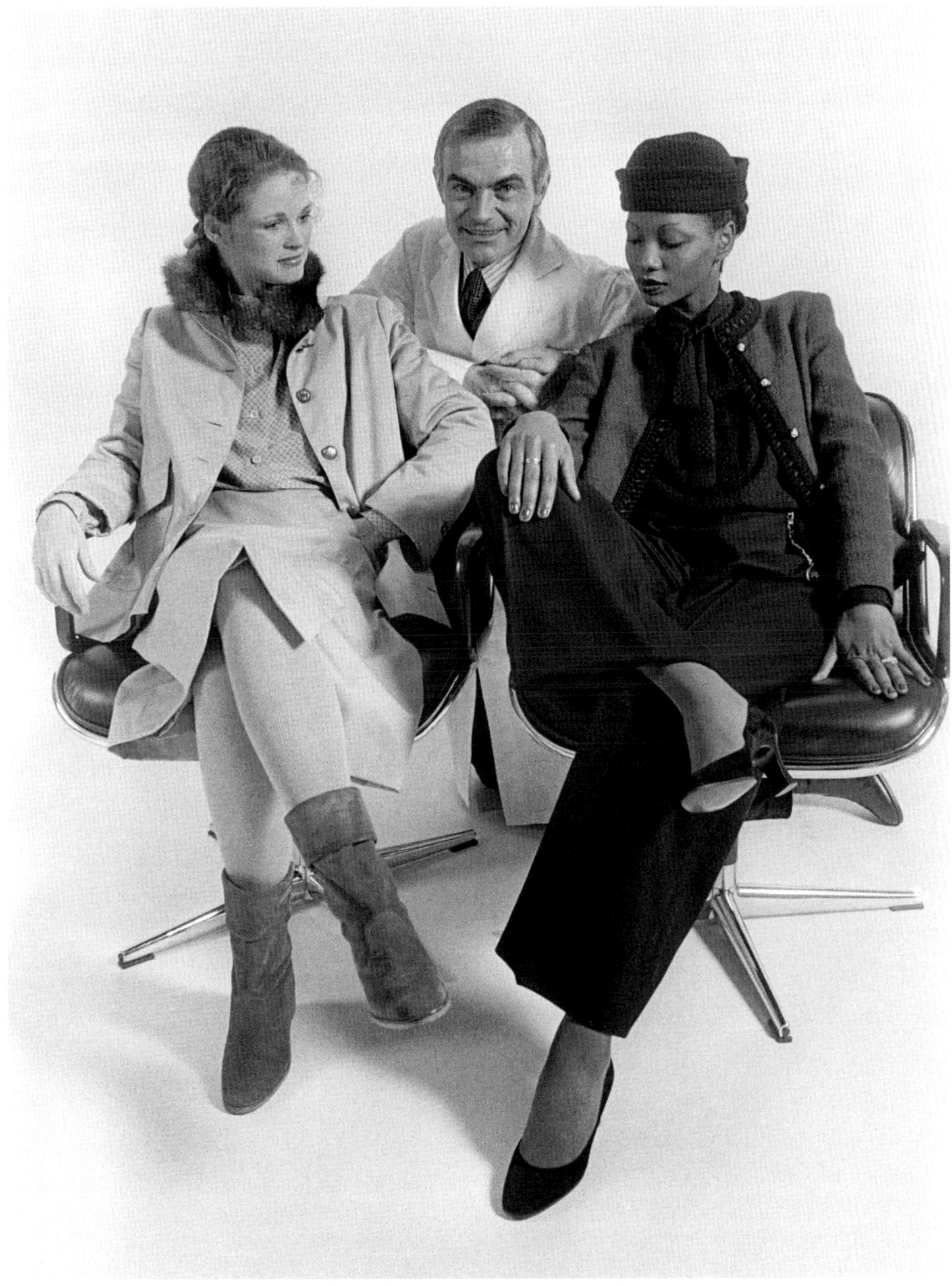

ABOVE: Chanel Fall 1978 Ready to Wear
Advance, Philippe Guibourge with two models,
including Mounia

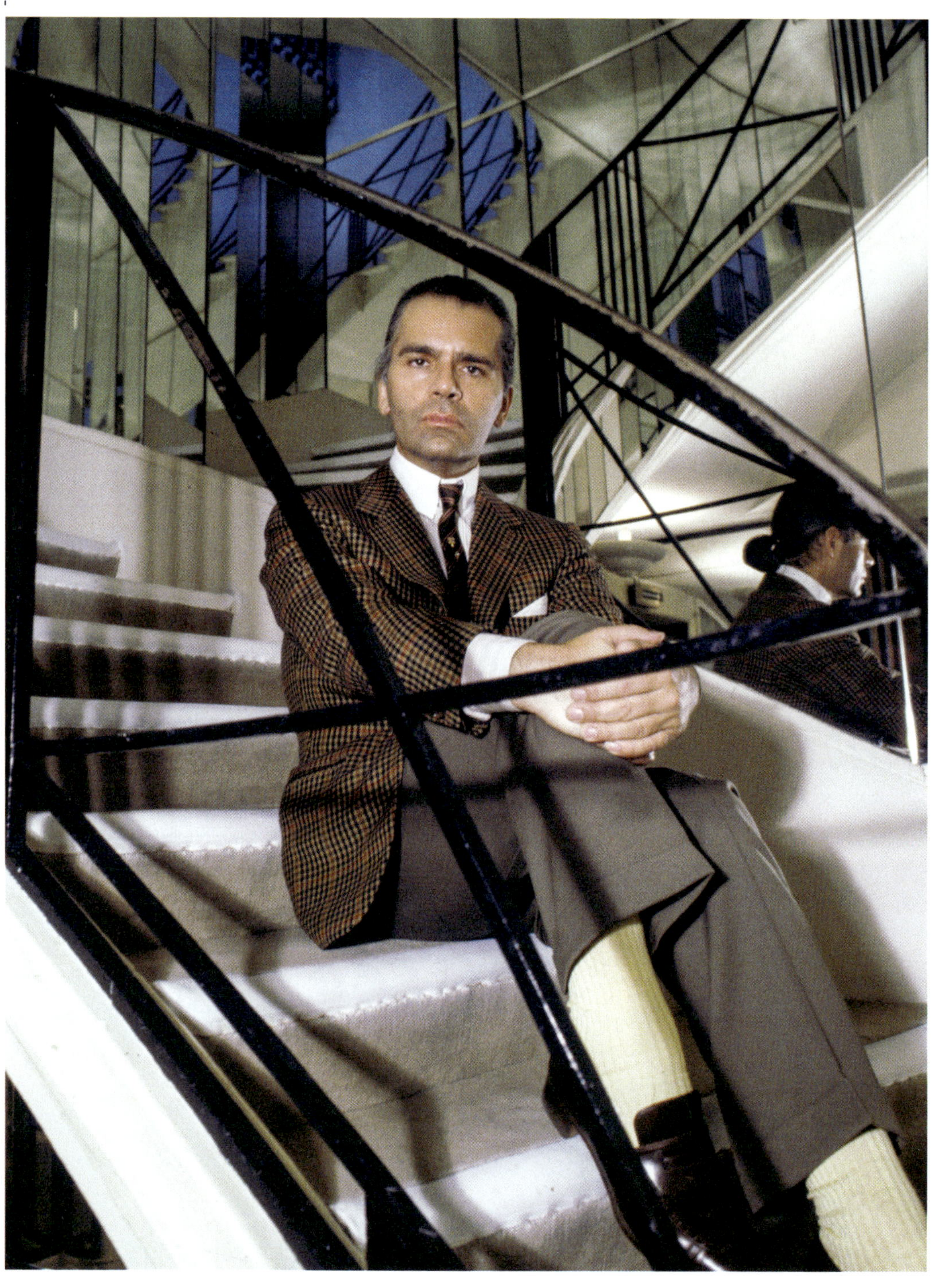

ABOVE: Stylist Karl Lagerfeld, posing on the
steps of the Chanel store, 1983, Paris, France

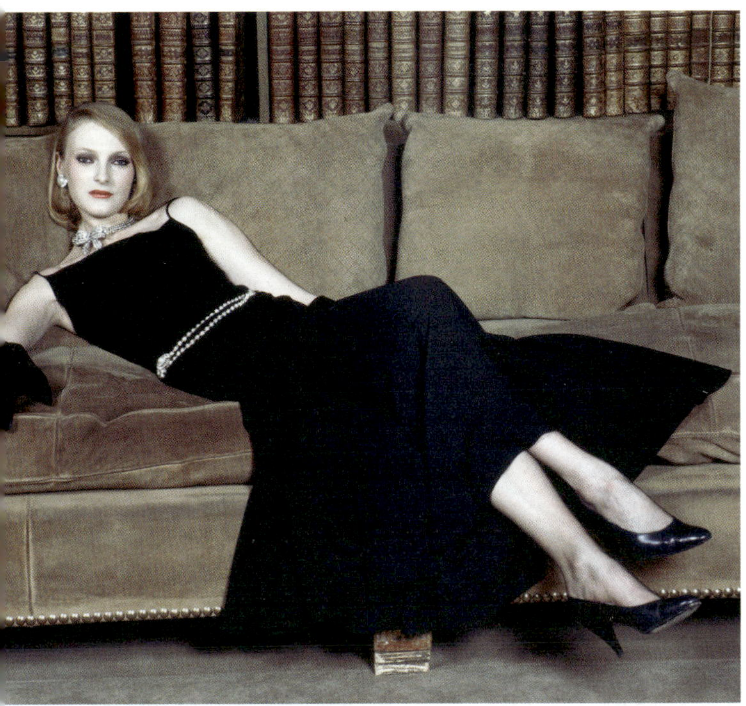

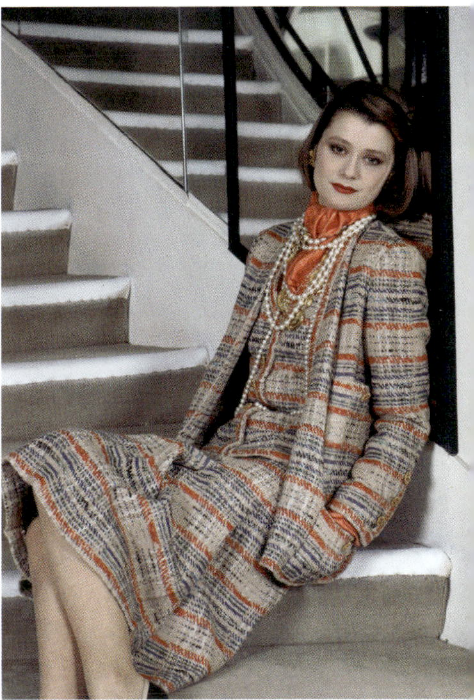

The rest is fashion history. Lagerfeld resurrected Chanel by going back to basics and using Coco Chanel's personal style and designs for inspiration. As his confidence grew he became more experimental and irreverent, a creative force of nature, prolific and powerful.

He once said that he didn't think Coco Chanel would have approved of the approach he took to the label; 'What I do Coco would have hated. The label has an image and it's up to me to update it. I do what she never did. I had to go from what Chanel was to what it should be, could be, what it had been to something else.'

Chanel and Lagerfeld was a match made in heaven, transforming Lagerfeld's own profile, as well as the fortunes of Chanel which is now a multi-billion dollar global empire.

'More than anyone I know, he represents the soul of fashion: restless, forward-looking and voraciously attentive to our changing culture,' said Anna Wintour, editor of *American Vogue*, when she presented him with the Outstanding Achievement Award at the British Fashion Awards in 2015.

This giant of the industry developed a personal style which was instantly recognisable even outside the fashion world. He hid his eyes behind sunglasses, contained his hair in a signature white ponytail, and covered his hands in fingerless gloves. He was also fond of a white shirt with a high, white, starched collar, usually worn with a black tie, jacket and jeans.

ABOVE: Spring 1983 couture collection, (L) the tank-top evening dress in black silk marocain (R) the tweed slouchy cardigan suit

THE LOWDOWN ON LAGERFELD

- Born 10 September 1933* in Hamburg, Germany, died 19 February 2019 in Paris, France.

- Moved to Paris as a teenager, with no formal training in fashion design, and got his break in 1954 by winning a fashion competition run by the International Wool Secretariat (now known as the International Woolmark Prize) in the 'coat' category.

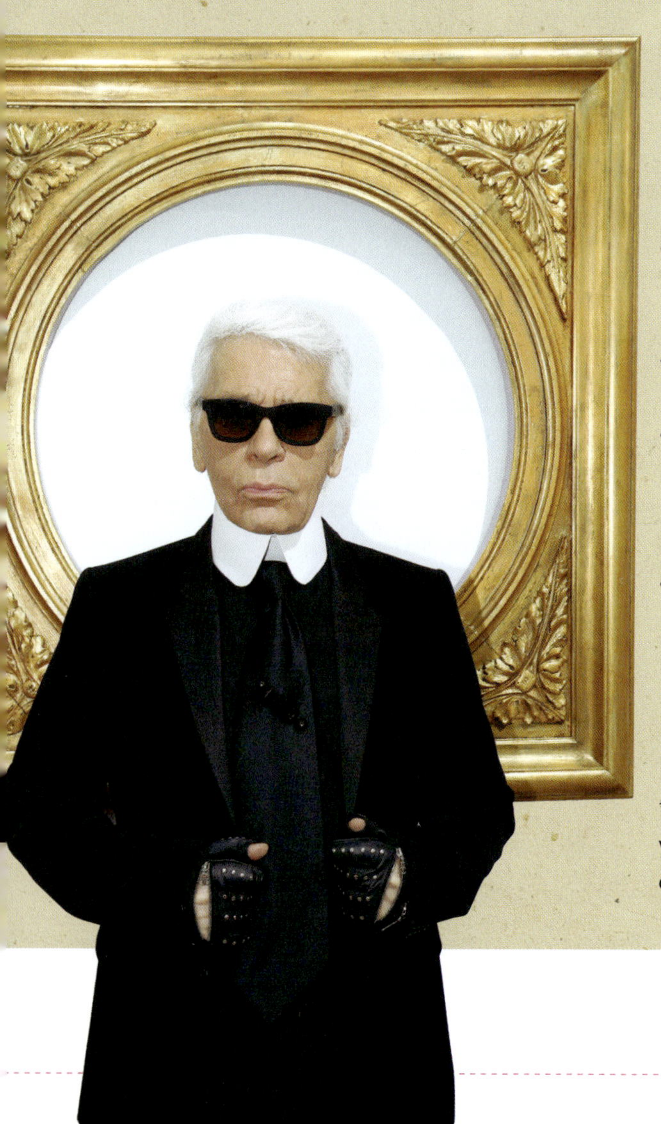

- He was first hired by Pierre Balmain, then later moved to Jean Patou, before freelancing in the emerging 'ready to wear' sector in the 1960s for companies including Krizia, Ballantyne, Charles Jourdan, and Chloé, where he stayed for over 10 years before joining Chanel where he had a lifetime contract.

- As well as his genius for fashion, Lagerfeld was a talented and respected photographer.

- He had an underground library at his home in Biarritz, France, which housed his collection of books, estimated to number 300,000 volumes.

- Fashion insiders knew him as the 'emperor of fashion' or 'Kaiser' in his native German.

- Mattel brought out a Barbie based on his look.

- He was devoted to his cat Choupette, a white Birman, who has her own maids, jewellery, and Instagram account.

- Fans of his work included Rihanna; Princess Caroline of Monaco; Christine Lagarde, the managing director of the International Monetary Fund and actress Julianne Moore.

* Lagerfeld would variously quote different birth years – frequently saying 1938 to knock five years off his age.

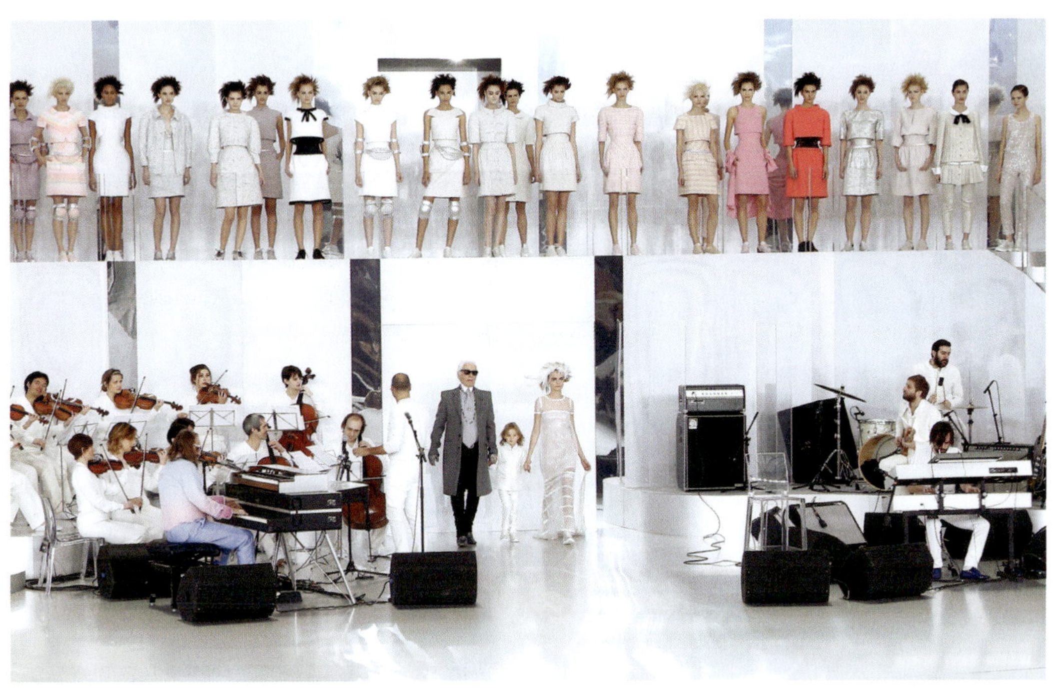

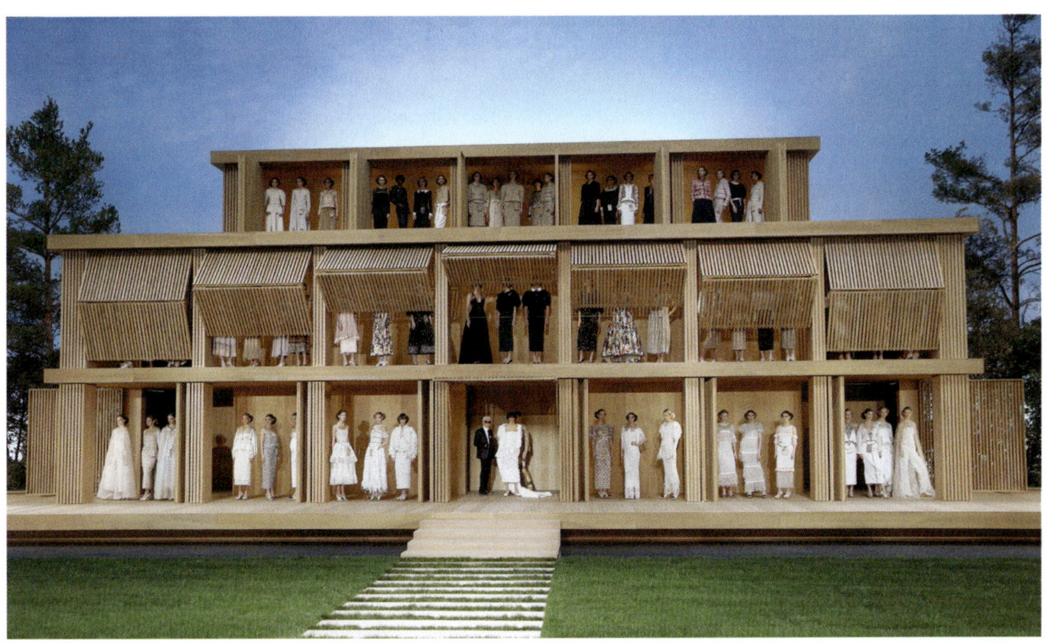

TOP: End of the Chanel show as part of Paris Fashion Week Haute-Couture Spring/Summer 2014

BOTTOM: End of the 2016 spring/summer Haute Couture collection show, Paris

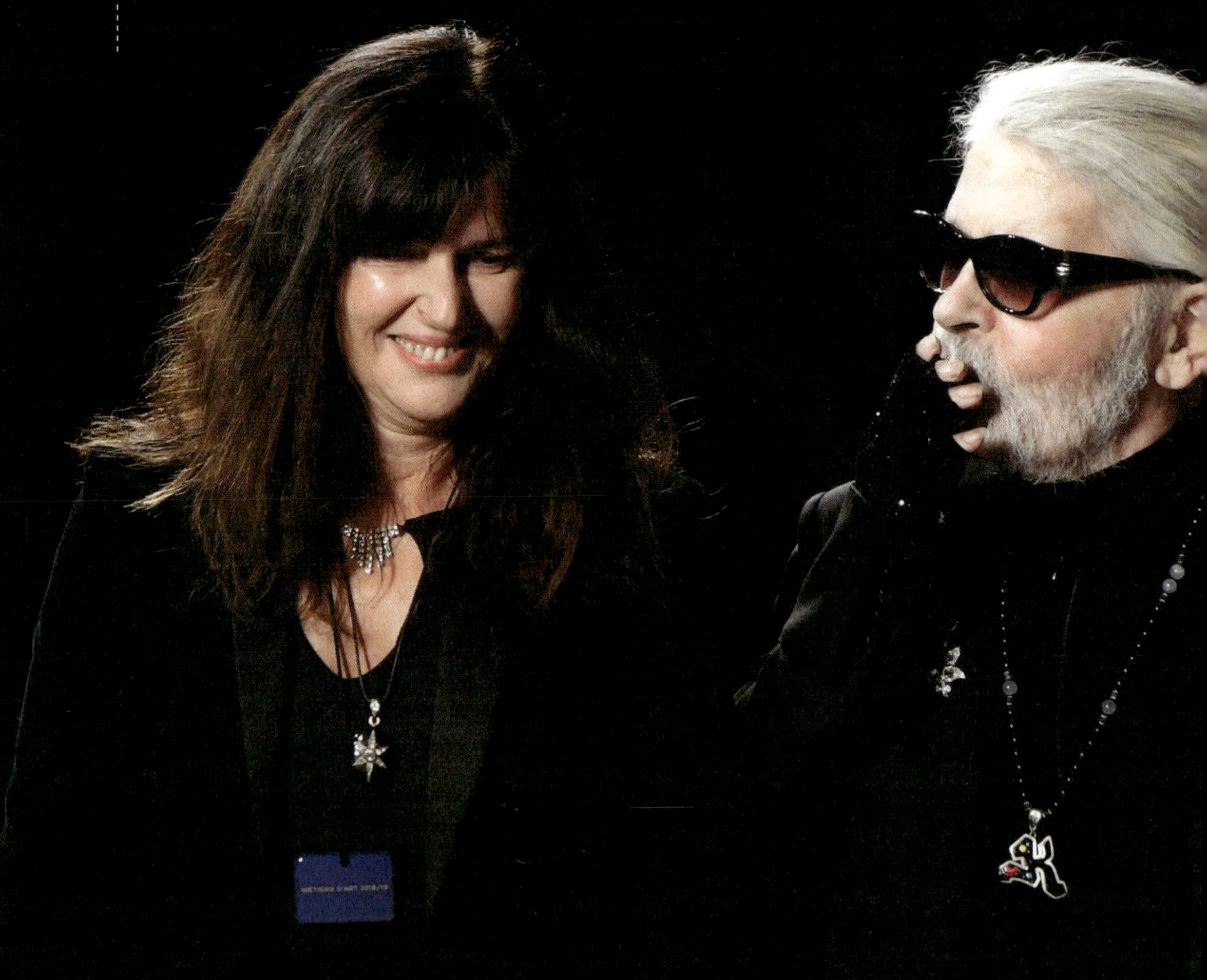

ABOVE: Karl Lagerfeld and Virginie Viard on the runway at Chanel Metiers D'Art 2018/19 Show, The Metropolitan Museum of Art, December 04, 2018, New York City

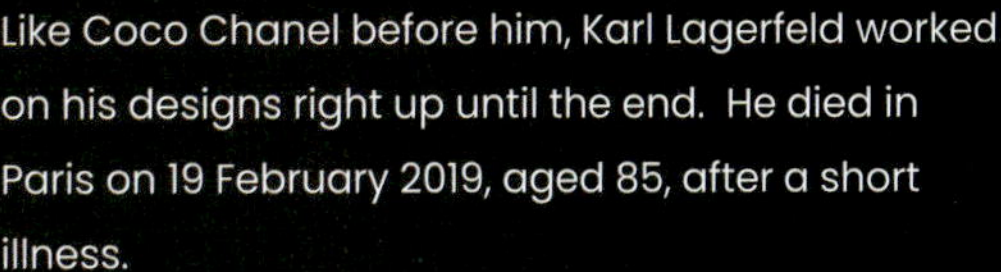

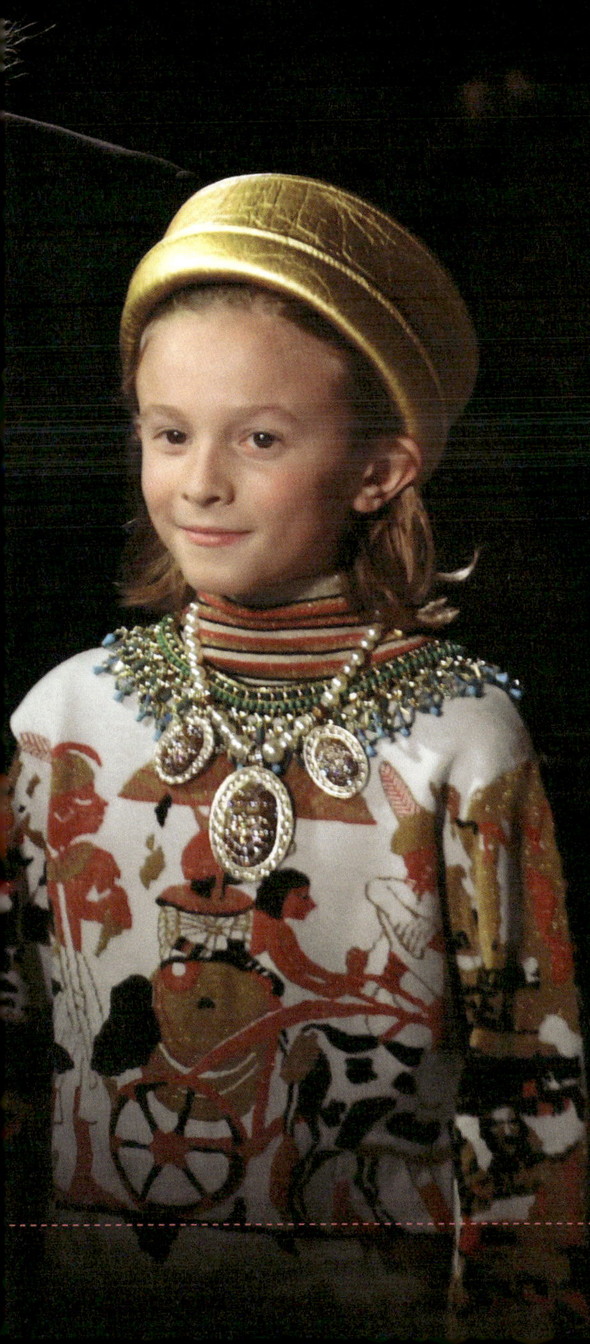

Like Coco Chanel before him, Karl Lagerfeld worked on his designs right up until the end. He died in Paris on 19 February 2019, aged 85, after a short illness.

His successor was Virginie Viard, who had collaborated closely with him at Chanel for over 30 years, latterly as creative studio director. Viard, who originally joined the Chanel Creation Studio as an intern in 1987, had been described by Lagerfeld as his 'left and right hand'.

In the late 1990s she had been appointed director of the Chanel Haute Couture Studio and shortly afterwards took additional responsibility for the Ready-to-Wear Studio. Announcing her appointment, Chanel said that its chief executive Alain Wertheimer, entrusted Viard with the 'creative work for the collections, so that the legacy of Gabrielle Chanel and Karl Lagerfeld can live on.' But there has been little word of her plans going forward as she keeps a low profile and has no social media presence.

This much we know.

Virginie Viard was born in 1962 and grew up in Lyon, where she later studied at Le Cours Georges fashion school, specialising in film and theatre costume. After a year in London, she took a job in Paris as assistant to costume designer Dominique Borg.

The internship at Chanel came next, in 1987, and she and Lagerfeld 'clicked'. The internship became a full time job and, realising her potential, Lagerfeld soon put her in charge of embroidery. Next came a five-year stint at Chloé, still under Lagerfeld's wing as he had begun working with the brand again in 1992. In 1997, she was named the studio director of Chanel and worked closely with Lagerfeld from then on, moving to 'ready-to-wear' in 2000. Her designs have been praised as fluid and fresh. She retains a 'rock and roll' vibe even now she has entered her 60s, with a penchant for grunge music. But for all that she had in common with Lagerfeld, she does not share his flair for making headlines. She's a far calmer character, almost retiring in comparison, but with a quiet strength. 'She's action versus talk,' actor and Chanel brand ambassador Kristen Stewart told *British Vogue*.

Following Lagerfeld's death and her appointment as Chanel's creative director, one of Viard's first big events was presenting the 2020 Cruise collection at the Grand Palais, in Paris. Lagerfeld had reinstated Coco Chanel's idea of the Cruise collection which involves largely 'travel inspired' clothes, presented outside the fashion world's seasonal schedule.

For her first solo collection, Viard staged a show in a Beaux-Arts style train station, very much in keeping with Lagerfeld's predilection for over-the-top runway sets. Chanel said that this train station set symbolized 'the promise of an adventure' as Viard began to bring her own ideas to the Chanel brand. More recently, *British Vogue* described her animal-inspired spring/summer 2023 Chanel couture showcase as having 'emerged triumphantly sophisticated'.

The legendary Chanel brand lives on – with, once again, a woman at the helm …

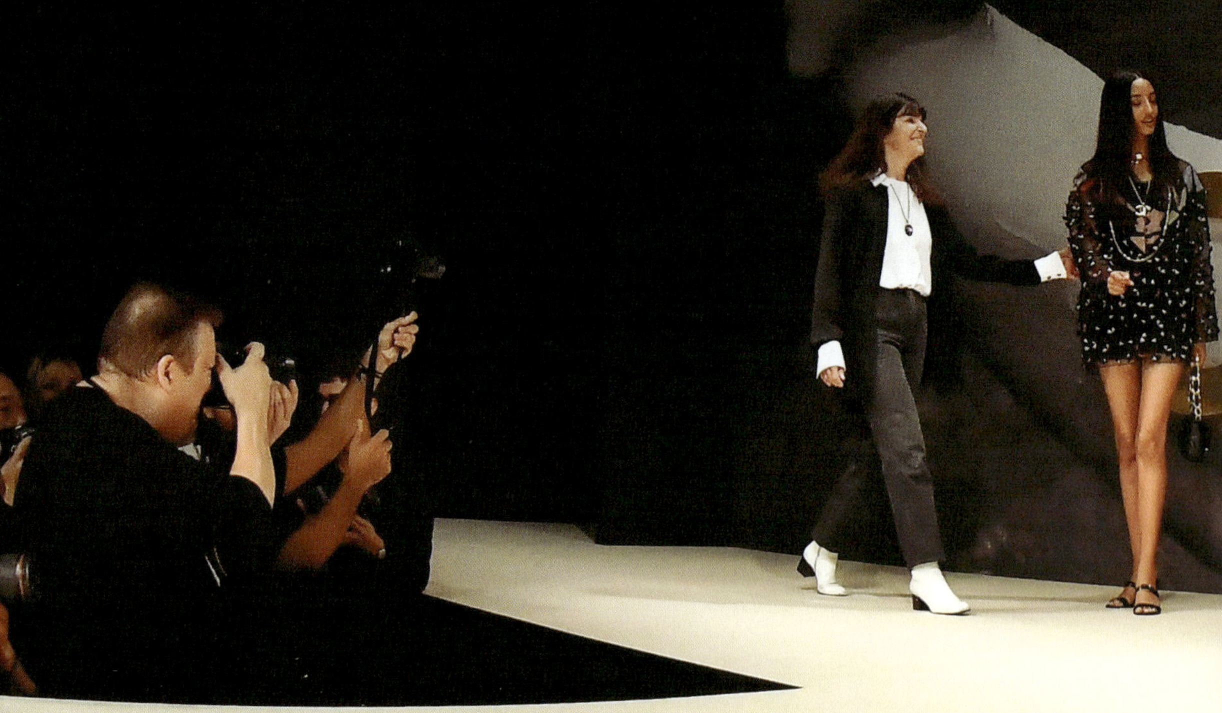

ABOVE: Virginie Viard walks the runway during the Chanel Ready to Wear Spring/ Summer 2022 fashion show, Paris Fashion Week, October 5, 2021

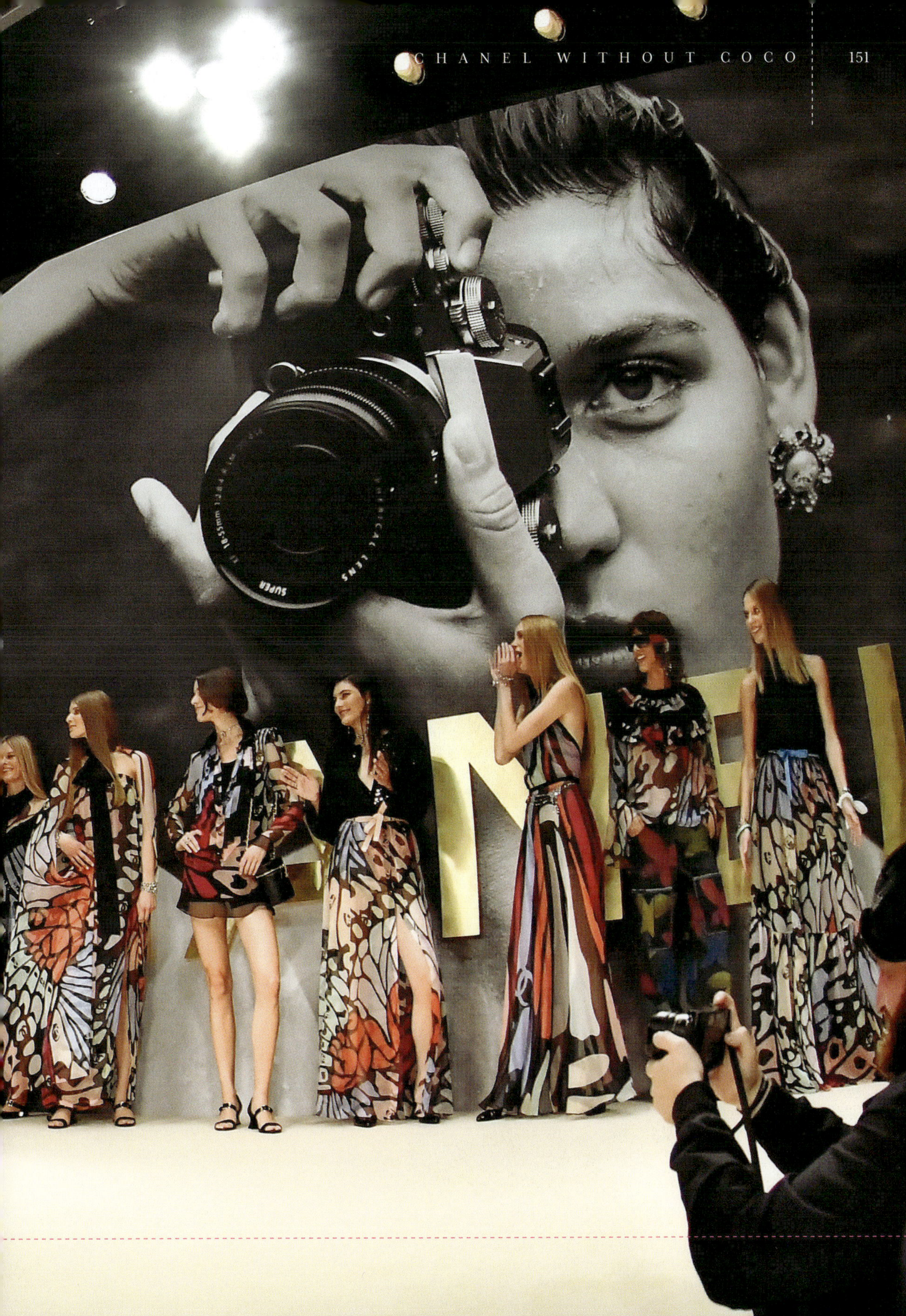

However, Viard's tenure came to an unexpected end in June 2024 when Chanel announced her departure after five years as creative director. The fashion house revealed that she would be leaving to 'pursue a new chapter in her personal life', bringing to a close an era that had seen her quietly steering one of fashion's most powerful brands. Industry insiders were taken by surprise, as there had been little indication that change was imminent. Chanel moved swiftly to reassure stakeholders that the house's creative vision would continue uninterrupted, with teams already in place to develop upcoming collections.

The search for Viard's replacement became one of the most closely watched developments in the luxury fashion world. Speculation ran rampant through industry circles, with names like Hedi Slimane, Pierpaolo Piccioli, and Sarah Burton circulating as potential candidates. The position represents not merely a job but a custodianship of one of fashion's most valuable and historically significant brands. Chanel's private ownership by the Wertheimer family meant that decisions could be made without the pressure of public shareholders, yet the weight of expectation remained immense.

In December 2024, Chanel ended months of intense speculation by announcing the appointment of Matthieu Blazy as its new artistic director, effective from June 2025. The Belgian designer, who had been serving as creative director of Bottega Veneta since 2021, brought with him a reputation for exquisite craftsmanship and a modern sensibility that resonated strongly with contemporary luxury consumers.

The fashion world now waits to see how Blazy will interpret the iconic codes of Chanel for a new generation.

ABOVE: Matthieu Blazy accept applause after the conclusion of the Bottega Veneta women's Fall-Winter 2024-25 collection presented in Milan, Italy, Saturday, Feb. 24, 2024

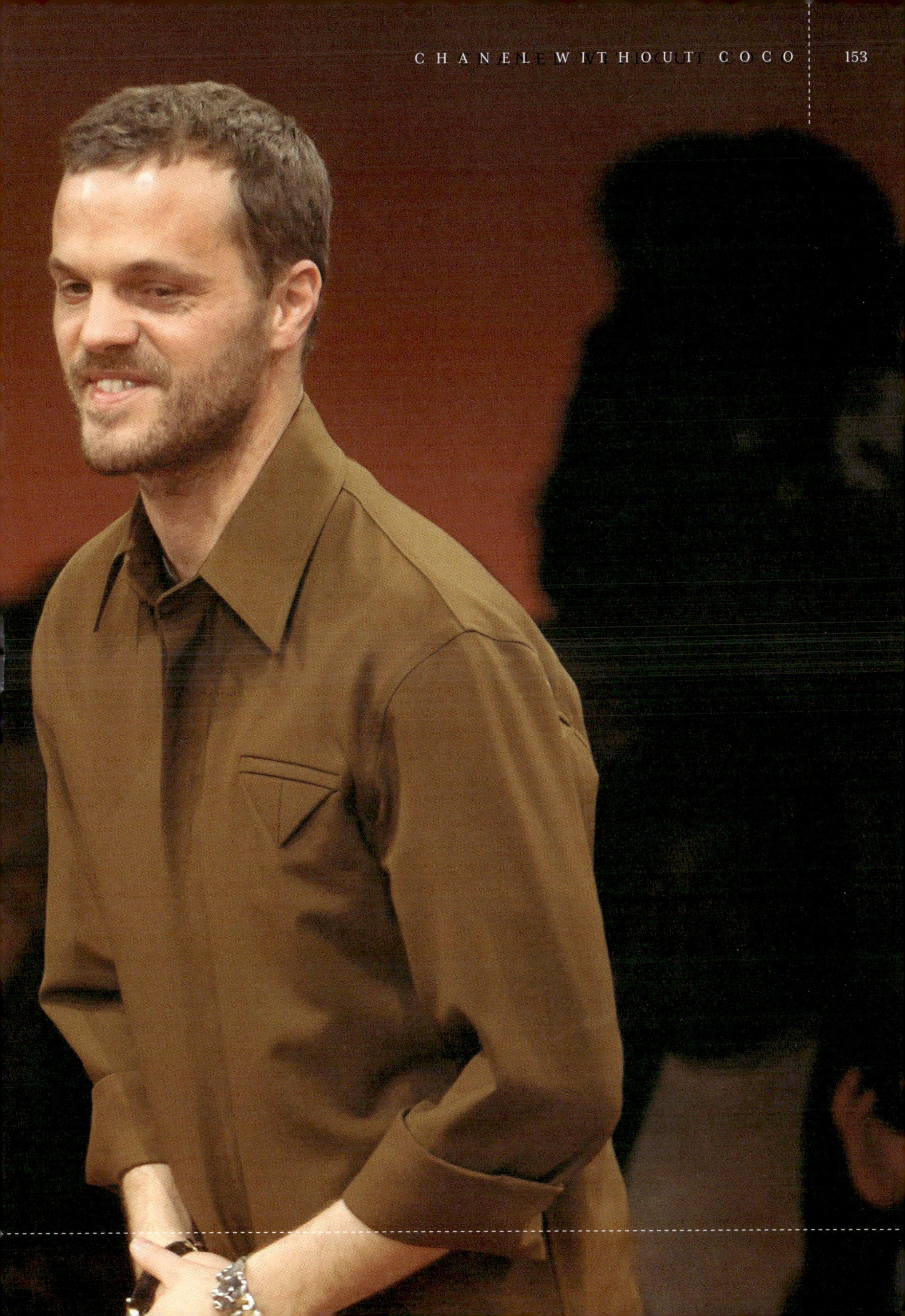

KEY DATES FOR CHANEL SINCE COCO'S DEATH

1985

Chanel acquires its first artistic craft house, button maker Maison Desrues. Keen to preserve specialist craft and manufacturing skills, Chanel goes on to gather other artisan workshops (Ateliers d'art) including Lemarie for feathers, Lesage for embroidery. Massaro for shoes and Maison Michel for millinery, all under the Paraffection umbrella subsidiary company.

1993

Chanel acquires the G&F Châtelain watchmaking manufacturer in Switzerland.

Creation of Chanel Fine Jewellery with the reproduction of the Comète necklace from the Bijoux de Diamants collection created by Coco Chanel in 1932.

1987

Creation of Chanel Watches. Its first design is the Première, which has a dial inspired by the shape of the Nº5 perfume bottle cap.

1990

Creation of the MADEMOISELLE watch, with a bracelet consisting of five rows of pearls.

1995

Launch of Rouge Noir nail lacquer.

1997

Opening of Chanel's fine jewellery boutique at 18 Place Vendôme.

1999

Chanel launches its first skin care line, Précision, and, following a licensing agreement with Italian eyewear company Luxottica, a line of sunglasses and eyeglass frames.

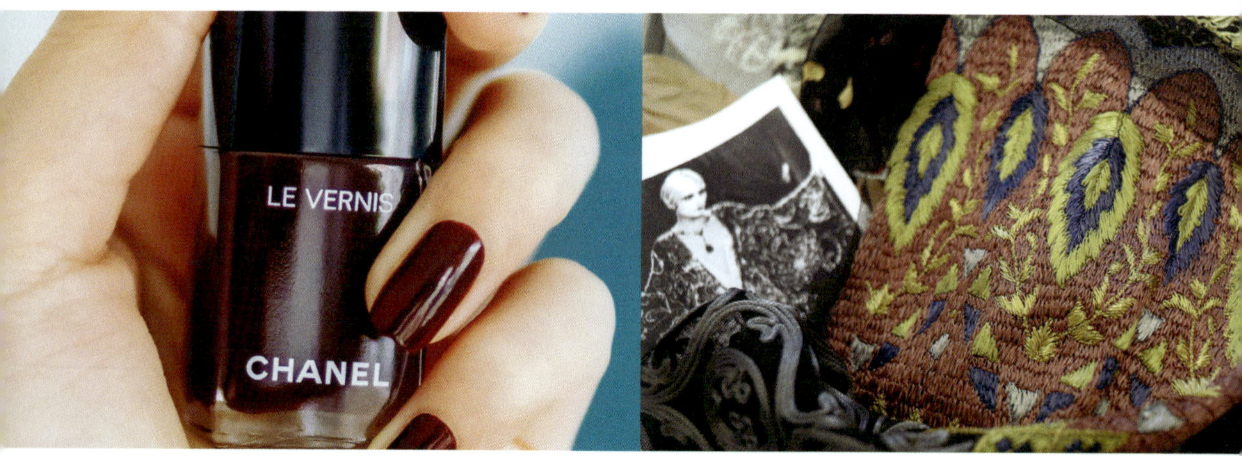

2000

J12, Chanel's first unisex sports watch is launched.

2019

Death of Karl Lagerfeld and appointment of Chanel's new creative director Virginie Viard.

2002

Chanel's Madison Avenue jewellery and watch shop opens in New York.

Chanel launches its now annual Metiers d'Art (Masters of Art) collection which pays tribute to its ateliers.

2007

Death of Jacques Helleu, Chanel's artistic director for fragrance, beauty, watches, and fine jewellery for over 40 years from 1965 to 2007 and the acknowledged driving force behind Chanel's iconic ad campaigns.

2001

Chanel acquires watchmaker Bell & Ross.

2013

Coco Chanel's apartment, together with the mirrored staircase which led up to it at 31 Rue Cambon in Paris, are designated as historical monuments following their acquisition by the French Ministry of Culture.

2018

Chanel relocates its global headquarters to London.

The use of fur and exotic skins is banned from Chanel collections.

2024

Matthieu Blazy appointed as Chanel's new artistic director, following Virginie Viard's departure.

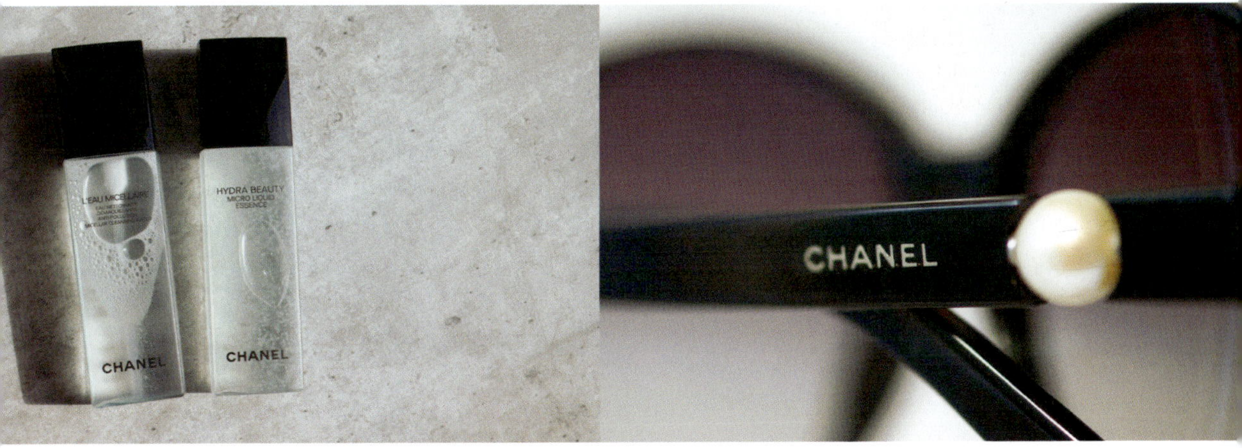

PERFUME PAR EXCELLENCE

Chanel's fragrances for men and women have been overseen by a succession of leading perfumers.

Ernest Beaux (1881–1961) was Chanel's first perfume designer, or 'nose', and the man who created the iconic Chanel No 5. After Beaux's retirement in 1952, Henri Robert (1899–1987) took over as chief perfumer and was responsible for Chanel's first men's fragrance Pour Monsieur and the now classic Chanel No 19.

Jacques Polge (1943–) from 1978 to 2015 became the third perfumer for the House of Chanel in 1978, creating Coco, Coco Mademoiselle, Allure, Chance, and Bleu fragrances. His son, Olivier Polge is the current head of the Chanel Perfume Creation and Development Laboratory, having taken over in 2015. As well as formulating the 2018 'parfum' version of Bleu de Chanel, he has so far created the new fragrance, Gabrielle.

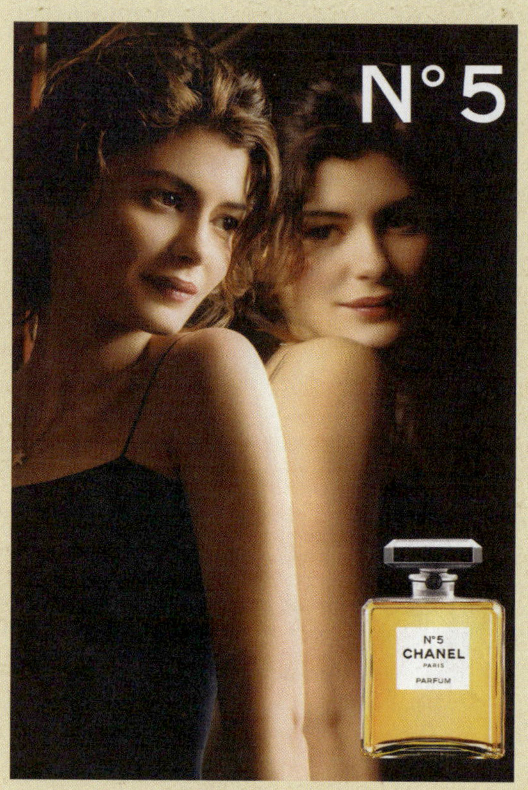

PERFUME LAUNCH DATES

1921 – Chanel No 5

1922 – Chanel No 22

1925 – Chanel Gardenia

1927 – Chanel Cuir De Russie

1928 – Chanel Bois des Iles

1955 – Pour Monsieur (first men's fragrance)

1970 – Chanel No 19

1984 – Coco

1990 – L'egoiste (men)

1996 – Allure

1998 – Allure Homme (men)

2002 – Chance

2001 – Coco Mademoiselle

2004 – Allure Homme Sport (men)

2007 – Les Exclusifs Perfume (A new line of perfumes whose names referenced the emblematic sites and creations of Coco Chanel and the House: 31 rue Cambon, Bel Respiro, 28 La Pausa, N°18, Coromandel, l'Eau de Cologne. Four reproductions of 1983, N°22, Gardénia, Bois des îles and Cuir de Russie rounded out this new collection, which sold exclusively in CHANEL boutiques).

2010 – Bleu de Chanel

2017 – Gabrielle

2018 – Les Eaux perfumes, a collection of fresh scents evoking destinations that were important to Coco Chanel.

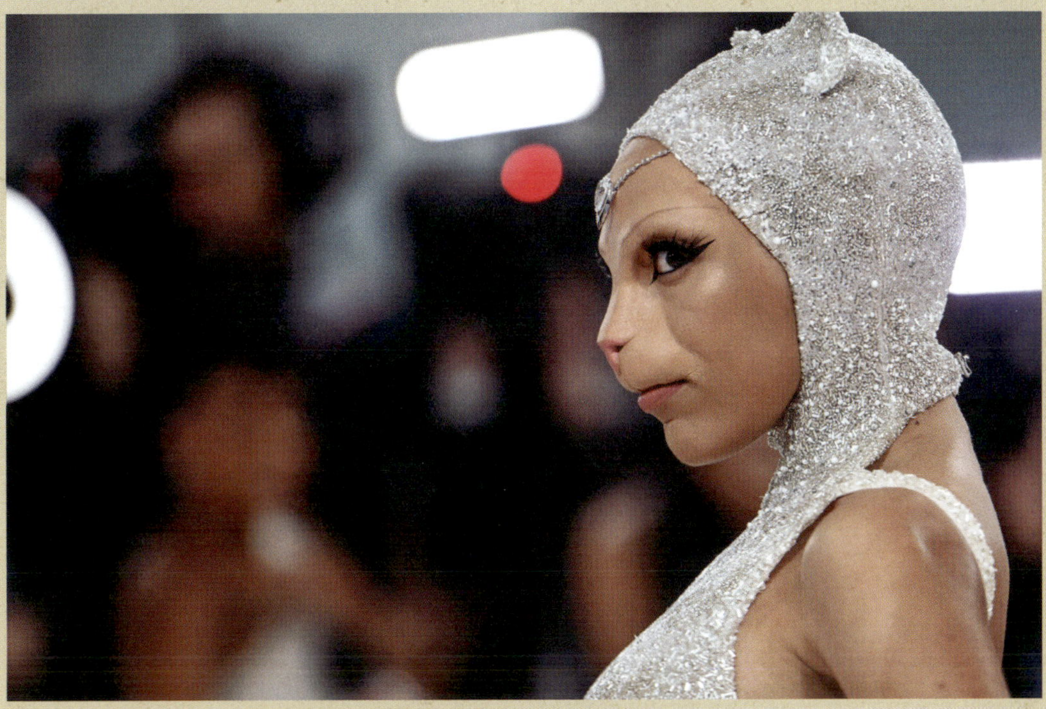

IN HONOUR OF KARL

The 2023 Met Gala fundraiser for the Metropolitan Museum of Art's Costume Institute celebrated the opening of the Costume Institute exhibition, ' Karl Lagerfeld: A line of beauty'.

The dress code 'in honour of Karl' led many of the gala's celebrity guests to model classic outfits from Chanel in his honour.

But others went in another direction and took his famous and beloved cat Choupette as their inspiration. Doja Cat wore facial prosthetics to give herself a feline appearance, while wearing a gown featuring cat ears. Actor Jared Leto went one step further by dressing entirely as a white cat.

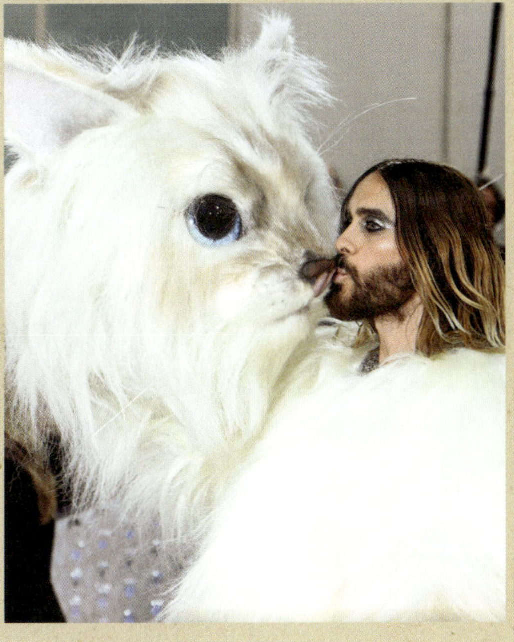

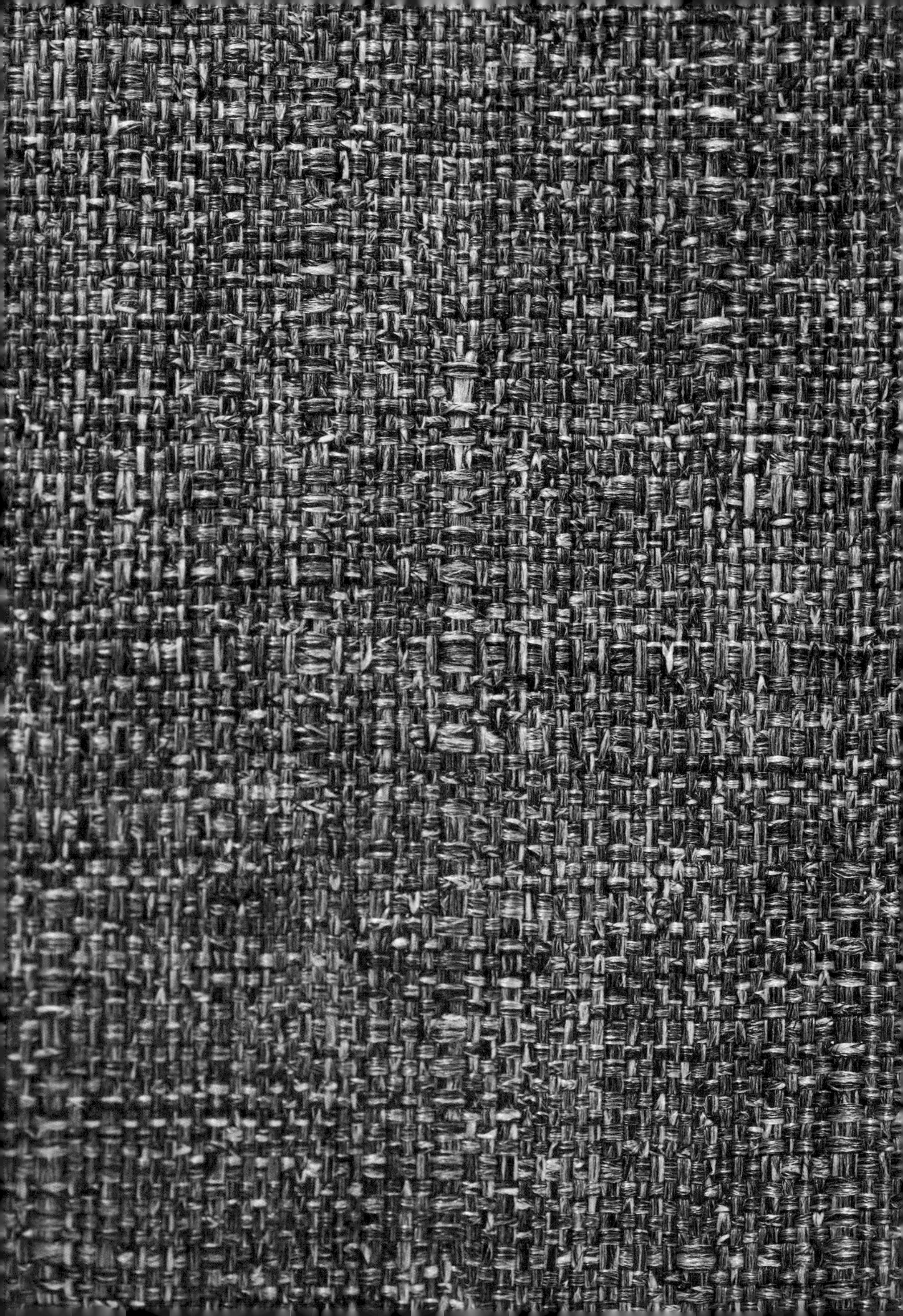